Study Guide

Caribbean History for CSEC®

Dr Dane Morton-Gittens
Veta Dawson
Rita Pemberton
Karl Watson

OXFORD
UNIVERSITY PRESS

Great Clarendon Street, Oxford, OX2 6DP, United Kingdom

Oxford University Press is a department of the University of Oxford.

It furthers the University's objective of excellence in research, scholarship, and education by publishing worldwide. Oxford is a registered trade mark of Oxford University Press in the UK and in certain other countries

© Dr Dane Morton-Gittens

The moral rights of the author have been asserted

First published in 2017

All rights reserved. No part of this publication may be reproduced, stored in a retrieval system, or transmitted, in any form or by any means, without the prior permission in writing of Oxford University Press, or as expressly permitted by law, by licence or under terms agreed with the appropriate reprographics rights organization. Enquiries concerning reproduction outside the scope of the above should be sent to the Rights Department, Oxford University Press, at the address above.

You must not circulate this work in any other form and you must impose this same condition on any acquirer

British Library Cataloguing in Publication Data

Data available

978-1-4085-2647-7

10 9 8 7 6 5 4 3 2 1

Paper used in the production of this book is a natural, recyclable product made from wood grown in sustainable forests.
The manufacturing process conforms to the environmental regulations of the country of origin.

Printed in India by Manipal Technologies Limited

Acknowledgements
The publishers would like to thank the following for permissions to use their photographs:

Cover photograph: Mark Lyndersay, Lyndersay Digital, Trinidad

Artworks: Cenveo, Jim Eldridge, Angela Lumley and David Russell

Photos: **p6**: Justin Kerr; **p9**: Duho' ceremonial seat, Taino, Republic of Haiti, 15th century (wood), Haitian School/Musee de l'Homme, Paris, France/Bridgeman Images; **p13**: Lanmas/Alamy; **p22** (L): Graham Watts/Alamy; **p22** (T): Pete Ryan/Getty; **p26**: Everett Collection/Mary Evans; **p37**: Reuters/Alamy; **p45**: Jorgen Udvang/Alamy; **p47**: Iconotec/Alamy; **p49**: Mansell/Getty; **p51**: Portrait of Toussaint Louverture (1743-1803) on horseback, early 19th century (colour engraving), French School, (19th century)/Bibliotheque Nationale, Paris, France/Archives Charmet/Bridgeman Images; **p53**: James P. Blair/Getty; **p54**: Creative Commons; **p56**: Sarah Rothwell/Flickr; **p57**: The Destruction of the Roehampton Estate in the Parish of St. James's in January 1832, 1833 (hand coloured litho), Duperly, Adolphe (1801-65)/Private Collection/Photo © Christie's Images/Bridgeman Images; **p60**: An Interior View of a Jamaica House of Correction, c.1830 (steel engraving), English School, (19th century)/Private Collection/© Michael Graham-Stewart/Bridgeman Images; **p62**: Getty/Hulton Archive/Stringer; **p65**: Wedgwood Slave Emancipation Society medallion, c.1787-90 (jasperware), Hackwood, William (c.1757-1829)/Private Collection/Bridgeman Images; **p68**: Classic Image/Alamy; **p72**: 19th era/Alamy; **p76**: Slaves Ladle Steaming Juice from Vat to Vat, Antigua, 1823 (print), Clark, William (fl.1823)/British Library, London, UK/© British Library Board. All Rights Reserved/Bridgeman Images; **p79**: Dov Makabaw Cuba/Alamy; **p80**: Prisma Bildagentur AG/Alamy; **p82**: Plantation Workers on arrival from India, mustered at Depot, c.1891 (b/w photo), English Photographer/Royal Commonwealth Society, London, UK/Bridgeman Images; **p84**: Getty/Christopher P. Baker; **p86**: Jon Malone/Alamy; **p89**: DEA/G.Dagli Orti/Getty; **p90**: Sandy Marshall; **p93**: The Caribbean Photo Archive; **p94**: Archive Farms Inc/Alamy; **p97**: Duncan Walker/iStock; **p99**: Ingenio Santa Teresa Agüica/British Library, London, UK/© British Library Board. All Rights Reserved/Bridgeman Images; **p100**: The Caribbean Photo Archive; **p103**: The Caribbean Photo Archive; **p105**: The Caribbean Photo Archive; **p107**: Allan/Three Lions/Getty; **p111**: Allen Morrison; **p113**: DOD Photo/Alamy; **p115**: clearing of Panama canal between 1879 and 1914 to link Pacific and Atlantic oceans under the leadership of FerdinanddeLesseps/Photo © Tallandier/Bridgeman Images; **p117**: Bettman/Getty images; **p119**: Digital Library of the Caribbean, George A. Smathers Libraries/University of Florida; **p120**: Luis Davilla/Getty; **p122**: Fidel Castro/Universal History Archive/UIG/Bridgeman Images; **p124**: BAY OF PIGS INVASION: Ten anti-Castro Cuban rebel prisoners land in Miami after their release by Castro, following the failed U.S. supported invasion of Cuba, May, 1961/Photo © Everett Collection/Bridgeman Images; **p127**: MARKA/Alamy; **p129**: Michael Dwyer/Alamy; **p131**: Rolf Richardson/Alamy; **p132**: The Library of Congress; **p134**: Digital Library of the Caribbean, George A. Smathers Libraries; **p138**: Express/Getty Images; **p140**: Aime Cesaire/Photo © Louis Monier/Bridgeman Images; **p142**: Val Wilmer/Getty; **p145** (L): The University of the West Indies; **p145** (ML): Pictorial Parade/Getty images; **p145** (MR): Richard Meek/The LIFE Images Collection/Getty Images); **p145** (R): Lennox Honeychurch; **p147**: adempercem/Alamy; **p149**: philipus/Alamy; **p151**: Alamy/Oliver Hoffmann; **p154**: Davide Agnelli/Alamy; **p157**: Grenville Collins Postcard Collection/Mary Evans; **p159**: PjrTravel/Alamy; **p160**: George Rinhart/Getty; **p162**: Digital Library of the Caribbean/University of Florida; **p164**: Dave G. Houser/Getty; **p166**: The National Gallery of Jamaica/Edna Manley Foundation; **p168**: Bruno Monteny/Alamy; **p170**: H. Armstrong Roberts/ClassicStock/Getty; **p172**: Bettmann/Getty; **p175**: PA Photo/David McFadden OR Monty Howell; **p176**: Sven Creutzmann/Mambo Photo/Getty

Although we have made every effort to trace and contact all copyright holders before publication this has not been possible in all cases. If notified, the publisher will rectify any errors or omissions at the earliest opportunity.

Contents

Introduction 1

Section A, Theme 1: The indigenous peoples and the Europeans — 2

1.1 Migration and settlement patterns 2
1.2 The Maya 4
1.3 The Taino and Kalinago 6
1.4 The Taino: art forms, beliefs and technology 8
1.5 The Kalinago: beliefs, art forms and technology 10
1.6 Gold, God and glory! 12
1.7 'The Columbian Exchange' 1: The impact of Europeans 14
1.8 'The Columbian Exchange' 2: The impact of the indigenous people 16

Section A, Theme 2: Caribbean economy and slavery — 18

2.1 European rivalry in the Caribbean 18
2.2 Tropical crops for Europe 20
2.3 The sugar revolution 22
2.4 The transatlantic trade 24
2.5 Personal experiences of enslavement 26
2.6 Physical layout and use of labour 28
2.7 Sugar production 30
2.8 Markets for sugar and rum 32
2.9 African cultural forms 1: shelter, dress, food and medicine 34
2.10 African cultural forms 2: language, music, dance and storytelling 36
2.11 Social relations: ethnic, gender and class 38
2.12 Social, political and economic consequences 40

Section A, Theme 3: Resistance and revolt — 42

3.1 Controlling the enslaved 42
3.2 Forms of resistance 44
3.3 Maroon societies 1: origins and development 46
3.4 Maroon societies 2: setting and culture 48
3.5 The Haitian Revolution 1: causes and events .. 50
3.6 The Haitian Revolution 2: the consequences .. 52
3.7 Major revolts 1: Berbice and Barbados 54
3.8 Major revolts 2: Demerara and Jamaica 56

Section A Practice exam questions 58

Section B, Theme 4: Metropolitan movements towards emancipation — 60

4.1 Effects of revolts on the emancipation process 60
4.2 Attitudes towards slavery 62
4.3 Anti-slavery movements 64
4.4 Amelioration 66
4.5 The British Emancipation Act 1833 68
4.6 Apprenticeship 70
4.7 Emancipation in British Caribbean territories ... 72
4.8 Emancipation in other Caribbean territories 74

Section B, Theme 5: Adjustments to emancipation (1838–76) — 76

5.1 Problems of the sugar industry 76
5.2 Attitudes to labour 78
5.3 Schemes of migration 80
5.4 Economic, social and cultural effects of migration 82
5.5 Emergence of free villages 84
5.6 Creation of a new society 86
5.7 Contribution of the peasantry 88
5.8 Crown Colony government 90

Section B, Theme 6: Caribbean economy (1875–1985) — 92

6.1 The Caribbean and the world economy 92
6.2 Decline of the sugar industry 94

iii

6.3 Resolving the crisis 96
6.4 Growth of Cuba's sugar industry..........................98
6.5 Growth and survival of alternative agriculture 100
6.6 Services and tourism 102
6.7 Industrial development factors 104
6.8 The effects of industrialisation 106

Section B Practice exam questions 108

Section C, Theme 7: The United States in the Caribbean (1776–1985) — 110

7.1 Reasons for the US interest in the Caribbean......110
7.2 Factors and conditions of US relations in the Caribbean 112
7.3 US foreign policy 1: Cuba, Puerto Rico and Panama...114
7.4 US foreign policy 2: Haiti, Dominican Republic and Grenada 116
7.5 US involvement: economic, political and cultural consequences...118
7.6 Policies of the Castro revolution 122
7.7 The US response...124
7.8 The impact of the Castro revolution 126
7.9 US involvement in the English-speaking Caribbean 128

Section C, Theme 8: Caribbean political development up to 1985 — 130

8.1 Early attempts at unification 130
8.2 The roots of nationalism.....................................132
8.3 The Moyne Commission 134
8.4 Political parties, adult suffrage and self-government 138
8.5 The movement to establish a federation 140

8.6 The failure of the Federation (1958) 142
8.7 Personalities involved in integration.....................144
8.8 Movements towards independence 146
8.9 Regional integration up to 1985..........................148
8.10 Alternatives to independence.............................150

Section C, Theme 9: Caribbean Society (1900–85) — 154

9.1 Social and economic conditions 1: housing 154
9.2 Social and economic conditions 2: cost of living and working conditions 156
9.3 Social and economic conditions 3: health...........158
9.4 Improving living conditions 1: organisations involved..160
9.5 Improving living conditions 2: government policies 162
9.6 Aspects of social life 1: community.....................164
9.7 Aspects of social life 2: visual and performing arts 166
9.8 Aspects of social life 3: architecture and housing 168
9.9 Aspects of social life 4: transport and communication...170
9.10 Aspects of social life 5: ethnic and race relations..172
9.11 Religious groups 1 174
9.12 Religious groups 2 176

Section C Practice exam questions 178

Glossary of key terms 180

Index 184

 Access your support website for additional content and activities here:
www.oxfordsecondary.com/9781408526477

iv

Introduction

This Study Guide has been developed exclusively with the Caribbean Examinations Council (CXC®) to be used as an additional resource by candidates, both in and out of school, following the Caribbean Secondary Education Certificate (CSEC®) programme.

It has been prepared by a team with expertise in the CSEC® syllabus, teaching and examination. The contents are designed to support learning by providing tools to help you achieve your best in CSEC® Caribbean History and the features included make it easier for you to master the key concepts and requirements of the syllabus. *Do remember to refer to your syllabus for full guidance on the course requirements and examination format!*

This Study Guide is supported by a website which includes electronic activities to assist you in developing good examination techniques:

- **On Your Marks** activities provide sample examination-style short answer and essay type questions, with example candidate answers and feedback from an examiner to show where answers could be improved. These activities will build your understanding, skill level and confidence in answering examination questions.

- **Test yourself** activities are specifically designed to provide experience of multiple-choice examination questions and helpful feedback will refer you to sections inside the Study Guide so that you can revise problem areas.

This unique combination of focused syllabus content and interactive examination practice will provide you with invaluable support to help you reach your full potential in CSEC® Caribbean History

 Access your support website for additional content and activities here: **www.oxfordsecondary.com/9781408526477**

Section A, Theme 1: The indigenous peoples and the Europeans

1.1 Migration and settlement patterns

LEARNING OUTCOMES

At the end of this topic you should be able to:

- Trace the migration patterns of early humans in the Americas.
- Identify in their original locations the different Caribbean cultural groups that existed.
- State the basic resources in the Caribbean.
- Understand what self-sufficiency means.

The Americas and the Caribbean

The Caribbean (the West Indies) comprises all islands and countries bounded by the Caribbean Sea or with specific historical, economic and political similarities. There are over 700 islands in the chain, subdivided into the Greater and Lesser Antilles and further into the Windward and Leeward Islands.

Migration into America

Archaeologists support the theory that early man entered the Americas around 13,500 years ago. Hunters and gatherers, following wild herds, crossed the Bering Straits ice bridge from Siberia into Alaska up to 10,000 years ago.

Artefacts confirm they moved south while hunting, reaching the southern tip of South America around 8,000 years ago, and settling around 5,000 years ago. Their staple crops were maize, cassava and potatoes. Villages were soon established and eventually developed into the great civilisations of the Maya, Aztec and Inca.

Moving into the Caribbean

The Taino and Kalinago were some of the earliest settlers in the Caribbean. They came from different areas. Archaeologists have, however, identified that many peoples preceded them by a few thousand years.

DID YOU KNOW?

Workers who came from India in the second half of the 19th century used to be referred to as East Indians, to distinguish them from the indigenous West Indian people. It is now customary to refer to them simply as Indian.

EXAM TIP

Make sure that you always read the examination questions and instructions carefully so that you understand exactly what the task is.

Figure 1.1.1 The Caribbean comprises the territories bounded by the Caribbean Sea.

The Europeans came after the Amerindians. The Spaniards came first in 1492, led by Christopher Columbus. They were followed by the English, French and Dutch. Africans came as enslaved people from the late 16th century and indentured Africans, Portuguese, Chinese and Indians between 1838 and 1845.

Cultural groups

Archaeologists believe that the earliest indigenous groups mixed farming, fishing and hunting and gathering. Their cultures were simple; they believed in animism and spirits.

The Taino evolved from another indigenous group. They migrated from the lower Orinoco, through Venezuela and Trinidad into the Caribbean (Figure 1.1.1). They had a well developed farming system based on cassava (manioc) cultivation. Leadership was hereditary and their culture and society was advanced.

The Kalinago migrated from the Amazonian basin to the Caribbean. Cassava was also important in their diet, but their leadership was based on war prowess. Contrary to common belief, they were not cannibals, but did consume blood from the heart of a slain warrior in the belief that this would give them his power. The Kalinago obtained their women from Taino raids, explaining the many similarities in Taino and Kalinago practices and language.

Resources

The South American and Caribbean's tropical rainforests provided humans and animals with food, clothing, shelter and materials for construction, industrial and medical uses. The land afforded stable ground for settlement, especially on the protected leeward coasts. Rivers provided water.

Historically, indigenous groups cultivated cassava, maize and potatoes and extensively used native fruits including guava, pawpaw soursop and sapodilla. Native hardwoods were used to make canoes, weapons, bowls and the *duhos* (ceremonial chairs; see Figure 1.4.1).

The indigenous people hunted agouti, deer, turtles and iguanas, and fished for lobster, conch and crabs. They made tools and weapons from bones, wood, stones and shells, pottery from clay, graters, mortars, pestles and spear heads from stone, and hooks and decoration from animal bones.

Early European settlers depended on the indigenous people's resources to survive.

DID YOU KNOW?

Abundant resources allowed the indigenous to be self-sufficient, using all parts of plants or animals and not needing any outside help. They used slash and burn, a method of farming that involves cutting down and burning the old vegetation before sowing new seed.

ACTIVITY

Identify three things that show that the Taino and Kalingo were not the first people to settle in the Caribbean.

KEY POINTS

- Early man migrated across the Bering Straits into America between 15,000 and 10,000 years ago.
- Early cultures included the Maya, Aztec, Inca, Taino and Kalinago.
- Indigenous culture was based on subsistence farming, hunting and fishing.
- Early people were self-sufficient.

SUMMARY QUESTIONS

1. Explain how and why the early migrants came into the Americas.
2. Describe the settlement patterns of the indigenous people in the Caribbean.
3. Explain how the Taino and Kalinago organised their societies.

1.2 The Maya

LEARNING OUTCOMES

At the end of this topic you should be able to:
- Locate the Mayan empire on a map.
- Describe the organisation of Mayan society.
- Explain the role of agriculture and trade in the Mayan economy.
- Assess the contribution of the Mayans to science, astrology and mathematics.

DID YOU KNOW?

The Maya made advances in writing and mathematics. Their civilisation was made up of a loose union of city-states.

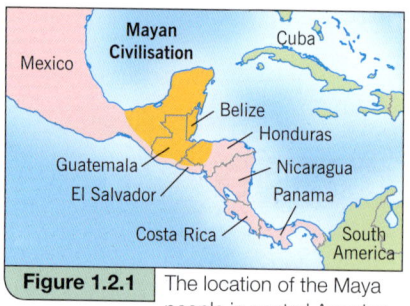

Figure 1.2.1 The location of the Maya people in central America.

EXAM TIP

Remember that the Mayan empire was continually expanding: communications, trade and roads were important.

The emergence of Mayan society

The Maya were the oldest of the three empires in Central and South America (the others were Aztec and Inca). Their empire stretched from Southern Mexico in the North to Nicaragua in the South and they flourished during the Classical Period, between 250 and 900 CE (Figure 1.2.1).

A network of city states

By 200 CE the Mayan people had evolved from small agricultural villages into city dwellers. These cities were political, religious and trading centres and comprised temples, palaces, plazas, religious pyramids and ball courts. Roads connected cities and runners carried news from one to another. During the Classical period there were over 45 cities with between 1,500 and 100,000 people. Cities included Coba, Copan, Tikal and Rio Azul.

Mayan society

Mayan society was stratified and everyone knew his place. The most powerful class included leaders called *ahaw* and *halach uinic,* and beneath them were *ah kinob,* priests, and *batabs*, nobles. *Pploms* were political officials who were also part of the military, and under them were labourers and skilled artisans such as farmers, architects, stone cutters and carpenters. War captives became slaves and servants in the lowest class.

The Maya were obsessed with building temples, which needed a large labour force. Great temples, elaborate pyramids and places were used for religious rites, burial chambers and living quarters for nobles. Houses were made of stone and clay and walls were painted.

Mayan society was patriarchal, so the man was dominant in the family. Babies were blessed by priests and their foreheads were flattened for beauty and intelligence. Looking cross-eyed was considered a sign of beauty. Men wore an *ex* (loin cloth) and *pati* (larger cotton shirts). Women were in charge of domestic duties. Married women wore jewellery and elaborate headdresses.

Religious beliefs

The spirit world was very important to the Maya; they believed in many gods which were good and evil and which controlled daily life. The ruler was semi-divine and was an intermediary between men and gods, interpreting events and messages of the gods. The Maya believed in an afterlife, but only those who were sacrificed went straight to heaven.

Religious activities included science, astrology and mathematics. Priests used them to forecast eclipses, and to decide when to plant and harvest. Priests practised divination, that is predicting the future. The chief priest, the *ahaucan*, was an advisor to the *ahaw* and decided which days would be sacred, for worship and festivals. The *chilane*, who had visionary power, and the *nacom*, who performed human sacrifice, were lesser priests.

The Maya invented a *haab*, a lunar calendar of 18 months, or *uinals*. The year was 365 days long and which had an extra 20-day month every five years.

Religious activities also included dancing and games, for example *pok-a-tok*, a ball game. The winners were heroes and the losers were sacrificed.

Political organisation

During the classical period city-states were run by nobles. Several **dynasties** rose and fell. The ruler of the Maya, the *ahaw*, lived in the city. Towns and villages round the city-state were administered by sub-lords, the *sajalob*, and represented by a chief, the *bhaah sahal*.

The *halach uinic* governed the city-state for the *ahaw*, and he was helped by a council of chiefs and priests known as *ah cuch cabob*. The *batabobs* were lesser chiefs responsible for the day-to-day running of a village. It was an inherited position. *Nacoms*, war chiefs elected for proving themselves in war, were part of the political system. They lived a regimented life, abstaining from alcohol and women, and assisted officials with the daily collection of taxes and planting of crops.

Agriculture

The Maya lived in tropical forests which were practically impenetrable. They drained swamps and built irrigation canals and terraces. Forests were cleared. Agriculture was the basis of their economy. Each farmer was allotted a piece of land to grow crops (*milpas*), with crop rotation used to keep the soil fertile. At harvest time the priests and nobles received a share as tribute. Food and grain were stored for times of scarcity in *chultuns,* underground dug-outs.

Economic patterns and trade

Crops were also grown, with shells, cocoa beans and precious stones used as money. Traded items included fish, squash, potatoes, corn, honey beans, fruits and raw materials such as limestone, marble, jade, wood, copper and gold. The *pploms*, the merchants, used the many waterways to carry goods throughout the city-states.

The Maya depended on a skilled and semi-skilled artisan middle class which produced jewellery, carvings, toys, weapons, paper, books and furniture.

Reasons for decline

By the 9th and 10th centuries Mayan Society had begun to decline. People abandoned the cities which became overgrown. The decline was caused by drought, environmental disaster and deforestation.

ACTIVITY

Undertake some research and identify Mayan inventions in mathematics, astronomy and writing.

KEY TERMS

Dynasty: a series of rulers who have inherited the title from a relative.

SUMMARY QUESTIONS

1. Describe the social and political organisation of the Mayans.
2. Explain how the Mayan economy was structured to meet the needs of an expanding empire.
3. Assess the role of religion in Mayan society.

KEY POINTS

- Mayan society was originally class-based.
- Each class had a specific role in society.
- Mayan city states were centres of their civilisation.
- Mayan life was controlled by religious beliefs and the priests.
- Mayan society was male-dominated.
- Trade was important to the Mayans.

1.3 The Taino and Kalinago

LEARNING OUTCOMES

At the end of this topic you should be able to:

- Identify the islands occupied by the Taino when the Europeans came.
- Explain why these groups occupied these specific islands.
- Describe the organisation of Taino society.

KEY TERMS

Patrilineal: descent through the father's line.

Matrilineal: descent through the mother's line.

The Taino move into the Greater Antilles

The Taino settled in the Greater Antilles between 250 CE and 1500 CE. They populated the island of the Bahamas, Cuba, Hispaniola (Haiti and the Dominican Republic) and Puerto Rico.

Taino society

Taino settlements ranged in number from small family units of 150 to as many as 4,000 people. The largest settlements were located in Cuba, Hispaniola and Puerto Rico. These islands were divided into provinces which were ruled by *caciques*, with sub-*caciques* governing smaller districts. Villages were ruled by a headman and had plazas and ball courts.

Taino society was made up of close family relations. Both **patrilineal** and **matrilineal** descent existed. The men prepared the land for agriculture, hunted and fished. The women did the planting, weeding, fertilising, harvesting, food preparation and they also made pottery. While men were naked women did wear a loin cloth. Some women wore beads and feathers. Both sexes painted their bodies. Monogamy was practised by the people, but the chief was polygamous.

The *cacique's* role was to organise the farming, hunting and storage of food. The *cacique* was an absolute leader and negotiated with other villages over disputes, treaties and to keep the peace. When a *cacique* became old he or she was strangled to death, wrapped in cotton and buried with ornaments. Because of the rules of heredity, it was not uncommon to have a female *cacique*, as in the case of Anacanoa in Hispaniola.

The Taino used a variety of plant dyes, especially *roucou*. Dyes were used on the body, cloths and pottery. Houses were round with thatched roofs, large houses had porches and the chief's home had several rooms. Taino made pottery that was not glazed, but there were markings and most vessels had rims for easy pouring. They were used to store food and as funeral urns. The Taino were excellent basket weavers and created a double-weaved wood and leaf basket to carry water.

The Taino loved festivities and celebrated weddings and the naming of babies. There was singing and dancing and instruments used included drums, pipes and gongs. They also played a ball game called *batos* and played on a field called a *batey*.

The Kalinago in the Lesser Antilles

The Kalinago were the last group to enter the Caribbean around the 13th century from the Orinoco region. They were still moving up the Lesser Antilles and had reached the Virgin Islands when Columbus

Figure 1.3.1 A stone Taino axe.

arrived in 1492. The Kalinago therefore settled the Lesser Antilles from Trinidad and Tobago to the Leeward Islands.

Kalinago society

Kalinago villages were small and built around a square or plaza. In these squares there was a central fire. All land was owned communally but canoes and ornaments were private property. Houses were small, oval and built of wood. The *carbet,* or meeting hall, was located in the middle of the village.

The Kalinago chief was called the *ubutu* (or *ouboutou*). He was chosen for his prowess, either for killing a number of Taino men or bringing back the head of a *cacique*. Competition for the position of chief led to rivalry and intrigue. The *ubutu* was the village commander and was assisted by the *ubutu maliarici*, his many lieutenants. There was also a commander of the canoes, the *naharlene* and a captain of the crew, the *tiubutuil*. To prove their prowess warriors went through an initiation rite that tested their power to endure pain.

Women and men lived separately but men were polygamous. Women were obtained from raids on Taino villages, and so there was a similarity in their language and culture. The women worked in the field planting and harvesting crops, and they also wove cotton, cooked the food and made pottery. It was a patriarchal society.

Men and women wore loin cloths and used plant dyes to colour them. They also painted and tattooed their bodies with dye. Ceremonies were common, especially for the birth of a child. Boys were initiated in the art of war at puberty when they would be separated from their parents. The *Itehwenne* was a religious festival which was held in the *carbet*. It lasted many days and involved a lot of drinking.

The Kalinago were potters. They used many different layers of clay, adding rims to give strength to the vessels and painted the pottery in different colours. They made strong hammocks and stools called *matoutou*. They preserved meat by drying and smoking it or soaking it in cassava juice.

The Kalinago were semi-nomadic and moved from island to island using large canoes. Villages were located near rivers or the sea to give easy access to waterways in times of raids. Because they were always preparing for raids, they were never in one place for long.

SUMMARY QUESTIONS

1. Explain the settlement patterns of the Taino and Kalinago in the Caribbean.
2. Describe the political organisation of the Taino and Kalinago.
3. Identify four ways in which the Taino and Kalinago were similar and four ways in which they were different.

DID YOU KNOW?

Both the Tainos and Kalinagos occupied Puerto Rico and Trinidad.

ACTIVITY

On a map of the Caribbean and South America, locate the original homes of the Taino and Kalinago. Trace their movements from these homes to the territories they occupied when the Europeans came.

EXAM TIP

Make sure you remember these names: a Taino chief was called a *cacique*. A Kalinago chief was called an *ubutu* or *ouboutou*.

KEY POINTS

- The Taino arrived in the Caribbean before the Kalinago.
- Taino society was organised for permanence.
- The Kalinagos were semi-nomadic.
- The Taino and Kalinago depended on the environment for shelter and sustenance.

1.4 The Taino: art forms, beliefs and technology

LEARNING OUTCOMES

At the end of this topic you should be able to:

- Describe the religious beliefs of the Taino.
- Identify the art forms of the Taino.
- Outline the main technological advances of the Taino.
- State the key music, dance and oral stories of the Taino.
- Explain how the Taino developed agriculture.

KEY TERMS

Shaman: a priest who claimed to be the only being in contact with a god.

Beliefs

The Taino respected and venerated nature and believed in a spirit world. *Zemis,* idols or gods made of gold, stone and bone, were placed around the person and homes of Tainos to ward off evil, sickness and war. Some of these protective spirits represented fertility while others gave strength.

Tainos believed in a sky god, a god of rain, sun and wind, an earth goddess and in a heaven where the soul went after death. The Taino stayed indoors at night because they believed that spirits, called *opia*, would come out and possess them. The *cacique* and **shaman** communicated with the spirits on behalf of the people. To pray, the Taino shaman would sniff *cahoba*, a powerful herb, which allowed him to travel to the spirit world and commune with the spirits.

Art forms

Taino art could be seen in all aspects of their daily life, from their homes to canoes. Their homes were built of hardwood with tightly woven thatched roofs. The roof was rectangular, gabled and conical.

Taino pottery was made from sand, ash and crushed shell. Potters used the coil method, layering wet clay in strips and moulding it with their fingers. They put stamped geometric motifs into the pottery. Dyes from plants were used to colour the variety of jars, bowls, cups and trays that were made.

Weaving was sophisticated and specialised. Cotton was used to make nets, hammocks and cloth. Women wove fast and produced fine cotton fabrics. Though baskets were made from cotton, green and dry palm leaves and grass were the main source materials.

Painting the body was a form of decoration but it also gave protection from the sun. *Roucou,* saffron, and berries were used as dyes. Ornaments, including jewellery made of bone, stone and gold were also worn. Other creative objects included ceramic items, decorative belts and sceptres, canoes and *duhos*, ceremonial chairs, which were decorated with carvings (Figure 1.4.1).

Technology

The Taino were good potters and weavers. They created a variety of tools including stone chisels, graters, hooks and cutting devices. They produced sophisticated cotton cloth and were skilled at making hammocks. They were known to have created stone works and good canoes. Goldsmiths hammered gold nuggets into plates which were then turned into ornaments.

Music, dance and storytelling

The Taino used a variety of shell or wooden musical instruments which included a wooden drum, gongs and reed pipes.

The main celebrations, which were the naming of a baby and the *cacique*'s wedding, included food, music singing and dancing.

The Taino had no real writing system though hieroglyphs were found in Cuba and Hispaniola. Stories were transferred orally and were religious in nature, for example legends of their creation and how the sun appeared.

Agriculture

The Taino were subsistence farmers who grew a variety of crops such as cassava, the chief crop, maize, sweet potatoes, yam, cotton, tobacco, pineapple, tania, peanuts and peppers. They grew these on plots of land called *cunucos*.

Men cleared the land but women planted, watered, fertilised and harvested the crops. A *cunuco* was worked for two to three years after which it was left fallow for the same period.

Both sweet and bitter cassava were cultivated. Women knew how to extract the poisonous bitter juice from the cassava which was used to make flour and the juice to make beer. They supplemented their diet by fishing, hunting animals like the lap, agouti and deer and gathering fruits from the forest.

Figure 1.4.1 A duho, a Taino ceremonial chair.

SUMMARY QUESTIONS

1. Describe the belief systems of the Taino.
2. Explain how Taino artforms were integrated into their daily lives.
3. Examine the methods used to provide food in Taino communities.

DID YOU KNOW?

A *bohio*, or Taino house, was made of a single piece of wood, which could be folded up for easy relocation.

EXAM TIP

Make sure that you can give examples of art forms from daily life, eg making *zemis*, canoes, baskets.

DID YOU KNOW?

A *cunuco* was a large mound of earth which was formed especially for farming. It would be packed with leaves which improved drainage and protected it from soil erosion.

ACTIVITY

Make a list of Taino activities that made use of the natural environment.

KEY POINTS

- The Taino belief system was based on nature and the spirit world.
- Taino art is reflected in all spheres of life.
- Taino tools were simple, but enabled them to produce high quality craftwork.
- The Taino were festive and used wooden and plant musical instruments.
- The Taino had a diversified agricultural system based on *cunuco* cultivation.

1.5 The Kalinago: beliefs, art forms and technology

LEARNING OUTCOMES

At the end of this topic you should be able to:

- Describe the religious beliefs of the Kalinago.
- Identify the art forms of the Kalinago.
- State key musical, dance and oral stories of the Kalinago.
- Outline the main Kalinago technological advances.
- Explain how the Kalinago developed agriculture.

DID YOU KNOW?

Maboya were evil spirits in Taino religion, but the Kalinago would wear them as small idols around their necks.

Beliefs

The Kalinago revered ancestral sprits, believed in a supreme creator and an afterlife. They believed that evil spirits roamed the earth making mischief. Malevolent spirits caused tragedies and death; to protect themselves Kalinago people kept a *maboya* to ward off evil. To keep the *maboya* happy cassava and fruit were given as offering.

The *boyez*, the priest, was very important and more influential than the *ubutu*. To help the sick the *boyez* inhaled tobacco to go into a trance so he could find out the cause. All illness was believed to be caused either by spirits or witchcraft.

When a person died, the body would be washed and painted and placed in a sitting position in the grave, which was usually in the family hut. Tools and ornaments were placed with the dead person, for the afterlife. They would be celebrated with singing and dancing. The dead were always with the living and it was believed that after three days they rose from the dead and entered the body of the youngest child.

Art forms

Kalinago art was simple. Houses were made of wood with thatched roofs. The *carbet* was built with foundation pillars, which made it strong, and also had a thatched roof, oval or rectangular in shape.

Like the Taino the Kalinago made pottery. It was intricate and made of terracotta. Vines, and stalks and leaves from the cocorite palm were used to make baskets, ropes and nets. Cotton was used to make loin cloths.

Body paint and dyes were very important to the Kalinago. They used *roucou*, red and orange dyes from the annatto plant. Dye was used not only in pottery and weaving but also for body decoration, protection against the sun and for camouflage. This last was useful in war and hunting, to avoid detection. It was considered a disgrace not to wear body paint.

The Kalinago knew the art of making cassava and sweet potato beer. A hanging basket called *matapis* was used to squeeze the juice out of cassava and sweet potato. This was left to ferment to create an intoxicating beer (Figure 1.5.1).

The art of war was well developed by the Kalinago. From puberty boys were put through gruelling training in pain endurance and fighting in preparation for battle.

Figure 1.5.1 A Kalinago hut showing a *matapi* squeezing out cassava juice.

Dance, music and storytelling

Kalinago festivities were very lively with dancing and singing. Birth, the first cutting of a child's hair, manhood initiation ceremonies and burial were all cause for celebration which could last several days and included eating, drinking and smoking. Kalinago drums were more advanced than those of the Taino.

The Kalinago also had oral traditions and many of their stories were religious. Stories of the afterlife included rewards for a warrior who had died honourably.

Technology

The Kalinago used similar tools to the Taino, but created superior weapons. Bows and arrows were skilfully made. The Kalinago knew how to apply both poison and fire to arrow heads. They were skilled canoe makers. They made sophisticated *pirogues*, fast canoes which could carry up to 100 people.

Agriculture

The Kalinago also grew cassava, sweet potatoes and a variety of crops. Their agricultural practices were similar to those of the Taino. Their main crop, however, was arrowroot which was important for its starch content. They also grew plantain and other root crops. Like the Taino, the women did all the work in the field. To supplement their diet the men would also hunt and fish.

SUMMARY QUESTIONS

1. What role did the *boyez* play in the Kalinago religious system?
2. How and why was *roucou* used?
3. Name three items used by the Kalinago. State the uses of each item.
4. Explain three features of Kalinago society which indicate the importance of war for the Kalinagos.

EXAM TIP

Make sure that you can describe features of Kalinago life other than their preparations for war.

DID YOU KNOW?

The Kalinago were active traders as they moved from island to island.

ACTIVITY

Identify five differences and five similarities between the Taino and Kalinago under the following headings: beliefs, art forms, music, technology and agriculture.

KEY POINTS

- The Kalinago believed in ancestral spirits.
- Kalinago art was similar to that of the Taino.
- Kalinago society was organised for war.
- Agriculture was the work of women in Kalinago society.

1.6 Gold, God and glory!

LEARNING OUTCOMES

At the end of this topic students should be able to:

- State the reasons for Europeans exploring beyond their borders.
- Discuss the importance to Europeans of gold and wealth.
- Explain why Christianity was such a major force in colonisation and exploration.
- Describe the factors that led to Spain's involvement in exploration.

KEY TERMS

Mercantilism: an economic theory of the 1500s and 1600s emphasising wealth and the belief that a nation increased its wealth and became economically independent by increasing exports and restricting imports.

The Renaissance: a movement of the 1300s that saw the revival of classical art, architecture, literature, and learning. It originated in Italy and later spread throughout Europe.

EXAM TIP

Remember to focus on the main factors that led Europeans to explore beyond their borders.

The age of exploration

Islam's spread into Europe between the 14th and 15th century led Christian crusaders to repel the invaders from the Holy Land. As Europeans ventured into the Middle East they came across wonders that led them to explore further, into Asia.

The Crusades and expanding trade resulted in a flood of information entering Europe. This led to **the Renaissance** which began in the middle of the 14th century. Old Greek and Roman works, ancient maps and Islamic mathematics propelled Europeans to invent a wide range of useful tools which included ship and navigation improvements such as the compass, quadrant, hour glass and sundial. Ships were made sturdier and new styles of sail added.

As European trade expanded in the 15th century the demand for luxury goods increased. Asia was the source of these goods so merchants from Venice, Genoa and Florence ventured there to obtain silks, spices, ivory and gold. As demand and profits grew, merchants wanted to increase the volume of trade and find a safer and faster route to Asia. Geographers, topographers and intellectuals discussed ways to do so.

Demand for gold

European countries depended on gold to finance wars, pay armies and pay off debts. Kings wanted their treasury filled with gold since those who had it were powerful and influential. As increased trade brought more gold, nations wanted more. Gold from West Africa was pouring into Europe and the promise of gold from Asia was very enticing.

Gold had become a medium of exchange and nations were dependent on it. This led to the economic system called **mercantilism** (see also 2.1). In addition to gold, silks, spices and other Asian products also brought wealth. A country that controlled foreign lands and resources had power over its rivals.

Spread of Christianity

The Roman Catholic faith was the main religion in Europe. The church dominated every aspect of people's lives. Roman Catholic leaders became patriotic and militant in their battle to expel the Moors from Granada, the Turks from Eastern Europe, and to spread Christianity.

Catholic nations wanted to push Christianity beyond the borders of Europe. There was no separation of church and state and thus the church was influential in state decisions. Missionary work was more than just spreading the word of Christ. The new crusade would unite all the lands they found and vanquish pagans and heathens. The Pope directed Catholic rulers to conquer foreign lands in the name of the Church. Nations vied to be the leading Christian state to bring 'souls' to Christ. The Church too gained from expansion as it obtained wealth from conquered lands, thus increasing its power.

Glory for self and Spain

Nations wanted to prove themselves powerful and nationalism as well as patriotism pushed them to expand and gain glory. Ownership of new land and wealth meant victory and power over others. Those that pursued a colonial agenda strived for glory, power and influence in Europe.

In 1469 Isabella of Castile and Ferdinand of Aragon united their kingdoms through marriage; in 1492 they achieved unity for the country by expelling the Moors from Granada in Southern Spain. To capitalise on their victories they envisioned an Empire to gain glory and power. Spain also needed to rebuild its economy, pay off the conquistadores and its creditors after the crusades. Expansion also meant accumulation of gold and wealth. Spain and Portugal were in a race to get to the East and dominate the rich spice market, and acquire the gold that was central to the European monetary system. Spain saw itself as the model Catholic country which would spread Christianity and civilisation. Nationalism and patriotism was spreading in Spain and a military campaign, if successful, would prove Spain's power.

Figure 1.6.1 Sturdier ships with new styles of sails made for speedier voyages.

DID YOU KNOW?

The Moors were a mixed Berber and Arab people of Islamic faith who originated in Morocco and who had settled in Andalucía, Spain, in the 700s CE.

The Portuguese Prince Henry the Navigator did not go out on exploration voyages. He earned the title because of his sponsorship of explorers and navigators.

SUMMARY QUESTIONS

1. Describe two inventions that emerged from the Renaissance.
2. Explain why gold and accumulation of wealth were important to Europeans.
3. Explain why the Roman Catholic Church was influential in European affairs.
4. State four factors which influenced Spain's involvement in voyages of exploration after 1492.

ACTIVITY

Draw a timeline showing the chronology of inventions used in exploration during the 1400s.

KEY POINTS

- The Crusades, expanding trade and the Renaissance were key to the age of exploration.
- Accumulation of gold led to a nation's prosperity and the push to colonise.
- The Roman Catholic Church's mission to spread Christianity contributed to expansion.
- A country's prestige, power and glory lay in controlling more land and having an Empire.

1.7 'The Columbian Exchange' 1: The impact of Europeans

LEARNING OUTCOMES

At the end of this topic you should be able to:

- List the ways in which the European presence impacted on the indigenous people.
- Describe the factors that led to the economic collapse of the indigenous people.
- Explain how colonisation brought about the demographic destruction of the indigenous people.
- Identify cultural changes which European contact brought to the indigenous people.

DID YOU KNOW?

In 1972 a historian, Alfred Crosby, coined the term 'Columbian Exchange' in a book that focussed on the biological changes resulting from the voyages of Christopher Columbus.

KEY TERMS

Encomienda: a grant by the crown to a conquistador or official enabling him to demand tribute from the Indians in gold, in kind, or in labour. In turn he was required to protect them and instruct them in the Christian faith.

Genocide: the killing of a whole people. The Spanish committed genocide against the Taino.

The impact of the Europeans on the indigenous people

When the Spanish rediscovered the Americas in 1492, little did people know that it spelled the destruction of the indigenous way of life. Europeans brought with them a different culture, technologically superior weapons and machinery, new agricultural products such as wheat, barley, oats (Figure 1.7.1), and animals such as cattle, sheep, pigs and goats. They also brought germs such as smallpox which decimated populations, and of course Christianity, which superseded indigenous belief systems.

Demographic collapse

In 1492 it was estimated that the indigenous population numbered around 40–60 million; within 30 to 40 years, however, nearly 95 percent were dead. At the same time thousands of foreigners from Europe were pouring into the Americas, as migration changed the demographic landscape.

Europeans were immune to the many diseases that evolved in Europe; the isolated indigenous population, however, were not. Diseases like smallpox, typhus, influenza, and measles once contracted spread rapidly among the indigenous people who had never encountered these diseases and did not have a cure for them.

The decline of the indigenous people was exacerbated by European mistreatment including overwork, enslavement under the ***encomienda*** system, war and displacement of people from their homes. Settlements were destroyed and forests cleared. The destruction led to forced migration, food and labour shortage and ***genocide***. With reduced populations cities were abandoned and forests took over; animals no longer hunted increased in numbers.

Colonisation

The Empires of Spain, Britain and France all pursued power through conquest. They used superior technology and weapons to impose their will on conquered people and European civilisation and the Christian religion to expand the empire and obtain resources.

The colonial systems were foreign to the indigenous people. In addition to the *encomienda* system, *repartimento* demanded that all indigenous people over 18 years provide a week's service for pay. In return they Christianised the indigenous people, a further means of exercising control.

In their colonial drive the Europeans used tricks, alliances and force to dominate the Americas. The indigenous people met them with diplomacy, and Stone Age tools.

Cultural impositions

Many families and communities were forced off their land and found it difficult to adapt to the new foreign systems. Extended family life patterns were disrupted. Europeans replaced their towns and cities with Spanish towns, forts, administrative buildings, churches, haciendas and plazas.

The indigenous people believed in the spirits of nature. They were now forced to convert to the Roman Catholic faith. In many cases they were made to follow European traditions instead of their own.

Indigenous people were seen as inferior 'pagans'. They were forced to wear European clothing, eat European food and learn European languages. They were now governed by a distant, invisible and demanding monarch. The guidance they had formerly sought from their traditional ruler was no longer available.

This cultural imposition led in time to a new mixed race, the *mestizo*, and of language — the development of creole.

Economic destabilisation

The indigenous people had worked their land as a community but With the arrival of the Europeans staple crops like maize and manioc were neglected. Indigenous people were forced off their land to areas which were not economically viable and the food they produced was consumed by the Europeans. Hunting grounds were destroyed and fish stocks depleted. European animals like cattle, horses, sheep and goats were allowed to graze on indigenous crops or trample them. The indigenous people could not supply the labour needed for the new intense plantation, which led to the introduction of enslaved Africans.

Figure 1.7.1 The Europeans brought new agricultural plants such as wheat, barley and oats.

EXAM TIP

Distinguish between the *encomienda* and *repartimento*, both tools of social and economic control used by the Spanish against the indigenous people.

ACTIVITY

Draw an outline map of the Atlantic world. Show by the use of arrows the different items exchanged in the contact between Europeans and indigenous people.

SUMMARY QUESTIONS

1. Explain five factors that led to the demographic decline of the indigenous people after 1492.
2. Discuss five ways in which Spanish colonialism caused the destruction of the indigenous way of life.
3. Explain five ways in which the *encomienda* and *repartimento* systems impacted on the indigenous economies.

KEY POINTS

- The Europeans brought more misery than good for the indigenous people.
- 'Guns, germs and steel' led to the destruction of the indigenous people.
- The conquest and submission of the indigenous people was all part of the European colonial enterprise.
- The Europeans destroyed indigenous culture and replaced it with Western-style systems.
- Indigenous-based communal sharing was destroyed for *encomienda* plots and plantation systems.

15

1.8 'The Columbian Exchange' 2: The impact of the indigenous people

LEARNING OUTCOMES

At the end of this topic you should be able to:

- Identify the ways Europeans have benefitted from indigenous knowledge.
- List indigenous crafts that have been adopted by Europeans.
- Describe indigenous foods and foodways that have had a global impact.
- Explain how indigenous labour facilitated European colonisation of the Americas.

Impact of the indigenous people on the Europeans

Though the European impact on the indigenous people was significant, the indigenous people's contribution was wide ranging with many of their inventions still in use in the world today.

Items introduced by the indigenous people include the zero, the almanac and calendar system from the Maya (Figure 1.8.1), canoeing, kayaking, tug-of-war and many ball games (the rubber ball was introduced by the Olmec). Snowshoes, hammocks, tipis, smoking tobacco, drinking chocolate and chewing-gum were all known to the indigenous people. Certain place names including Haiti, Tobago, and Palmiste are indigenous names.

Europeans benefitted from indigenous knowledge of the environment and used local people as guides during exploration and marine activity. Indigenous knowledge of herbs and their uses was heavily relied upon by the Europeans and indigenous food prevented the invaders from starving. In addition some crops, like potato and cassava, were taken to Europe and other European colonies where they became staples.

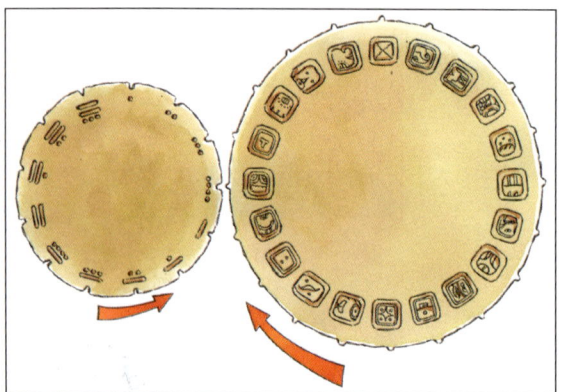

Figure 1.8.1 The Mayan calendar. The two circles show how two of the years were counted. The day shown is 4 Ak'bal. If you imagine the wheels turning as indicated by the arrows, tomorrow's date will be 5 K'an.

Introduction of craft

Many of the crafts produced by the indigenous people have relevance today. The design of indigenous homes has been incorporated into modern architecture, for instance in circular rooms and *adobe* walls.

Different styles of pottery were introduced to the Europeans. Indigenous beadwork and turquoise jewellery are high-fashion items even today. The indigenous people were skilled in the art of melting gold and creating jewellery. Cotton was used to create fine cloths. Baskets and hammocks are popular items and basket weaving is still practised today. Dyes from different plants are increasingly used for colouring and flavouring food as the demand for organic products increases.

Introduction of agricultural products

The indigenous people domesticated a number of species of flora and fauna which have been added to our diet. Products grown included peanuts, squash, pumpkins, tomato, avocado, pineapples, guavas, beans and vanilla. For generations the people had experimented with maize or corn and were growing it for a variety of purposes, including making bread and pop-corn. Potatoes which were grown by the Inca in the Andes, were taken back to Europe where they became a main staple of the people. Cassava or manioc

DID YOU KNOW?

In the field of language North America Indians created sign-language to communicate and trade. Today it is universally used to communicate with the hearing impaired.

was cultivated to make flour, beer and for the meal pepper-pot. In the Caribbean cassava is the basis of a number of cuisines. Corn and cassava were used to facilitate European colonisation in Africa.

For the wealthy, cocoa was cultivated to make a warm beverage. It became a major plantation crop for export to Europe.

Tobacco was cultivated and harvested for its medicinal and religious purpose. It was taken as snuff, chewed and smoked in pipes. The habit was transferred to Europeans and is still in use, though now widely considered unhealthy.

A number of animals were also domesticated which we use today, including the llama. The indigenous people were expert at extracting honey from bees without being stung.

Provision of labour

In the beginning the indigenous people showed the Europeans how to grow crops for survival. Trackers showed them how to hunt and where to find resources.

At first labour was voluntary. By the 16th century, however, Europeans had enslaved the indigenous people and forced them to work on *encomiendas* or on plantations. They grew crops, extracted resources like gold and silver and would dive for pearls. In this way they contributed to the wealth of European empires.

Diseases and adaptation to the tropics

Europeans who came to the Americas faced the sweltering heat and suffered from deficiency diseases, malnutrition and dehydration. There has been speculation that syphilis was introduced to the Europeans, but some historians question this: there is evidence to show that the disease existed in Europe before 1492. New to the Europeans, however, was *chagas*, an infectious disease spread by bloodsucking insects.

Europeans began to realise the medicinal value of local plants. With the help of the indigenous people Europeans learned about the nutritive and medicinal value of fruits and plants. For example, cocoa was used as an anaesthetic and the bark of the willow tree, which contains salicylic acid, a main ingredient for aspirin, was used to reduce fever and pain.

SUMMARY QUESTIONS

1. Explain three ways in which the indigenous people impacted on Europeans.
2. List four inventions or contributions of the indigenous people.
3. State six ways in which cassava has impacted on our diet.
4. Identify three indigenous sources of modern medicine.

DID YOU KNOW?

Adobe is a form of building material used by the Indigenous People to construct buildings. It is made with clay, sand, straw and water. Adobe bricks are put in the sun to dry before using.

ACTIVITY

Draw up a table with two columns. In the table write down the different contributions, European and indigenous people, side by side.

KEY POINTS

- The Indigenous contributed significantly to science, sports, clothing and everyday life.
- Cultural practices from home design to pottery, jewellery and toys are still common today.
- A variety of flora and fauna were domesticated by the indigenous and are key staples of life.
- Indigenous labour was the building block of European prosperity and development.
- Though they had few diseases, the Indigenous contributed to medical knowledge.

Section A, Theme 2: Caribbean economy and slavery

2.1 European rivalry in the Caribbean

LEARNING OUTCOMES

At the end of this topic you should be able to

- Distinguish between piracy, privateering and buccaneering.
- Describe the different European settlement patterns.
- Explain how warfare in the Caribbean undermined Spanish wealth and power.
- Discuss strategies used by European nations to attack Spain's monopoly claim.

KEY TERMS

Bull: often in the term 'papal bull': an edict or law issued by the pope. The term comes from the Latin *bulla*, a seal.

The challenge to Spain

The 1494 Treaty of Tordesillas signed between Portugal and Spain divided the world between the two nations (Figure 2.1.1). This papal **bull** angered the English, French and Dutch, who did not accept the treaty and chose to challenge Spain's monopoly by:

- exploration into the Americas
- attacks of pirates, privateers and buccaneers
- organising illegal settlements in areas that the Spanish were not occupying and trading illegally with Spanish colonists
- war in the Americas, including the Seven Years' War (1763) and the War of Jenkins' Ear (1739).

By the 1780s Spain was no longer a powerful nation in the Americas and was considered the 'lame duck' of Europe.

Piracy, privateering and buccaneering

Attacking Spanish settlements and treasure ships transporting the wealth of the Americas to Spain was dangerous, but could mean huge profits. Raids were organised at bases such as Port Royal, Jamaica and Tortuga in Hispaniola. They were of three types:

- by pirates, robbers on the high sea, who came from several countries.
- by privateers, persons hired or authorised by a government to attack vessels during wartime. Two famous privateers were John Hawkins and Sir Francis Drake, cousins who were supported by Queen Elizabeth of England. Two famous raids were the attack in 1570 on the Isthmus of Panama capturing Spanish ships carrying silver. In 1554 the French privateer Francois Le Clerc sacked Santiago, Cuba.
- buccaneers, specialist pirates with larger and more violent crews. They attacked Spanish shipping and settlements in the Caribbean. Some famous buccaneers included French Jean-Davis Nau and Henry Morgan.

Establishing settlements

The Spanish concentration on Central and South America and the Greater Antilles left nearly all North America and the Lesser Antilles open to foreign settlement. From 1559, under the policy of 'no peace beyond the line' (a new agreement had superseded the Treaty of Tordesillas), Europeans claimed 'effective settlement'. This meant that any European nation which could set up a colony and keep it from

Figure 2.1.1   The Treaty of Tordesillas (1494): the dotted line shows how new conquests were to be shared by Spain and Portugal.

18

being attacked or destroyed would break the Spanish monopoly. The Spanish retained the right to destroy these settlements.

The first settlers were smugglers who used coves and bays as bases from which to trade illegally. By 1600 waves of English, French and Dutch settlers had begun to grow crops to be sold in Europe.

West India Companies were set up to encourage people to come out and form companies. Early settlers were encouraged to build a community and produce crops like tobacco, cotton, indigo and cocoa.

Snatching colonies

A country that could wrestle a colony away from the Spanish was able to weaken Spanish monopoly. Associated with this was the theory of **mercantilism**: a country must take from others or be left out.

Oliver Cromwell had a plan, the 'Western Design', to drive Spain out of the Americas. Admiral Penn and General Venables attacked and took Jamaica in 1655.

French pirates had established a base at Tortuga in 1625, which became the colony of Saint Domingue in 1660.

War

During many wars the English, French and Dutch took advantage of Spanish preoccupation to attack Spanish colonies and occupy territories. By treaty arrangements, ownership of occupied territory was confirmed.

The Dutch were more interested in trade but between 1630 and 1640 the Dutch West India Company settled Saba, Curaçao, St Martin and St Eustatius. The Dutch War of Independence (Eighty Years War 1566–1648) was part of the Dutch campaign for independence from Spain. This led the Dutch to become very active against Spanish colonies in the New World.

Illegal trade: breaking the monopoly

European illegal traders, interlopers, took advantage of the long time it took Spanish ships to bring supplies.

One of the most important products demanded by colonists was slaves, and the extra numbers demanded were supplied by illegal traders such as Francis Drake and John Hawkins. In many cases Spanish governors were ignored when they protested—demand was too great. If interlopers were caught, however, they were punished severely.

SUMMARY QUESTIONS

1. Explain four ways in which the English, French and Dutch challenged the Spanish in the Caribbean.
2. State the differences between piracy, privateering and buccaneering.

DID YOU KNOW?
'Buccaneer' originally meant men who smoked meat over a wooden frame, a *boucan*.

EXAM TIP
Make sure you can explain how countries like England and France wrested colonies away from the Spanish.

DID YOU KNOW?
The dates of the main Anglo-Dutch wars were 1652–4, 1665–7 and 1672–8.

ACTIVITY
Draw a map of the Caribbean and colour code the territories owned by different European nations during the 1700s.

KEY POINTS
- Spain was challenged by the English, French and Dutch by piracy, illegal settlement and war
- There were three types of raids on the Spanish: piracy, privateering and buccaneering
- Mercantilism was an economic system that formed the basis for operations against Spanish colonies.
- Several European wars fought in the Caribbean undermined Spanish monopoly.
- Europeans exploited the desperation of Spanish settlers by illegally trading with them.

2.2 Tropical crops for Europe

LEARNING OUTCOMES

At the end of this topic you should be able to:

- Explain why certain crops were planted in the Caribbean for export
- List the territories that grew cotton, cocoa and coffee.
- Describe the process of tobacco production and sale.
- Describe the development of the logwood and mahogany industries.

DID YOU KNOW?

Tobacco was not perishable, nor bulky. It did not need much land, nor large labour forces. Large profits could be made by planters.

KEY TERMS

Indigenous: belonging by birth, or occurring naturally in a region.

Planting the colonies

In the 17th century merchant houses employed lord proprietors to organise colonies and recruit colonists to grow profitable crops. Luxury goods like tobacco, cotton, cocoa, coffee, indigo and timber were in high demand, suited to the tropical climate of the Caribbean and were not perishable.

Early settlers faced hardships, hurricanes, disease and drought, and attacks from the Spanish and Kalinago. They also had to grow food crops to survive; crops like cassava and maize became very important.

Tobacco

Tobacco was first introduced by the **indigenous** people to the Europeans. Demand increased as smoking or taking snuff became fashionable. For a short period in the 1600s 'tobacco was king'.

By the mid-17th century cheaper but better quality Virginian tobacco flooded the market. Prices dropped and tobacco planters moved to sugar cultivation.

Cotton

Christopher Columbus noticed the cotton garments worn by indigenous people. As a commercial crop, cotton was first grown by the English colonists in St Christopher and Barbados in the 1620s and by the French in Martinique, Guadeloupe and St Christopher. With greater demand output grew between 1625 and 1645. Sea Island cotton, the major variety grown, was of high quality, soft and much prized.

Cotton degraded more quickly than tobacco and sugar and it required more labour. Competition from American cotton caused prices to drop. With the changeover to sugar some planters gave up on cotton. Where it continued to exist in the 18th century, pests like the boll weevil and chenille severely damaged the industry.

Cocoa

First used by the Mayan and Aztec elite as a beverage, cocoa was carried by Cortez to Spain in 1528. It soon became popular in Europe in the 1600s, not only as a beverage, but as confectionery. By 1657 chocolate houses were opening up in London and Paris.

Cocoa was introduced to Trinidad by the indigenous people and cultivated under Spanish rule, especially after 1783 when it was an export crop. Under British rule, there was a significant swing to sugar cultivation which offered huge profits. Large-scale cocoa cultivation occurred from 1870 when tea and confectionery became fashionable in Europe. Several Caribbean countries diversified into cocoa production when the market for sugar declined in the late 1800s and early 1900s. The cocoa industry in the Caribbean declined when competition from producers in Africa and Asia caused prices to fall and the industry was plagued by diseases and pests.

Cocoa production soon spread to areas like Africa and Asia and this competition, coupled with blight and diseases, caused cocoa to decline.

Coffee

First introduced into Martinique in 1720 and from there to Jamaica in 1728, the popularity and demand for coffee grew in the 18th century, putting it in competition with tea (Figure 2.2.1). Production in St Domingue overtook that of Martinique. After the revolution Cuban coffee became important.

Logwood to mahogany

Logwood

Logwood was produced in Belize (then British Honduras). The first lucrative period was between 1600 and 1780, after which a glut caused a price slump and a collapse of the industry.

Mahogany

This hardwood was important for furniture and construction and became lucrative in the 1600s and 1700s. In 1724 enslaved Africans were brought in to cut mahogany and by the 1770s they were doing the bulk of the work. Mahogany was a seasonal job, with the enslaved spending months in the forest housed in makeshift tents.

The workforce included gangs of armed huntsmen, axe cutters and cattlemen who were organised in gangs to locate, cut and transport trees. They were unsupervised for extended periods. The relationship between planter and enslaved in the mahogany works had a stronger element of trust because of the nature of the process of mahogany harvesting.

There was division of labour, with women relegated to the domestic sphere. Belize lumber production continued to be prosperous well into the 1700s.

Figure 2.2.1 Blue Mountain Coffee from Jamaica is still one of the most highly prized brands.

EXAM TIP

Pay attention to the ways in which the needs of different crops affected the production methods and use of labour.

ACTIVITY

Describe the organisation of labour in the mahogany woods.

KEY POINTS

- Tobacco, cotton, cocoa, coffee, logwood and mahogany were developed as commercial crops in the Caribbean.
- Tobacco was one of the first major crops demanded due to the fashion of smoking and taking as snuff.
- Sea Island cotton was a prized material produced in the Caribbean.
- Coffee introduced by the French was popular in the 1700s; Blue Mountain is still highly prized.
- The organisation of labour in the logwood and mahogany industries found in Belize was different from sugar and other crops.

SUMMARY QUESTIONS

1. State three reasons why tobacco cultivation was popular among early settlers.
2. Explain why cocoa and cotton did not become major commercial crops in the Caribbean in the 1600s.
3. List the territories that produced cocoa and coffee in this period.
4. Compare the production processes for logwood and mahogany with sugar.

2.3 The sugar revolution

> **LEARNING OUTCOMES**
>
> At the end of this topic you should be able to:
>
> - Identify the factors that caused the change from tobacco to sugar production.
> - Explain how Dutch involvement assisted the development of the sugar industry.
> - Define the sugar revolution.
> - Assess the impact of the sugar revolution on Caribbean society and economy.

> **KEY TERMS**
>
> **Sugar revolution**: the transformation that came over Caribbean society as a result of the change from tobacco to sugar production.

> **DID YOU KNOW?**
>
> It was the Dutch who learned the process of sugar production from the Portuguese at Pernambuco, Brazil. They transferred that knowledge to the English and French planters in the West Indies.

The move to sugar

The sugar cane plant is a tropical plant, indigenous to the South Pacific. It was taken to India, and then Arab traders brought it to the Middle East. Europeans introduced it to the New World.

The term '**sugar revolution**' refers to the changes which occurred in the Caribbean as a result of the change of crop from tobacco to sugar (Figure 2.3.1). Caribbean society and economy were transformed by changes in the size of plantations, land-use patterns, demand and price of land, the nature and quantity of labour, the composition of the population, marketing procedures, capital investments, profit generation, social and political organisation.

Figure 2.3.1 Tobacco plants and sugar cane: when tobacco prices fell and the crop became less profitable, planters changed to the production of sugar.

The change from tobacco

By mid-17th century tobacco faced competition from Virginia and South Asian tobacco. This resulted in a glut and prices dropped.

Sugar cane was non-perishable, not bulky and easily transported. It required a large acreage to be profitable, which caused an increase in demand and prices for land.

The production of sugar was labour-intensive, resulting in the import of large numbers of workers, enslaved Africans. West Indian society changed from being a small population of white planters and indentured labourers to a large population of whites and mainly blacks. The white class were socially and politically dominant and the enslaved Africans were at the base of the hierarchy. A new trading pattern, the 'triangular trade', emerged, linking Europe, Africa and the Caribbean.

The Dutch contribution

The Dutch provided capital, expertise, credit and goods, enslaved labour, shipping and markets so they could get the sugar industry under way. When the Dutch were expelled European entrepreneurs and companies replaced them.

Impact of the sugar revolution

Tobacco only needed a small labour force, usually indentured. With the changeover to sugar, however, much more labour was needed. Sugar production needed labour to plant, harvest, store and transport the crop. Indigenous and indentured labour were neither sufficient nor suitable. African labour, was cheap and easily available.

As the sugar industry expanded, so did the demand for enslaved Africans. This resulted in a horrific, but lucrative, trade in people.

> **EXAM TIP**
>
> When answering questions on the sugar revolution, focus on the transformation of society and economy.

ACTIVITY

Copy and complete the table below to make a comparison between tobacco and sugar production.

	Tobacco production	Sugar production
Land		
Labour		
Capital		
Social structure		
Population size		
Population structure		

SUMMARY QUESTIONS

1. Give three reasons for the change from tobacco to sugar production.
2. Explain the role of the Dutch in the development of the sugar industry in the Caribbean.
3. Explain three ways in which the sugar revolution impacted on the Caribbean and its urban centres.

KEY POINTS

- Sugar originated from the Pacific region and came to the West Indies via the Dutch.
- There were a number of major changes that occurred with the change of crop.
- Labour and capital demands of sugar production were different from those of tobacco.
- Growing demand and high prices stimulated the Caribbean sugar industry.

2.4 The transatlantic trade

LEARNING OUTCOMES

At the end of this topic you should be able to:

- Describe West African Societies and Kingdoms before the advent of Europeans.
- Discuss the organisation of the transatlantic trade in Africans.
- Explain how and why Africa became involved in the transatlantic trade.
- Describe the experiences of the captured.

DID YOU KNOW?

As a result of the slave trade, the famous brass work of the Oyo, or their 'lost wax' process of brass making, was lost.

West African societies

Before 1600 West Africa had three great empires: Ghana (830–1250), Mali (1230–1600), and Songhai (1340–1591). These empires were politically stable and were based on trading in salt, gold and kola nuts with North African Berbers. Yam, millet and vegetables were cultivated, goats and sheep were raised. Skilled craftsmen produced fine wood, ivory and metal items. The belief system was based on ancestor worship and Islamic beliefs.

Forest societies

After 1500 major kingdoms evolved in the forest regions: Benin (1500–1750), Oyo (1450–1750), Dahomey (1700–1850) and Asante (1700–1874). They were all involved in the trade in captive Africans. They were skilled farmers growing root crops like yam and reared goats, pigs and fowl. They were skilled craftsmen, especially in pottery, weaving and metalwork and traded with the north and west. They practised ancestor worship and their political systems were organised for war.

Organisation of the trade of captive Africans

The voyage to West Africa took from two to six months. Companies organised ships, crew, provisions and trade goods for the journey. Ships left ports like Bristol, Liverpool, London in England, and Nantes

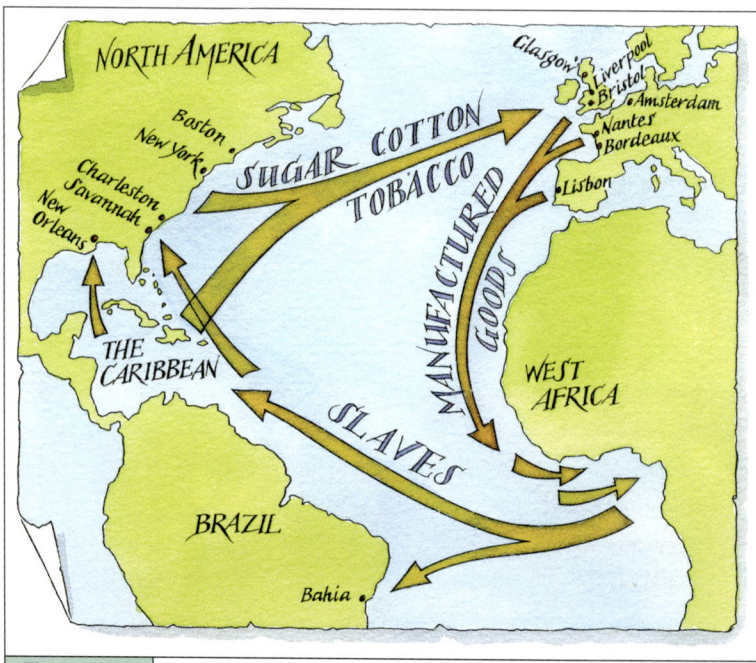

Figure 2.4.1 The triangular trade between Europe, Africa and the Caribbean.

and Bordeaux in France. Items used to purchase Africans included pots and pans, cotton and woollen items, mirrors, cheap jewellery, firearms and alcohol.

Trading on the West African coast

Captives were obtained through raids, prisoners of war, barter, debt and criminals. On the West African coast 'factories' or forts were established to collect, organise and process captives and protect or secure the trade on the coast. A 'factor' was responsible for overseeing the administration of the fort.

The captured Africans would be marched to the coast in a **coffle** while middle men would pay bribes and taxes to rulers for safe passage. The captives were washed and branded and kept in the 'barracoons' until the ship was ready. Then they were taken in small boats to the waiting ship to be brought to the Caribbean.

The Middle Passage

Captives were crammed together and chained on floors below deck for the six to eight-week journey. They became disoriented and fearful and some attempted suicide. They endured abuse, poor ventilation and sanitation, brutal treatment, disease, hunger, thirst and lack of exercise but they did make attempts to resist. During stormy weather or emergencies, in order to lighten the ship, weak, sick and dying captives were thrown overboard.

The Caribbean port

On arrival in the Caribbean the captives were washed and prepared for sale. After purchase the captives were sent to the plantation where they went through a 'seasoning' period, during which they learned what to do on the sugar estate.

ACTIVITY

Write a paragraph that explains what is meant by 'the triangular trade'.

SUMMARY QUESTIONS

1. Describe the organisation of three West African civilisations in 1600.
2. List Europeans items that were used to purchase captive Africans.
3. Describe the experience of a captive from capture to arrival at the fort.
4. Explain why the middle passage can be described as 'the most horrible' stage of the triangular trade.

DID YOU KNOW?

A famous factory was Elmina, a coastal fort in what is now Ghana. This was a Portuguese slave fort built in 1482 and seized by the Dutch in 1637.

KEY TERMS

Coffle: an Arabic word meaning a line of captive people fastened by the neck or feet.

KEY POINTS

- There were major civilisations in West Africa with established economic, social and political advancements.
- The Atlantic trade was organised as a triangle, linking Europe, West Africa and the Caribbean.
- European products, for example pans, alcohol, jewellery and guns were traded for Africans.
- The West African stage included the factory, middlemen and an intricate system of payments and bribes to get the coffle to the coast.
- The Middle Passage was a horrific experience for the captives who suffered sickness, atrocious conditions and death.

2.5 Personal experiences of enslavement

LEARNING OUTCOMES

At the end of this topic you should be able to:

- Outline the life experience of Olaudah Equiano.
- Describe the 'seasoning' process of new enslaved arrivals.
- Give an account of the daily life of enslaved Africans on a sugar plantation.
- Identify the strategies used to keep order on a plantation.

Olaudah Equiano

Born in an Ibo village in what is now Benin in 1745, Olaudah Equiano was the son of an Ibo slave trader. At 11 years of age he was kidnapped and sold into slavery in Barbados and then sold to a Virginian planter. In 1754 he was bought by a British naval captain, Henry Pascal, who renamed him Gustavus Vassa.

As an enslaved seaman Equiano learned to read and write and became a Methodist. He was freed for war service and re-enslaved and sent to Montserrat in 1762, but bought his freedom in 1766. He travelled to England and worked with Granville Sharp and Thomas Clarkson in the abolition movement.

Figure 2.5.1 Olaudah Equiano told and published his own story, one of the first enslaved to do so.

DID YOU KNOW?

Equiano published his enslaved experience in his autobiography of 1789 *The life of Olaudah Equiano the African*.

Arriving on the plantation

On arrival on the plantation the 'seasoning process' began. The captives were branded and their names changed. They had to learn the planter's language and religion. Each was given a ration of clothes and food and attached to an experienced enslaved African who outlined the work routine, job allocation and expected behaviour.

Life on the plantation

Plantation life was hard: the work routine started at day break and ended at nightfall. The enslaved were divided into field workers, domestic workers and artisans. Field workers were further divided into gangs which did back-breaking work in the hot sun all day under a whip-yielding driver.

During the 'dead season' the enslaved weeded, manured, hoed, did building maintenance, cut lumber and other odd jobs. The 'crop season' (November to July) was the busiest time for field and factory workers and working hours were extended. The enslaved cut cane, carried it to the mill and worked in the boiling house. Domestic workers served in the Great House.

The enslaved lived in poorly ventilated barracks or huts made of wattle and mud and thatched roofs. They were allocated provision grounds to supplement their food rations. Sunday was free so the enslaved could tend to plots, sell in the market or attend church.

Maintaining order

Planters employed a variety of controls to keep the enslaved in place.

- Physical: a host of punishments and tortures were applied, from the whip to the wheel, and death. Public punishments instilled fear and obedience.
- Legal: the Spanish, English, French and Dutch produced detailed legal codes to keep the enslaved in their place.
- Social: a racial class system kept the enslaved subordinate. Whites were superior and blacks inferior. Divisions were created among the enslaved to help assert white control.
- Culture: African culture was deemed obscene and savage.
- Religion: the teachings of the European churches reinforced European superiority and African inferiority
- Psychological: the enslaved were brainwashed into believing that every aspect of their culture was inferior.

> **DID YOU KNOW?**
>
> The French enslaved laws were called the *Code Noir* and instituted in 1785.

> **EXAM TIP**
>
> Make sure that you understand the subtle mechanisms of control.

> **ACTIVITY**
>
> Do some research to find out about other enslaved experiences, for example those of Mary Prince, Ottobah Cugoano or Zamba Zembola.

> **SUMMARY QUESTIONS**
>
> 1. State three ways in which the life story of Olaudah Equiano adds to your understanding of the trade in enslaved Africans.
> 2. Give three reasons why the 'seasoning process' was difficult for a new enslaved African.
> 3. Describe the life experience of an enslaved person on a sugar estate.
> 4. Explain the mechanisms used by planters to control their enslaved workers.

> **KEY POINTS**
>
> - Olaudah Equiano was an enslaved African whose life was recorded so we can see what slavery was like.
> - The 'seasoning process' trained the new enslaved how to function in the routine of plantation life.
> - The enslaved were classified into groups, with each allocated specific responsibilites.
> - Planters controlled their enslaved by physical, social, **psychological**, economic and legal means.

2.6 Physical layout and use of labour

LEARNING OUTCOMES

At the end of this topic you should be able to:

- Describe the layout and land use pattern of a typical sugar estate.
- Identify the buildings and their location on a sugar estate.
- Explain the division of labour on a sugar estate.

KEY TERMS

Arable: used to describe land that is suitable for ploughing and growing crops.

Chattel: personal property. Chattel slaves, along with their children and grandchildren, were regarded as the property of the owner.

The design of a plantation

A typical sugar estate averaged 80 hectares (about 200 acres). Most of the **arable** land was dedicated to sugar cultivation, with the rest of the land used for provision grounds, pasture and woodland. Buildings included the grain house, accommodation for white employees, houses for the enslaved, hospital, jail, animal pens and factory buildings.

Woodland

Woodland contained trees and brush that provided lumber used for the construction of buildings, barrels and carts, and fuel for the factory and domestic uses.

Fields

The plantation was divided into three to five fields and sub-divided into plots of between and 2 and 8 hectares (five and 20 acres). Fields were laid out in rows or grids with centre access for carts (Figure 2.6.1).

Figure 2.6.1   A plantation: after the field was hoed into rows or grids, the cane cuttings were planted.

The factory

The factory consisted of the mill where cane was crushed, the boiling house where sugar was crystallised, the distillery where rum was made, the curing house where the hogsheads were placed for curing sugar and the trash house where cane trash was stored for fuel. Also included were workshops where artisans made and repaired equipment.

The quarters of the enslaved

Dwellings of the enslaved varied. In some territories they lived in individual huts, in others they lived in barracks. These were often built by the enslaved themselves and arranged in rows. They had earth floors and were usually located downward from the Great House.

The Great House

The planter and his family lived in the Great House, the largest dwelling on the estate. It was constructed of wood and cut stone and usually had two stories. Its large rooms, which included a hall, dining rooms, a sitting room and banquet hall, were built to allow a breeze to blow through and were surrounded by a veranda.

The division of labour

Women made up a large percentage of enslaved Africans brought to the Caribbean. Since women and men were seen as **chattel**, there was no real division of labour: the focus was on their ability to work.

Women could be found in all the enslaved gangs. Up to 44 per cent of enslaved Africans in Barbados field gangs were women. The only areas where men were preferred was in the factory and in skilled jobs.

The majority of enslaved domestics were women. They were worked 24 hours a day cooking, cleaning, serving tables, carrying water, looking after the planter's children, as healers, midwives and sometimes religious elders. They were more open to abuse at the hands of planters and their wives. Women were not encouraged to have children until after 1808 when the slave trade ended.

> **DID YOU KNOW?**
> The Great House was located on elevated ground so the planter had a good view of the estate and could respond promptly to an emergency.

> **EXAM TIP**
> Remember the strategic and functional location of all the buildings on the estate.

> **ACTIVITY**
> Arrange to visit a former sugar estate in your territory. Make a sketch map of the layout.

> **SUMMARY QUESTIONS**
> 1. List the buildings to be found on a sugar estate and state what each was used for.
> 2. Describe how land was used on a typical sugar estate.
> 3. Explain the considerations that governed gender roles on a sugar plantation.

> **KEY POINTS**
> - Sugar estates were organised to be self-sufficient.
> - Woodlands were important for fuel and lumber.
> - Fields were broken up to maximise sugar production.
> - The factory was the main centre of sugar production.
> - The planter's home showed the wealth of the plantation.
> - Sugar estates maximised both male and female labour.

2.7 Sugar production

LEARNING OUTCOMES

At the end of this topic you should be able to:

- Describe the processes involved in the manufacture of sugar: planting, boiling, curing and rum production.
- Identify other labour responsibilities of enslaved Africans on the sugar estate.

DID YOU KNOW?

Planters did not usually replant new canes but used the stems or cuttings (ratoons) from the old cane. This was called ratooning.

Planting

Two methods of sugar planting were:

- trenching (the main method): long trenches were dug and cane cuttings laid on them. Fertiliser was added, and the cane covered with soil, leaving the cuttings sticking out.
- holeing: holes were dug between 10–20 cm and 0.5 m square (five to nine inches deep and five feet square). Fertiliser was added and the cane placed in the hole.

The canes, which were weeded and fertilised, took between 14 and 18 weeks to mature.

Reaping

The field enslaved would cut the mature canes with cutlasses and machetes, close to the last joint, or knot, to allow for 'ratooning'. The leaves were cut off and stalks bundled and transported to the mill.

The mill

Caribbean planters used three types of mills: animal, water and wind. Mills operated with a three-roller vertical system: a central roller turned against two others. The cane was fed into the rollers, which crushed it. The extracted juice was sent to the boilers. The juice had to be processed within 48 hours or its sucrose content would be reduced.

The boiling house

Six copper boilers or kettles were fired up to boil the juice. Each boiler was smaller than the last, in descending order. Lime was added to the first boiler to allow impurities (scum) to rise to the surface to be skimmed off.

Skilled enslaved workers kept feeding the fire and turning the juice with a ladle. As the sugar liquid passed from one boiler to the next it thickened with evaporation. By the time it reached the last boiler the reduced syrup was thick and brown. It was taken off the fire and allowed to cool. Figure 2.7.1 shows the process of production. Rum was a by-product of the process, distilled from the dark brown syrup, the molasses.

The curing house

In the curing house the syrup was cooled in wooden troughs and placed in hogsheads which were then placed in a drip tray. Hogsheads had holes in the bottom to allow excess molasses to drip out. It was kept here for about a month, when the resulting muscovado sugar was taken to ships for transport.

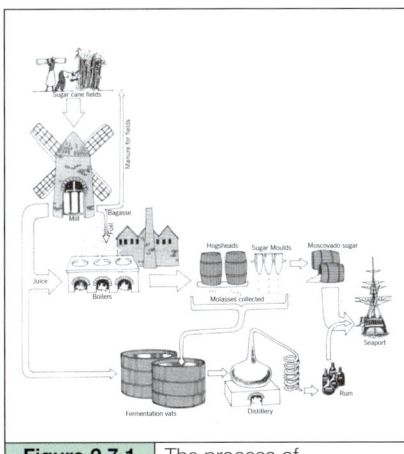

Figure 2.7.1 The process of sugar production.

Rum production

The molasses, scum and some cane juice were placed in a container and left to ferment. After a period the fermented liquid was heated, vaporised and reconstituted. In some cases yeast was added to speed up the fermenting process. The finished product was rum.

Maintenance

The enslaved were responsible for keeping plant equipment operational. Fields were kept clear of weeds and canes mulched and manured. The third gang (children and elderly people) swept the grounds and picked up garbage.

At the mill rollers had to be cleared of cane trash and lubricated. The different boilers had to be washed and the floor cleaned. The furnace had to be cleared of soot and ash. Fences, posts and carts were in constant need of repair.

Other estate tasks

Other jobs carried out by the enslaved were carrying water to different parts of the estate, cutting lumber for furnaces and boilers, making tools, repairing buildings and maintaining the estate. Blacksmiths and tanners were very important on the estate. The enslaved were also taken to towns as porters to carry purchases

Women and children cared for the animals; they collected milk, eggs and meat for the Great House. There were other jobs like footmen, coachmen, butlers, seamstresses, tailors and 'jobbing slaves', including prostitutes, sailors, fishermen and watchmen.

SUMMARY QUESTIONS

1. Outline the methods used to plant sugar.
2. List the types of mills to be found in the Caribbean.
3. Describe the sugar manufactuing process.
4. Explain the responsibilities of enslaved Africans outside the crop season.

DID YOU KNOW?

Muscovado or wet sugar was unrefined brown *sugar* with a strong molasses flavour.

EXAM TIP

Make sure that you understand the importance of timing in the sugar production process and the need for a strict schedule.

ACTIVITY

You are a sugar planter in the 1700s. Write a few journal entries detailing how sugar was produced on your estate.

KEY POINTS

- Planters used two planting methods: holeing and trenching.
- Sugar reaping involved putting cane stalks in bundles and loading them on to carts.
- The manufacture of sugar was an important process which involved skilled workers.
- Enslaved workers were responsible for keeping estate machinery in good working order.
- Enslaved workers were also engaged in jobs other than sugar production.

31

2.8 Markets for sugar and rum

LEARNING OUTCOMES

At the end of this topic you should be able to:
- Identify the markets in which Caribbean sugar and rum were sold.
- State the provisions of the Navigation Acts and explain their intent.
- Describe the problems encountered in making sugar and its by-products.

KEY TERMS

Imperial: describing countries that extended and exploited power over other states and acquired colonies, using military means to defend and control their interests.

Tariff: the duty or tax to be paid on imported or exported goods. The term may also mean the law that imposes the tax.

EXAM TIP

Remember that mercantile policy stimulated European rivalry in the century after 1660.

Control of trade and markets

The early sugar trade was controlled by the Dutch, who were the middlemen for planters. The Dutch bore the risks, provided expertise, gave credit and sold the sugar in European ports. As the industry became more profitable, the **imperial** governments sought to control the trade by placing legal restrictions on foreign involvement which targeted the Dutch.

Mercantilism

Mercantilism (see 2.1) was based on the theory that all trade should be monopolised by the mother country and foreigners excluded. Imports of foreign goods were discouraged and colonies were not allowed to develop industries.

The Navigation Acts

The British were the first to impose mercantilist laws aimed at breaking the Dutch monopoly. Known as the Navigation Acts, they were imposed in 1650 and 1651. The Acts stated that:

- all English trade was to be carried in English vessels
- foreign ships were banned from transporting goods from England or its colonies.

Later the **Tariff** Act of 1661 and Staple Act of 1663 ended Dutch control of trade in the region.

The Minister of Finance Jean-Baptiste Colbert passed French navigation laws in 1662, preventing foreigners from owning property in the colonies. Known as *L'Exclusif,* it was a legal system that targeted the Dutch monopoly.

Shipping

Ships carrying sugar and rum offloaded into warehouses. Agents took care of all shipping costs including freight, insurance and porterage charges, ship duties and warehousing.

On return ships carried supplies needed by the planters, including food, liquor, clothes, tools, equipment and machinery. All these were credited to the estate. All third party ships were banned from transporting goods from outside England, with the aim of removing the Dutch from any form of British trade.

The risks

There were many risks that planters and agents faced:

- fires, insurrection, natural disasters that slowed and/or reduced production.

- tropical storms, pirates, running aground and war resulting in the loss of a ship and its cargo
- dishonest agents who committed fraud and embezzlement causing losses to planters
- sudden price drop due to poor market conditions, low demand and glut
- insufficient, unsuitable and unreliable shipping causing delays and cargo rotting.

The profits

Planters and agents became rich from the sale of sugar and rum. During the 17th and 18th century planters in Barbados, Jamaica and St Domingue became rich overnight. The islands became so profitable that they were called the 'jewels of the empire' in England and France. Many planters were able, because of their wealth, to influence government policy.

Profits in sugar and rum depended on high prices. In the 17th and 18th century the population of Europe was growing, wages were higher than before and sugar had replaced honey as the major sweetener. Demand and prices were high. At one point sugar sold at a shilling a pound.

Imperial powers profited from sugar. Tariffs, duties and taxes brought significant revenue. Historian Eric Williams noted that sugar was so profitable that it fuelled the British Industrial Revolution.

Figure 2.8.1 An English coffee house, where merchants and plantation owners would meet to discuss their businesses and trade in the Caribbean.

DID YOU KNOW?

Many planters became so rich that they preferred being absentee owners, hiring managers to run their estates in the Caribbean while living an idyllic life in Europe.

ACTIVITY

You are a planter and have just received word that your ship has been attacked at sea. Write a letter to your agent detailing the problems that you now face.

KEY POINTS

- The sugar trade was first controlled by the Dutch after which merchants from the imperial countries took control.
- Mercantilism was a policy that protected the wealth of a nation.
- The Navigation Acts prevented foreign nations from taking a share of other nations' wealth.
- Shipping sugar and rum was organised by agents who took care of all the details.
- Planters could become bankrupt due to storms, devious agents and low price of sugar.
- Between the 1600s and 1700s planters and imperial states became rich based on good prices for sugar.

SUMMARY QUESTIONS

1. Define the term 'mercantilism'.
2. Explain how mercantilism was applied by England and with what consequences.
3. List the risks faced by planters in marketing sugar and its by-products.

2.9 African cultural forms 1: shelter, dress, food and medicine

LEARNING OUTCOMES

At the end of this topic you should be able to:

- Describe African cultural forms in the Caribbean up to 1838: shelter, dress, food and medicine.

DID YOU KNOW?

Homes built of mud or clay were called *tapia* houses. *Tapia* is a Spanish word meaning mud wall.

Shelter

West African enslaved people transferred some of their cultural ways and beliefs to the Caribbean. They had to build their own huts on the sugar plantation and they patterned these on styles from their native Africa (Figure 2.9.1).

Figure 2.9.1 | A palm-thatched hut on a plantation: one man is weaving a mat for a bed, and there are paw-paw, ochro, plantain pineapple, plantain and banana plants growing nearby.

Dress

West Africans wore many types of beautiful flowing garments, the best known of which is the *boubou* and the *dashiki*. They tried to recreate West African-style clothing from the cloth (duffield, kersey, osnaburg and linen) given to them by the plantation owners. They also made blankets, dresses and coats.

The enslaved used bright colours in their garments, especially green, yellow, red brown and blue. Women would use some of the cloth as a head tie. West African styles of braiding and plaiting hair were transferred to the Caribbean.

Food

West African food and foodways were transferred to the Caribbean with the introduction of some African food items such as millet, yam, plantain, bananas, rice, beans, okra, peanuts, peppers and pigeon peas (Figure 2.9.2).

Figure 2.9.2 Many foods common in the Caribbean today are African in origin.

Africans also adapted locally available items and seasoned them to make a variety of stews and pilaus. They also made dishes similar to those they had known in Africa, such as the salt fish fritter, and yam rice.

Medicine

West African medicine was closely intertwined with religion. Sickness was associated with bad spirits, while good health was associated with good spirits. It was for this reason the *obeah* or voodoo priest was important for helping the enslaved get better. He or she prescribed charms and potions and performed exorcisms to get rid of the spirit that caused sickness.

West Africans were versed in herbal medicine. They used different plants for different illnesses. Some with herbal knowledge served as 'doctors' and 'doctoresses' on the plantations. In the Caribbean, however, the herbalists had to experiment with the local flora. Roots and leaves were used to cure fever, congestion and problems in pregnancy. Aloe was used for the skin and purging the body. Many types of leaves were infused to make teas which were used as part of a meal or as a body coolant.

> **EXAM TIP**
>
> Note how, despite planter opposition, Africans were able to maintain some cultural practices.

> **ACTIVITIES**
>
> 1. Make a list of foods and plants that were introduced into the Caribbean from Africa.
> 2. Identify Caribbean dishes that have been influenced by West African cuisine.

> **SUMMARY QUESTIONS**
>
> 1. Explain why planters were opposed to traditional African cultural practices.
> 2. Describe three methods used by planters to prevent African cultural expression on a typical 18th century sugar estate and state their outcomes.
> 3. Explain five ways in which West African cultural practices remain visible in the Caribbean.

> **KEY POINTS**
>
> - Construction of homes for enslaved Africans reflected styles used in their native country.
> - African styles were replicated in the clothes and hairstyles of enslaved Africans.
> - West African food and foodways have influenced Caribbean cuisine.
> - Herbal medicinal practices in the Caribbean reflect West African traditions.

2.10 African cultural forms 2: language, music, dance and storytelling

LEARNING OUTCOMES

At the end of this topic students should be able to:

- Identify Africanisms in present-day language.
- List religions which are African in origin.
- Describe African influences on music, dance and song.
- Explain the African legacy in the Caribbean oral tradition.

DID YOU KNOW?

Some Afro-Caribbean folklore characters, like the Douyen and the Socouyant, come from the Fulani and Soninke people.

Language

Enslaved Africans came from different ethnic groups but they understood each other's language. The dominant language was that of the coloniser, but Africans incorporated their words and expressions to create the local creole or patois, for example *mumu*, from the Yoruba in Nigeria, meaning foolish, *all yuh*, and *junbie*, in Angola, a ghost.

Religion

Enslaved Africans believed in multiple gods and goddesses, benevolent and malevolent spirits, and that the spirits of their ancestors would guide them. People used good and evil spirits to help or hurt and believed that their ancestors watched over and protected them. Ancestors had to be fed constantly. This became part of their religious rites.

Gods and goddesses controlled nature and rewarded or punished the people. Death was a transition to the next life and the enslaved believed that the soul entered a new baby. Many enslaved believed that when they died their soul would return to Africa. Important spiritual rites included the naming of a baby, weddings, a wake for the dead and burial rites.

In enslaved society the obeah or vodun priest was important. He or she said prayers to ward off evil, heal the sick, exorcise the possessed, create charms and potions to ward off witchcraft and identify bad people. The Orisha, Vodun, Santerya and Shango Baptists are examples of African-inspired religions.

Music

Enslaved Africans used music in all spheres of life, for recreation, communication and a way to draw people together in solidarity. There were work songs, celebratory songs and songs used at wakes and funerals. Planters were afraid of African music and banned it as they believed it would be used to plan revolts. Africans were permitted to play their music at plantation celebrations, for example Christmas, crop-over, weddings, funerals, wakes and church services.

Drums were very important in African music for invoking the ancestors, stimulating dancing and singing and communicating over long distances. Musical instruments included rattles, flutes, banjos, tambourines and percussion instruments like the *sansa* from Jamaica, the *tamboo bamboo* from Trinidad and the *tambrin* from Tobago. Africans also incorporated European instruments into their music.

Dance

Dancing accompanied music and enslaved Africans used their free time to dance and sing. Both men and women danced, sometimes separately or together, at all festivities and rites.

Dancing included a lot of intricate foot, waist and wrist work. Dances included Bongo, performed at wakes, Limbo, Bélé and John Canoe, or Junkanoo (Figure 2.10.1).

Figure 2.10.1 Many dances have their origins in Africa.

Storytelling

The spoken word was important to Africans who used it to transfer vital information to the next generation. This was called the oral tradition, which allowed them to keep their history, culture, values and language alive. **Griots** would sing, recite poems or act out themes around a fire. Many used imagery and analogy to teach young people life lessons, values, morals and skills.

Enslaved people continued this tradition on the plantation and used it to keep the people together in solidarity, rally them for a cause and inform them about events on the island. The most famous stories that have survived are the Akan stories of Anansi the trickster spider. These stories taught important moral lessons which were used to guide the young generation to develop acceptable habits.

SUMMARY QUESTIONS

1. Identify five African features in Caribbean creole languages.
2. Describe three religious practices that reflect African influences.
3. Identify the aspects of African culture which were banned by planters and explain the reasons for the ban.

KEY TERMS

Griot: a West African storyteller and musician who keeps the oral tradition alive, telling stories and histories to music.

DID YOU KNOW?

In Trinidad the *griot* or *djeli* evolved into the 'chantwell' singer and then into the modern day calypsonian.

EXAM TIP

Pay special attention to the role of story telling in African Caribbean culture.

ACTIVITY

Create your own story, song or poem as the griots did. In your choice make sure to have a moral lesson that can impact the next generation in a good way.

KEY POINTS

- Different African inputs are visible in Caribbean creole languages.
- The spirit world was important to the enslaved Africans.
- African culture was kept alive in the Caribbean through music and dance.
- Dance was an important mechanism of communication for enslaved Africans.
- Storytelling was an important medium of transfer and preserver of African traditions, values and morals.

2.11 Social relations: ethnic, gender and class

LEARNING OUTCOMES

At the end of this topic you should be able to:

- Identify the role of ethnicity in social relations.
- State the factors that determine gender roles and relations.
- Explain the significance of class in Caribbean social relations.

DID YOU KNOW?

The 'one-drop rule' stated that anyone who had one drop of African blood was considered black and inferior.

Ethnic relations

The enslaved were made up of different ethnic groups, for example the Dahomey, Asante, Igbo and Coromantee. In Africa some ethnic groups were at war but many worked together to attain freedom in the Caribbean.

Planters tried to mix ethnic groups on an estate, to reduce communication and resistance. This was not altogether successful. There were occasions, in Jamaica for example, where ethnic groups revolted to create their own society.

The Europeans competed for colonies, but were united in their contempt for Africans and supported each other against African resistance movements.

Class

Caribbean social class was a complex system where people were grouped according to colour, race and status. In the social pyramid whites were automatically placed at the top, coloureds in the middle and blacks at the base.

Within each group there were divisions which were largely influenced by status. This status determined the power wielded by each group and was determined by occupation: the governor, colonial officials and large planters were at the top of white society, professionals and white employees in the middle and poor whites at the base.

For the coloured group, legal status determined class position. For free coloured, colour, especially gradations of colour, and occupation were important. Coloured workers were ranked with enslaved Africans.

Among the Africans, colour and occupation on the estate influenced class and status. Coloured enslaved were usually employed in the Great House. Enslaved domestics, skilled artisans and drivers enjoyed higher status than field workers, as did doctors and midwives.

Gender

Look back to 2.6 for information on how men and women enslaved were employed.

Both men and women cultivated the provision grounds and sold in the Sunday market, but the majority of market vendors were female. As chattel, enslaved men had no power over their family, so the responsibility for caring for children fell on women.

In white society there was a clear division between men's and women's work. Men were administrators, planters, managers and professionals. Women were ascribed domestic roles of running the house, management of domestic workers, organising social events, church and charity work.

Social structure

Figure 2.11.1 shows the structure of plantation society.

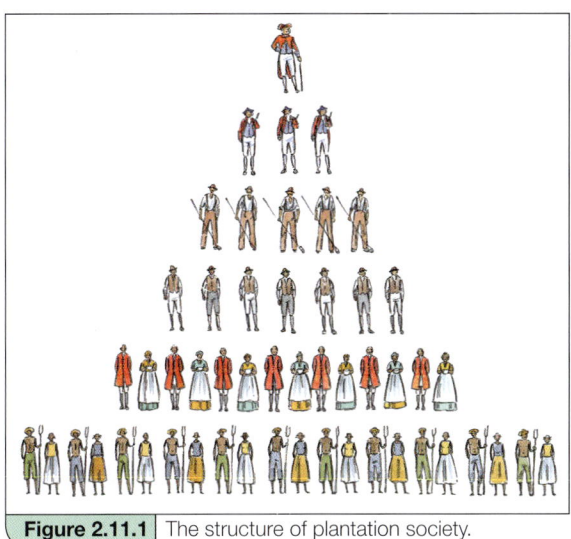

Figure 2.11.1 The structure of plantation society.

Legislation

The planter's responsibility was to baptise, feed, clothe and provide medical care for the enslaved men and women.

Enslaved men and women had no legal rights. Enslaved Africans could not own property, get married, move around freely, meet in numbers, beat drums, practise their culture or give testimony in a court of law. The laws provided for different punishments including lashes, torture and death. There is more information on slave laws in 3.1.

Interaction

Whites interacted on the estate as employer and employee, for example the planter and his overseer. Social interaction beyond this was limited, as whites kept the social lines clear. White and black interaction was limited to celebrations or Sunday market.

ACTIVITY

Copy and complete the following table to make notes on the benefits and responsibilities of planters and enslaved that were set out in the slave laws.

Responsibilities		Benefits	
Planters	Enslaved	Planters	Enslaved

EXAM TIP

Pay close attention to the sub-divisions within the different sections of the plantation social pyramid.

SUMMARY QUESTIONS

1. State the ways in which planters sought to prevent Africans from uniting to resist enslavement.
2. Explain how gender roles were allocated in slave society.
3. Why were the free coloureds located in the middle class of Caribbean society?
4. Assess the impact of race, class and colour on Caribbean social relations.

KEY POINTS

- Many different ethnic groups existed in Caribbean islands.
- Class in the Caribbean was based on race, colour and status.
- Both enslaved women and men worked on an estate; jobs were based on strength, not sex.
- The social structure of society resembled a pyramid with whites at the top and enslaved at the base.
- Whites and the enslaved had limited contact on the estate other than through their jobs.

2.12 Social, political and economic consequences

> **LEARNING OUTCOMES**
>
> At the end of this topic you should be able to:
> - Define creolisation.
> - Explain how demographic changes affected social relations.
> - Assess the impact of economic forces on social relations.
> - Identify the role of land ownership in determining status and privilege in society.

> **KEY TERMS**
>
> **Demography**: the study of a population.
>
> **Huckster**: a person who sells small articles, either door-to-door or from a stall or small store.
>
> **Syncretic**: a combination of different cultural forms to create something entirely new. Syncretic religions have integrated parts of other religions into their rituals.

> **DID YOU KNOW?**
>
> The creole language of the Netherlands Antilles is called *papiamento*.

Creolisation

The mixing of different ethnic and racial groups in the Caribbean merged cultures to create indigenous forms. A creole originally meant anyone born in the Caribbean and was associated with second-generation enslaved people, but has come to represent the blending of different cultures, especially European and African to create something new. This is visible in the different ethnic mixes, language, music, dance, food, religion and festivals of the region.

At the time Europeans looked down on Creoles as inferior to them, an attitude that also applied to whites born in the Caribbean.

Ethnic demography

The original indigenous populations were joined by Europeans and then enslaved Africans, whose presence created an imbalance that changed the face of the Caribbean. In most islands the white population was never more than ten per cent; the mixed population moved between ten and 20 per cent. While whites were located in both urban and rural areas, the free coloured population was urban-based, except in Trinidad, where they were rural.

Land ownership

The Europeans introduced private land ownership into the region. Land owning became a symbol of status and privilege in society. In an attempt to confine land owning to whites, land was sold in large blocks at high prices and there were restrictive land owning and inheritance laws.

Enslaved men and women could not own land and, until the 1800s, nor could white women. Free blacks and coloured people recognised the importance of land ownership and sought to acquire land.

Culture

Caribbean culture emerged from the varied cultures that came to the region. Hybridisation is evident in language, food and foodways, **syncretic** religions such as Shango or Vodun, music, such as calypso, reggae and zouk, and in celebrations and festivals such as Carnival.

Free and enslaved

Freedom was essential to attaining social status during the period of enslavement. This status empowered free people over enslaved men and women. Free black and coloured men and women sought to emulate the dress and lifestyle of whites, who in turn used restrictive laws on dress and carrying arms to prevent it.

Small traders and vendors

Enslaved men and women cultivated crops such as corn and yam and reared animals that they sold at Sunday markets (Figure 2.12.1). This activity led to the development of an important internal marketing system on which planters came to depend.

Hucksters, as they were called, used their earnings to buy their freedom, or manumission, acquire land and/or luxury goods and attain some measure of independence.

Figure 2.12.1 A market in Antigua: markets were an important, not just for the produce sold, but for the contact they enabled between enslaved men and women.

West India regiments

From early settlement militias were established when regular troops could not be posted in every colony. The men chosen came from indentured labourers, freedmen and planters. By an act of the local assembly a force was created composed of able-bodied white men aged between 12 and 65. Under them were subordinate trusted mixed race and enslaved men. The militias comprised infantry with a small group of artillery. They were responsible for their own uniforms and arms.

Normally blacks and coloureds were banned from carrying arms, but because of a shortage of white males, enslaved black corps were raised in time of invasion or revolts when extra defence was needed.

The right to vote

Each Caribbean territory (except Guyana, St Lucia and Trinidad) was run by a local assembly, which comprised the Governor and elected members. Qualification to vote and run for office was based on colour, wealth and property. This excluded all the enslaved and all women. Free blacks and coloured people were not allowed to vote or hold office, even though many had property and wealth.

EXAM TIP

Remember that the defence was based on white and black military corps.

ACTIVITY

Using pictures and charts, produce a poster that shows the different cultural syncretic forms that emerged out of slavery.

SUMMARY QUESTIONS

1. Define creolisation and explain the factors that led to its development in Caribbean society.
2. Describe the methods used by whites to maintain control in Caribbean society.
3. Explain how enslaved men and women were able to attain a level of independence during enslavement.

KEY POINTS

- Creolisation was the creation of new cultural forms in the Caribbean that enriched language, food, religion, music and festivals.
- The population of the Caribbean became more diversified in the time of sugar and enslavement.
- Land was in the hands of the whites who tried to control it.
- Being free determined status and position in the Colonies.
- Huckstering empowered enslaved men and women and developed a local economy.
- Local and foreign militias protected the islands.
- Only white males had the right to vote and run the island.

Section A, Theme 3: Resistance and revolt

3.1 Controlling the enslaved

LEARNING OUTCOMES

At the end of this topic you should be able to:
- Identify the various forms of control used in the Caribbean.
- Describe each form of control.
- Assess the overall success of these means of control.

The need to control

Plantation society was based on fear. The white owners feared uprisings by the enslaved population which outnumbered them. To prevent this, control of the enslaved population was absolutely essential. This was done in a variety of ways.

Legislation

Spanish slave laws were based on the *Siete Partidas*, a slave code to which new laws were added to deal with the Spanish West Indian colonies.

The French *Code Noir* set out the status of the enslaved and regulated ownership and sale. It set limits for punishment and laid down minimum conditions for food and housing. It granted a right to legal trial and some civil rights. Britain did not have a slave code: each colonial assembly made its own regulations. In spite of the many laws, enslaved workers did have some basic rights, which were extended over time.

Psychological control

Planters also used subtle mechanisms of control which involved convincing Africans of their inferiority. Images would be shown of the enslaved working under the command of whites. Detailed definitions of 'white', 'coloured' and 'black' were used, teachings which were supported by the church. Public punishment put psychological pressure on enslaved people to conform to planter orders.

Economic control

Plantation society was paternalistic: planters were responsible for their enslaved possessions, providing them with housing, issuing them with rations and controlling their use of time.

The working day was drawn out to benefit the planters and free time was limited. Time spent on provision grounds, where the enslaved grew crops largely for themselves, was restricted and meeting time was specified. Most of the earnings of 'jobbing' slaves—slaves who did additional work as, for example, carpenters, went to planters. The aim was to control and limit the opportunities open to enslaved men and women to obtain extra earnings.

Social control

Planters implemented mechanisms of social control by creating classes and affording status within the system of enslavement. So some groups were privileged: domestics enjoyed better living conditions, food and dress than field workers and felt themselves superior. Drivers enjoyed status among the enslaved because they

DID YOU KNOW?

Many planters came to depend on the produce of the provision grounds.

were feared. Doctors, 'doctoresses', skilled workers and midwives were valued by planters and afforded status within enslavement. Planters instituted a system of rewards which brought enhanced status to those enslaved who brought information or defended the master or his property.

In this way the planters tried to prevent the enslaved Africans from uniting and the distinctions helped to prevent some enslaved men and women from participating in resistance activities.

Ideological control

Ideological control meant projecting the basic idea that Africa was the uncivilised 'dark continent' and that Africans were inferior. European values were said to be the norm. The idea that Africa was 'negative' and Europe 'positive' was underscored in teachings in schools and in church.

Physical control

Punishment was an important agency of control. Planters were brutal and each plantation had a prison. Repeat offenders were put on a treadmill, flogging was common (Figure 3.1.1), as were public hangings, torture and mutilation. Public punishment had an important psychological value beyond the physical, to discourage disobedience and enforce acceptance of planter dictates.

Figure 3.1.1 Flogging was common on the plantations.

Cultural control

Planters exerted control by exploiting divisions within the enslaved community: Creole versus African-born, lighter versus darker, mulattoes versus African. Planters also sought to make Africans more open to control by **deculturisation**, that is banning them from singing their songs and performing their traditional dances, worshipping their traditional gods. Resisting this control became an important strategy for enslaved.

> **EXAM TIP**
>
> Remember that control was exercised through overt and covert means.

> **ACTIVITY**
>
> List the methods used by planters to punish disobedient enslaved workers. Do some research to find out the offence that would result in each punishment.

> **KEY TERMS**
>
> **Deculturisation**: the attempt to make people give up a culture that is considered inferior and accept one that is projected as superior.

> **SUMMARY QUESTIONS**
>
> 1. Explain why planters saw controlling enslaved men and women as a necessity.
> 2. Describe three strategies used by planters to control enslaved men and women.
> 3. Assess the success of the measures used by planters to control enslaved men and women.

> **KEY POINTS**
>
> - Planters engaged in a range of mechanisms to control enslaved workers.
> - Fear of revolts drove planters to implement brutal punishments.
> - Brutal punishments instilled fear in the enslaved men and women, forcing them to obey the planters.

3.2　Forms of resistance

LEARNING OUTCOMES

At the end of this topic you should be able to:

- Identify the different types of resistance strategies.
- Describe the characteristics of each type.
- Assess the impact of each strategy.

KEY TERMS

Maroons: derives from *cimarron*, a Spanish word which originally meant an escapee. It then came to mean 'living on a mountain top'.

Resistance

African resistance began from the time of captivity in Africa, on the ship crossing the Atlantic and continued on the plantations in the Caribbean. This resistance took several forms: insurrectionary and non-insurrectionary.

Insurrectionary resistance

Armed attack

Revolts, or insurrections, were more common among newly arrived Africans, who were very impatient with enslavement. Some revolts were spontaneous and were sparked by an immediate event or perception of injustice. Others were planned, some over extensive periods of time. Examples of planned uprisings were the revolts in Berbice (1763), Haiti (1791), Barbados (1816), Demerara (1823) and Jamaica (1831).

Marronage

The first **Maroons** were enslaved Africans who escaped from the Spanish in Hispaniola and Cuba, and from French and Dutch plantations in the Guianas. The term comes from the Spanish term for an escapee, *cimarron*. The Maroons grew into large communities while the plantation system was still fully established in the Caribbean. There is more information on the Maroons in 3.3 and 3.4.

Arson

Canefields and estate buildings were prime targets for rebellious enslaved men and women. This strategy brought significant losses to plantation owners. Recognising their vulnerability to arson, slave laws specified punishments for destruction of plantation property, and if caught, rebels were usually hanged. Nevertheless, in many revolts estate buildings were destroyed and canefields set on fire (Figure 3.2.1).

Non-insurrectionary resistance

Go-slow, or malingering

Workers played up to the prejudices of the planters and pretended to be stupid or not understand instructions. This enabled them to delay, be careless and be slow in production.

Feigned sickness

Workers would avoid work by pretending to be ill or prolonging the symptoms of an illness.

Sabotage and poisoning

Incidents of sabotage were most often used when planters were on high alert, making open rebellion difficult. Estate machinery, tools, animals, buildings and canefields were targeted. Sometimes animals were maimed or let loose to damage the young cane plants. Enslaved domestics used their knowledge of plants to slow-poison planters, add itchy plants to clothing and linen or over-starch clothes to make them uncomfortable.

Some enslaved African men and women engaged in individual resistance strategies that were not always visible. These included resistance by idleness, deliberate carelessness, running away, pretending to be ill, pretending not to understand, mocking planters (especially in song) and working within the system.

Figure 3.2.1 Extensive crops were an easy target for rebellious slaves.

Working within the system

Some enslaved enslaved men and women chose to use opportunities to work against the system while still working within it. Ways of doing this included using their earning power as jobbing slaves, on the provision grounds or as market vendors to accumulate funds, which would then be used to purchase freedom for themselves or their children, to purchase animals or luxury goods, or save for the future. Others collaborated with the planters and would reveal plots or risk their lives to save planters and their families, in the hope of being rewarded with freedom. Enslaved men and women also protested against injustice.

Female resistance

Some women used their relationship with planters to maximise benefit for themselves or their offspring. Some would extend the breastfeeding period for as long as possible or take advantage of their monthly periods to escape work. Mothers resorted to abortion or infanticide to prevent their offspring entering enslavement.

The role of women as market vendors was important as it enabled them to pass messages between different communities. They were important links in the resistance network.

DID YOU KNOW?
In Tobago, enslaved men and women marched to the governor's residence to protest against injustices.

EXAM TIP
Remember that all resistance was active.

ACTIVITY
Using research at your local library, archive or museum, identify a revolt of enslaved men and women in your territory. Describe the course and outcome of the revolt.

SUMMARY QUESTIONS
1. Give five reasons why enslaved men and women resisted enslavement.
2. Describe five resistance strategies used by enslaved men and women.
3. Assess the success of any three methods of resistance.

KEY POINTS
- Resistance to captivity and enslavement began in Africa.
- Captives on the ship also resisted captivity.
- In the Caribbean, enslaved men and women used a variety of strategies to resist.

3.3 Maroon societies 1: origins and development

LEARNING OUTCOMES

At the end of this topic you should be able to:

- Identify the factors which facilitated the development of large Maroon communities.
- Explain why large communities did not develop in the smaller island units.
- Describe Maroon communities in Jamaica and Suriname.

KEY TERMS

Mandatory: compulsory.

DID YOU KNOW?

Each island had its famous Maroon leaders. In Jamaica there was Cudjoe and Quao; in Dominica, Balla and Jacko; in St Vincent, were the 'Black Caribs' Chatoyer and Duvallé.

Maroon societies: new communities

Running away and joining or forming Maroon communities was an important resistance strategy for enslaved Africans. Marronage occurred in all territories as enslaved Africans sought freedom in hideouts such as caves, forests, mountains or unoccupied territories.

Life in Maroon communities was organised around the recollection of life in West Africa, allocation of responsibility to all members and the cultivation of food to sustain the group. Supplies of food, weaponry and essential items were supplemented with stores taken in attacks on plantations. Loyalty to the group leader was **mandatory**.

Mainland and Island Maroons

Particular physical features favoured the development of Maroon communities. These were dense forests crossed by wide rivers, difficult mountain terrain and extensive areas of unoccupied land far from settlements. This meant that large Maroon communities developed in the mainland territories and larger island units; smaller communities existed on the smaller islands.

Wars and treaties

The first Maroons in Jamaica escaped during the English attack in 1655. Their numbers were increased by other rebels and runaways and by captives from raids on plantations. Maroons practised guerrilla warfare: sniping and ambushing from cliffs and trees, using decoys and forest roadways to track their enemies and piling stones on cliffs overlooking the roadways and letting them loose on unsuspecting soldiers.

Their frequent attacks on estates made life difficult for plantation owners in Jamaica, where several Maroon wars were fought. Ultimately peace was made with the Maroons by treaties that gave them rights to extensive areas of land, but demanded guarantees that they would not harbour any further runaways.

Maroon leaders were very important in holding their communities together. Two examples are Cudjoe and Nanny.

Cudjoe of Jamaica

Cudjoe was a Coromantee and skilful guerrilla fighter who escaped during a revolution in Jamaica in 1690 and formed a Maroon camp. Members raided plantations taking livestock and encouraging enslaved men and women to join them. Planters employed armed bands and organised troops to beat back the Maroons. Cudjoe and his brothers, Johnny and Accompong, fought years of battles with the British troops and held them off. They built permanent settlements in Cockpit Country (Figure 3.3.1). In 1739, after 80 years of conflict, the British signed a peace treaty with Cudjoe and the western Maroons, giving them 2,500 acres of land. There were further conflicts and in 1796 the Maroons of Trelawny were defeated and banished from Jamaica.

Nanny of the Maroons

Nanny was a sister of Cudjoe. She had been enslaved and became an active leader in the Maroon community who settled in the north east of Jamaica. She became famous for her understanding of tactics in the fight against the colonial power. She is now one of the National Heroes of Jamaica.

> **DID YOU KNOW?**
> Peace treaties were also made with Maroon leaders Chatoyer of St Vincent and Jacko of Dominica.

> **EXAM TIP**
> Notice the spelling of 'Maroon' and its associated abstract noun 'marronage'.

Figure 3.3.1 Cockpit Country in Jamaica, where Maroon settlements were established.

> **ACTIVITY**
> List the terms of the peace treaty signed by the British authorities with the Maroon leaders in Jamaica.

> **SUMMARY QUESTIONS**
> 1. Describe the features which facilitated the development of Maroon communities in the Caribbean.
> 2. Name the territories in which large Maroon communities developed during enslavement in the Caribbean.
> 3. Describe the organisation of Maroon communities.
> 4. Explain the role played by any one Maroon leader in his or her community.

> **KEY POINTS**
> - Marronage occurred in all territories with enslaved Africans.
> - Marronage was facilitated by favourable physical conditions.
> - Maroons attacked plantations, frustrating planters and forcing the signing of peace treaties.
> - Maroon leaders played important roles in their communities.

3.4 Maroon societies 2: setting and culture

LEARNING OUTCOMES

At the end of this topic you should be able to:

- Define maritime marronage.
- Locate the areas in which this practice was prevalent.
- Describe the problems faced by maritime Maroons.

DID YOU KNOW?

Individual enslaved men would run away from the plantation and wait around the ports, hoping for employment on a ship.

KEY TERMS

Maritime marronage: use of the sea as the means to escape to freedom.

Life as a Maroon

Life for the new Maroon communities was always risky, but those in mainland settlements had a greater chance of maintaining their freedom than those on small island territories. Although they were free from enslavement, life in the Maroon camps on the small islands was not easy. They were often forced to shift locations to avoid capture by planters and soldiers. Their numbers were small and they were short of weapons, ammunition, food and clothing. They gathered what food they could from the forest and from small temporary garden plots. Women and children had to follow the men as the camps moved.

Maritime marronage

Forested areas were vital for protecting new Maroon settlements. If an island had forests, there was the opportunity to make canoes and escape by sea. This **maritime marronage** was a problem for plantation owners in several territories. In St John, St Thomas and St Croix orders were issued that trees should be felled to prevent them being used by the enslaved, and laws were passed determining the size of boats that could be owned. Owners were legally bound to take certain measures, for example removing the bung when the boat was not in use, to prevent enslaved fugitives from stealing canoes.

In spite of this, the enslaved Africans were resourceful and resilient and many did manage to escape by sea. From Barbados Maroons escaped to Tobago, St Vincent and St Lucia. From Tobago there was maritime marronage to Trinidad. From Trinidad there was maritime marronage to Venezuela. These ventures depended for success on whether or not the receiving territory remained uncultivated: if it did, the communities not last long. Governors wrote to the governors of the receiving territories asking for the return of escapees, usually to no avail. Freedom seekers also sought employment on ships as their means to escape. Planters posted 'Wanted' notices at the ports to prevent captains from employing runaways.

Retaining traditions

Jamaica has the last Maroon settlements on the islands (Figure 3.4.1). Trelawny Town has been deserted ever since the defeat of the Trelawnys (see 3.3), but the early Maroon camps of Moore Town, Charles Town, Scotts Hall and Accompong still survive, and descendants of the Maroons still live there. In Jamaica tourists now visit the villages, special festivals are held there and in other places the sites of Maroon camps form part of national parks. Maroon settlements in Suriname have remained intact to this day and continue to reflect the traditions of West African communities.

Figure 3.4.1 Descendants of some of the early Maroon communities still live in the region.

DID YOU KNOW?

The Surinamese maroon population totals about 65,000 and is located in six communities in the territory.

EXAM TIP

Remember the factors which helped to keep the Maroon communities together.

ACTIVITY

Using a map of the Caribbean, locate the areas where large Maroon communities developed.

SUMMARY QUESTIONS

1. List the factors that facilitated maritime marronage.
2. Describe the problems faced by maritime Maroons.
3. Explain the response of planters to maritime marronage.

KEY POINTS

- Maritime marronage existed where unoccupied land was close to plantation territories.
- Maritime marronage continued only as long as the receiving areas remained unoccupied.
- Maritime marronage was more common between the units of the Lesser Antilles.
- Employment on ships offered another opportunity for escape to freedom.

3.5 The Haitian Revolution 1: causes and events

LEARNING OUTCOMES

At the end of this topic you should be able to:

- Describe conditions in St Domingue before the rebellion.
- Describe the leaders of the rebellion.
- Assess the impact of the leaders on the rebellion.

DID YOU KNOW?

'Man is born free, and everywhere he is in chains' wrote Jean-Jacques Rousseau. Voltaire urged his countrymen, 'Whatever you do, trample down abuses, and love those who love you'.

The situation in St Domingue

The French Caribbean colony of St Domingue comprised half of the island of Hispaniola (which had originally been called 'Haiti' by the Taino Indians). Spanish settlers focused on Santo Domingo, leaving the other half of the island open to French occupation (Figure 3.5.1). The French imported thousands of enslaved Africans to cultivate sugar, coffee, cotton and cocoa on the plantations in the territory they called St Domingue. France made huge profits from the plantation crops.

Figure 3.5.1 The island of Hispaniola during the Revolution, showing the border between the French-occupied territory (here called Saint Dominique) in the west and the Spanish in the east. The dotted line shows the border before the Revolution, the broken line the border after 1844.

Divisions of class and colour were very marked between whites, mulattoes and blacks. The whites felt that the French government did not allow them enough power over their own affairs and demanded elected assemblies like those in the British colonies. White social groups were *grands blancs* and *petits blancs*, who were contemptuous of the mulattoes and those who were opposed to the restrictive laws and denial of particular political rights, and forbidden from holding posts in the militia and membership of the assemblies.

Influence of the French Revolution

In France the middle classes were becoming wealthier but they had no political power. Scientists, artists and writers were upset with the incompetence of the royal government. Labourers and peasants faced high taxes and rents, expensive food, and they were landless. Some of the educated class articulated a need for 'Liberty, Equality and Fraternity'.

These social, financial and political causes sparked a revolt which led to the French Revolution of 1789. The coloured people of the French

West Indies insisted that political liberty was their right as well, for while they were admitted to the National Assembly in France they were not in St Domingue. Discontent among the oppressed enslaved population mounted to the point of revolt.

Vincent Ogé

The coloureds, led by Vincent Ogé, took up arms against the whites and were defeated in 1791 by the planter forces. Ogé and his supporters were executed.

Dutty Boukman

The enslaved used the cover of vodun ceremonies to spread their plans across the island. They were led by Dutty Boukman who made successful attacks on plantations in 1791, taking the whites and the French troops by surprise. Eventually, however, Dutty Boukman was captured and put to death.

Toussaint L'Ouverture

Toussaint L'Ouverture was an enslaved domestic worker who became a coachman. He organised and led the enslaved population of Haiti against European nations, defeated and expelled the British in 1798.

Figure 3.5.2 Toussaint L'Ouverture: L'Ouverture was a title that he gave himself. It meant 'the opener of the way', the man who could break gaps in the enemy lines.

EXAM TIP

You should be able to identify the leaders of the Revolution in Haiti in the correct chronological order.

SUMMARY QUESTIONS

1. Describe the social classes which existed in San Domingue before the outbreak of the Revolution.
2. Explain the factors which led to the Haitian Revolution.
3. Discuss the role of the leaders in the Haitian Revolution.

ACTIVITY

Make posters of the leaders of the Haitian Revolution and attach pen portraits to them.

KEY POINTS

- Disaffection existed within the ranks of all social groups in St Domingue.
- Developments in France, especially the French Revolution, facilitated the revolt.
- Leaders of the enslaved Africans played an important role in the success of the revolt.

3.6 The Haitian Revolution 2: the consequences

LEARNING OUTCOMES

At the end of this topic you should be able to:

- Explain the course of the Haitian Revolution.
- Describe the features of Toussaint's rule in Haiti.
- Analyse the impact of the Haitian Revolution.

DID YOU KNOW?

The drain on the economy of the payments demanded by France had an effect on the territory that is still evident today.

Haiti under Toussaint: 1801–2

Toussaint managed to get the former enslaved men and women back to work on the ruined estates. He made treaties with foreign governments, built roads and public buildings. He tried to encourage trade, but estate production was low and the European nations did little or no trade with St Domingue. Toussaint had great trouble raising the money for reconstruction and he had to abandon some of his plans. He then decided that St Domingue must become independent.

The French invasion

Napoleon Bonaparte wanted to regain France's lost colony and raised a large naval expedition under General Le Clerc, which, after months of brutal fighting, wooed some of Toussaint's forces and gave him no choice but to accept a dangerous peace with France.

Toussaint gave up his leadership and went home to his estate to live in peace with his family. He was tricked, however, captured and imprisoned in France, where he died in 1803.

The declaration of independence

The independent republic of Haiti was declared on 1 January 1804. In 1844 the Spanish-speaking half of the island became the independent Dominican Republic.

Dessalines

Jean-Jacques Dessalines was the next ruler, until 1806, when he was assassinated. He was succeeded by Henry Christophe, who spent considerable sums of money building the palace of Sans Souci and the fortress La Ferrière (Figure 3.6.1).

Political consequences of the Revolution

Post-Revolutionary Haiti suffered from lack of trade, lack of money, and lack of rulers with vision. Wars wrecked the country, as leaders sought to overthrow each other. The republic was split between the black Christophe ruling the north, and the mulatto Pétion in the south. Despite unification in 1820 under Pierre Boyer, the bitterness continued. Haiti gained its freedom, but became choked in anarchy.

Haiti was not allowed to link its trade and economy into the European economic system. France demanded that Haiti pay a heavy compensation for the loss of investment caused by the Revolution.

Social and economic consequences

The export economy was totally destroyed. The system of administration remained disorganised and governments remained unstable. Basic needs—healthcare, education, public buildings, roads—could not be met effectively. With no proper land management system for decades, people settled everywhere, even on steep mountainsides, cutting down large numbers of trees for fuel. Many of the large population of over 8 million were forced to eke out a living from the land, creating an environmental disaster.

Other European powers feared the ripple effect of the Haitian Revolution on the enslaved population in the region. They refused to trade with Haiti, further crippling its economy.

The wider Caribbean

Haitians continue to seek refuge in other Caribbean states (Dominican Republic, Bahamas, Cayman Islands, Turks and Caicos) but they face entry restrictions in many of these territories. Other Caribbean governments were afraid of the Haitian experience and what that meant for plantation communities, and in the modern era afraid of the financial burden that Haitians would place on their treasuries.

On the other hand, during enslavement, the Haitian Revolution was a symbol of hope to enslaved populations in the Caribbean.

Figure 3.6.1 The impressive fortress of La Ferriere, Haiti, built by Henry Christophe.

> **EXAM TIP**
>
> Make sure that you are familiar with the social, political and economic consequences of the Revolution.

> **ACTIVITY**
>
> List the ways in which Haiti was affected by the Haitian Revolution.

> **KEY POINTS**
>
> - Toussaint faced many difficulties after the Revolution.
> - The French invasion had a major impact on the course of events.
> - The international response to Haiti had a lasting effect on the independent territory.

> **SUMMARY QUESTIONS**
>
> 1. Explain the facts which contributed to the success of the Haitian Revolution.
> 2. Assess the impact of the French Revolution on the outbreak of the Haitian Revolution.
> 3. Examine the impact of the Haitian Revolution on the wider Caribbean.

3.7 Major revolts 1: Berbice and Barbados

LEARNING OUTCOMES

At the end of this topic you should be able to:
- Explain the causes of the revolts in Berbice and Barbados.
- Assess the consequences of these revolts.
- Compare the causes and consequences of these revolts.

Berbice, 1763

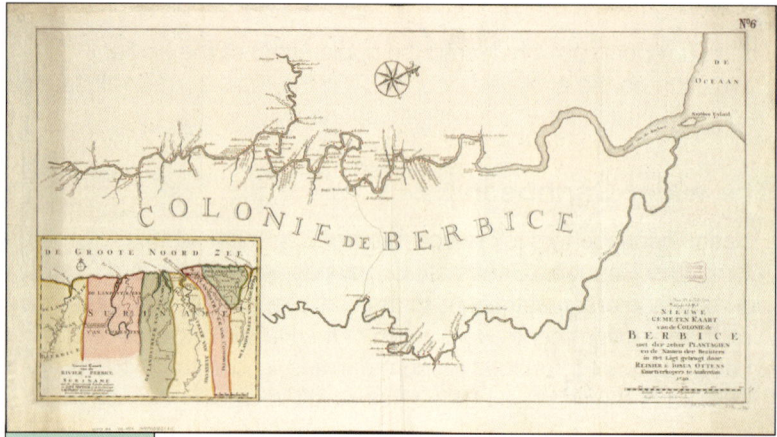

Figure 3.7.1 An old map showing the location of the Dutch colony of Berbice. The territory is now part of Guyana.

Causes and course

On 27 February 1763 a rebellion broke out in the Dutch colony of Berbice (Figure 3.7.1). Earlier there had been three lesser insurrections. Led by Kofi, Atta and Akara, enslaved Akans from West Africa, rebels forced the white population to flee and gained control of the colony for more than a year.

The underlying cause was shortage of local and imported food supplies for the growing enslaved population and Spanish restrictions on the Orinoco fisheries. Brutality was the immediate cause, however, and the eight most notorious planters were identified. The large number of newly arrived Africans who were impatient with enslavement was an additional and crucial factor. At the time of the revolt, the white population had been shaken by an earlier series of disturbances (in 1749, 1752 and 1762), and an epidemic of dysentery which raged in the colony between 1756 and 1765.

The insurgents drove out the whites, occupied estates, seizing arms and ammunition to equip their followers. Looting, burning and killing whites caused panic as confused whites fled to safety in Demerara. Those who were caught were killed.

The insurgents were organised along military lines. Kofi was 'Governor of the Negroes of Berbice', and they adopted European military ranks. By March 1762 whites were confined to the malarial swampy areas of the mouth of the Canje River, but by June the insurgents were losing ground.

DID YOU KNOW?

Kofi is sometimes spelled Coffy, Cuffy, or Kofi, a name that tells us that he originally came from Ghana in West Africa. He and his fellow leaders were Akans, a group from that region.

Coffy was virtual ruler of Berbice from 23 February until 17 December 1763.

From December, the whites had reorganised themselves and with the assistance of indigenous Indian forces, loyal Africans, the Dutch in Suriname, Demerara, Essequibo and St Eustatius and the British, a strong counter-attack was launched. Disunity and ethnic differences weakened the insurgents who burned estates and fled to the forests. Beset by food shortages, disease, poor planning and a strengthened opposition insurgents surrendered; some gave assistance to the whites. The rebellion ended with the capture of Atta in April 1764.

Consequences

124 insurgents were condemned to death. Before his death Atta was tortured by burning at the stake. 16 Africans and coloureds who had assisted the whites, including the leaders Akara and Goussari, who betrayed Atta, were rewarded with freedom and sent to Holland. Many planters were ruined and enslavement was reimposed on the colony.

There was unrest among the enslaved populations of Demerara where the planters fled to safety downriver. There were tensions in Essequibo and fears that the rebellion could spread to Suriname.

Barbados, 1816

Bussa's rebellion broke out in St Phillip, Barbados in April 1816. It spread to the parishes of Christ Church, St John, St Thomas, St George and parts of St Michael, engulfing more than half of the island.

Causes and course

The Haitian Revolution, abolition of the trade in enslaved Africans and increased abolitionist pressure signalled an era of change which planters in the Caribbean resisted. They refused to implement improving measures and became hostile to imperial orders and more brutal to their enslaved charges. Sensing the changed mood and realising that something was happening, the radical enslaved felt that this was a good time to act.

The chief organiser of this planned revolt was Bussa, assisted by several poor free coloureds. There were leaders on every estate who recruited supporters who were told about the success of Africans in Haiti. The revolt was timed to coincide with the Easter festivities, the harvesting period when the height of cane provided cover for their activities. Planters were most vulnerable at this time.

Consequences

The revolt lasted only four days, but it caused significant losses to planters. Damage to property was estimated at £175,000 and 25 per cent of the sugar cane crop was burnt. 144 rebels were executed, 70 sentenced to death and 123 to transportation. Some argue that over 1,000 enslaved Africans were killed. The revolt had a regional impact, the system of British colonisation was shaken and St Lucia, St Vincent and Demerara declared martial law as a protective measure.

EXAM TIP

Revolts have multiple causes but the most powerful underlying cause is the desire for freedom.

ACTIVITY

Do some research to make a poster to illustrate the role of Bussa in the Barbados Rebellion of 1816.

SUMMARY QUESTIONS

1. Examine the causes of the Berbice revolt of 1763 and the Barbados revolt of 1816.

2. Describe the factors which affected the outcomes of the Berbice and Barbados revolts.

3. Compare the consequences of the Berbice revolt and the Barbados rebellion.

KEY POINTS

- There were aggravated pressures on the enslaved in Berbice and Barbados which sparked revolts of the enslaved Africans.
- Revolts were often planned well in advance.
- Leaders of revolts selected strategic opportunities to launch their attacks.
- Rebellions were brutally put down but their consequences spread beyond their locations.

3.8 Major revolts 2: Demerara and Jamaica

LEARNING OUTCOMES

At the end of this topic you should be able to:

- Explain the causes of the Demerara revolt.
- Identify the role of the missionaries in the Jamaica revolt.
- Assess the consequences of these revolts.
- Compare the causes and consequences of the these revolts.

Demerera, 1823

The colony of Demerara in South America had been ruled by the Dutch, but in 1823 it was under British rule. A rumour that the King (George IV) had freed the enslaved Africans but that the authorities in Georgetown were blocking this sparked the revolt of 1823. On 18 August 1823 enslaved attacked and captured many managers and overseers. In a few days some 13,000 enslaved were in open rebellion. Soldiers were quickly brought to the scene and over 100 enslaved were killed.

Figure 3.8.1 The Demerara River has always dominated the landscape. The former colony is now part of Guyana.

Consequences

The rebellion was suppressed. 47 rebels were hanged and others were flogged or imprisoned. Blame was put on the Reverend John Smith who was arrested and charged with having stirred up the rebellion. He was found guilty and condemned to be hanged, but he died in prison before the sentence could be carried out.

Jamaica, 1831

The most violent revolt involving religious activity and impatience of enslaved Africans occurred in Jamaica in 1831. Also called

DID YOU KNOW?

William Knibb was an English Baptist minister and missionary in Jamaica.

the Baptist War, the rebellion was organised by Samuel Sharpe, a deacon in the Baptist church. As in Guyana, it was believed that freedom had been issued by the king but that the Jamaican authorities were keeping it back.

Sharpe planned a strike after the Christmas holiday, to force managers to pay wages to enslaved workers. Violence broke out on 27 December and spread to all the estates in the western parishes. Canefields and estate buildings were set on fire causing considerable damage until the militia arrived and crushed the rebellion. About 500 enslaved Africans were executed and over 100 flogged.

Consequences

Missionaries and preachers were blamed for the uprising. Sharpe was among those slaves hanged, but men like William Knibb were also arrested on charges of inciting rebellion. Baptist and Methodist chapels were destroyed and the homes of preachers and ministers were raided. A Reverend Bleby was tied to a post and covered with tar and feathers.

These cases of violence and persecution in so many parts of the British West Indies were used by the humanitarians in Britain to emphasise the need for urgent action on the question of ending the system of enslavement.

Figure 3.8.2 The destruction of Roehampton Estate, Jamaica, during the uprising.

EXAM TIP
The main success of the revolts lay in the quickening pace of the humanist campaign to end enslavement.

ACTIVITY
Prepare a short biography of Samuel Sharpe.

KEY POINTS
- Enslaved people were determined to fight for their freedom.
- The revolts were stimulated by events within and outside the Caribbean.
- Planters directed their hostility towards the missionaries
- The revolts contributed to the final ending of enslavement.

SUMMARY QUESTIONS

1. Explain why planters were so willing to blame missionaries for the revolts in Demerara and Jamaica.
2. Describe the course of the Jamaica rebellion.
3. Explain how planters in Jamaica responded to the imagined threat from the missionaries.

Section A Practice exam questions

SECTION A: Multiple-choice questions

1. If you were a Mayan living before the arrival of the Europeans and had a **milpa**, you would most likely
   - a farm it
   - b eat it
   - c wear it
   - d sit on it

2. Identify the political features that were common to the systems of government of the Tainos, Mayans and Kalinagos:
   - i   there were rules of inheritance
   - ii   there was a tribute system
   - iii women could become rulers
   - iv   religion played a integral role

   - a i, ii and iii only
   - b i, ii and iv only
   - c ii and iii only
   - d i, ii, iii and iv

3. European exploration in the fifteenth century was possible because of the following reasons or factors
   - i   the Renaissance
   - ii   improvements in cartography
   - iii imperial funding
   - iv   winds

   - a i, ii and iii only
   - b i, ii and iv only
   - c ii and iii only
   - d i, ii, iii and iv

4. Which of the following BEST defines the term '**slave society**'?
   - a The culture of the enslaved is the major culture.
   - b The society is prejudiced against enslaved people.
   - c The obeahman is the key figure in society.
   - d The majority of the population is enslaved people.

5. The MAIN reason for the switch from logwood to mahogany in Belize in the 1770s was:
   - a collapse of the industry because of a drop in the price
   - b discovery of synthetic and other plant dyes
   - c deforestation due to lack of replanting
   - d finding the mahogany was much easier

6. Identify the by-product of sugar that was also exported from the British Caribbean to Europe.
   - a Molasses
   - b Rum
   - c Wine
   - d Crystals

7. Which of the following was NOT considered a negative experience for enslaved people on a typical eighteenth-century sugar estate in the Caribbean?
   - a Provision ground system
   - b Working in the factory
   - c Working in the fields
   - d Demotion to the fields

8. Which of the following was NOT a method used by planters to control enslaved Africans?
   - a Economic
   - b Political
   - c Psychological
   - d Social

9. Which of the following were problems encountered by maroons in smaller islands?
   - i   They often had to move camp.
   - ii   They were small in numbers.
   - iii They were short of weapons and food.

   - a i and ii only.
   - b i and iii only
   - c ii and iii only
   - d i, ii and iii

10. Which of the following was a political problem faced by Haiti after the revolution?
    - a The economy was disorganised.
    - b The governments were unstable.
    - c There were tensions between blacks and coloureds.
    - d Europeans refused to trade with Haiti.

SECTION A: Additional practice questions

1

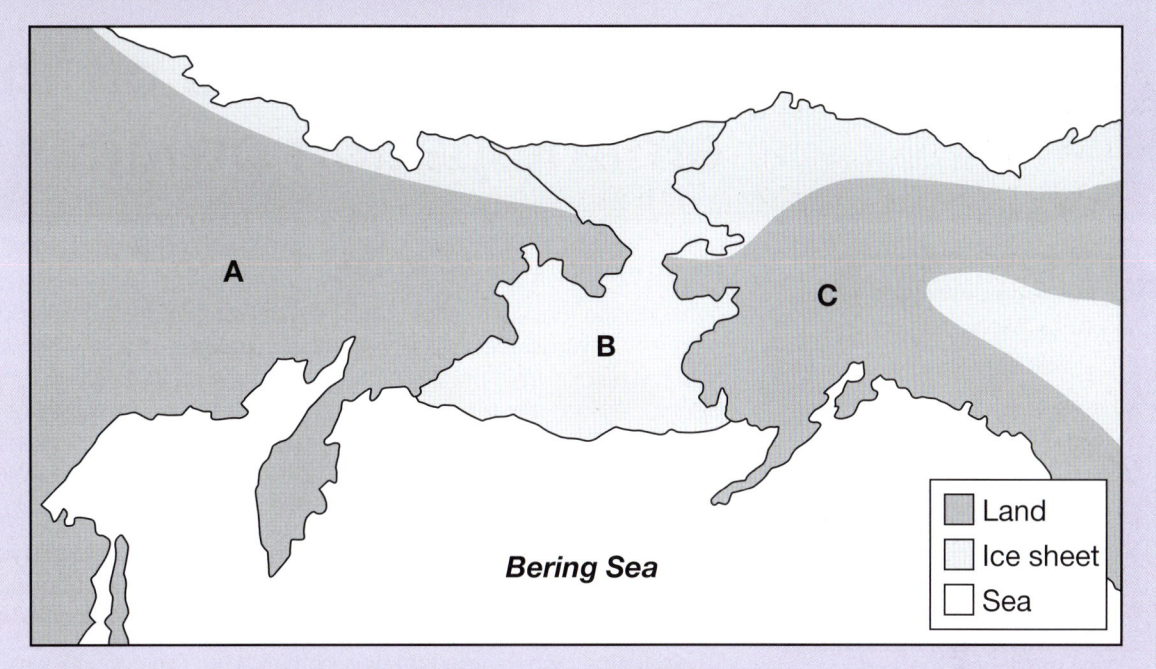

Bering Sea

Legend: Land / Ice sheet / Sea

Copy and complete the map above: name the areas A, B and C and, using arrows to connect A to B and B to C, illustrate the migratory route of the Amerindians from the Old World to the New.

2 a Describe the activities which took place in the following buildings on a typical eighteenth century sugar estate:
   i   the mill
   ii the boiling house
   iii the curing house.
b State any TWO factors that could cause a disruption in the process of sugar production on a typical eighteenth century sugar estate.

3 During the second half of the 1700s the British Caribbean colonies experienced rapid population growth which resulted in the African population becoming 10 times larger than the European population. Planters used a variety of measures to control the African population.

a What caused the rapid growth of the African population in British Caribbean?
b What measures were used by planters to control the African workers?
c In which 3 territories did major revolts occur during the 1800s?
d What impact did these revolts have on the emancipation process?

Further practice questions and examples can be found on the online support website.

59

Section B, Theme 4: Metropolitan movements towards emancipation

4.1 Effects of revolts on the emancipation process

LEARNING OUTCOMES

At the end of this topic you should be able to:

- State the outcomes of the 19th century revolts.
- Classify the effects into positive and negative.
- Explain their overall impact on the process of emancipation.

Negative effects on slavery

Although the long-term effect of the revolts across the territories was progress towards eventual emancipation, we have seen in Theme 3 how the revolts were brutally suppressed, with cruel deaths for the leaders. Across plantations there was an immediate tightening of security and harsher measures for enslaved workers, which included the use of the treadmill. Figure 4.1.1 shows a treadmill in use, with one enslaved worker being used to force others.

Not surprisingly, the planters and commercial classes were alarmed at the revolts, because of the threat to their interests. The uprisings confirmed the belief that enslaved Africans could not be trusted.

To plantation owners freedom was unthinkable. Their priority was to protect their investment by suppressing the revolts and keeping the plantations operational and profitable.

Figure 4.1.1 A treadmill in use. Notice how enslaved were used to punish their colleagues.

The effect on political opinion in Europe

Positive effects on the emancipation process

One way in which people in Britain were made aware of slavery was the sight of enslaved blacks. In London and other cities during the eighteenth century it was common to see retired planters walking through the streets accompanied by enslaved black attendants. Some of these planters, who had been the penniless younger sons of English families, boasted of their new status by parading with theis new status symbol. Aside from these well dressed and well fed enslaved Africans, there were many destitute, some fugitive, blacks in Britain.

In 1764, The Gentleman's Magazine estimated that there were about 20,000 black people in London alone.

The growing number of enslaved Africans in Britain prompted some English people to question the country's laws to establish whether enslavement was legal in Britain and whether racially based limitations on freedom could be imposed on people. Does British law permit the enslavement of others on British soil? Is there any limit to the freedom of a man in England because of his race? The first Englishmen to agitate publicly against slavery by taking these issues before the courts was Granville Sharp, who was joined by Thomas Clarkson, James Ramsay and William Wilberforce. They worked together to make the public aware of the evils of slavery and demanded the abolition of the British slave trade.

The 1772 case of James Somerset served to raise awareness of the whole issue of slavery. Somerset was an escaped enslaved African who had been brought to England by his master. He had been reclaimed by his former master, but Granville Sharp worked hard to prove that, following a similar case a few years earlier, the laws of slavery did not apply on English soil. Sharp's lawyers stressed the point that no man could be a slave in England, and showed that the laws of England were separate from those of the colonies. After much hesitation, the Chief Justice Lord Mansfield delivered his historic judgement, concluding 'Whatever inconveniences may follow this decision, I cannot say this case is allowed or approved by the laws of England; and therefore the black must be discharged.' Very simply, this meant that as soon as any enslaved person set his foot on English ground, he or she was free.

Increased support for abolition

The uprisings gave great encouragement to the abolitionists, but it was a long time before the actual trade in slaves could be abolished. The West India interest was still too powerful. The violent overthrow of the ruling classes in the French Revolution and the cry to disrupt the established patterns of society with 'Liberty, Equality and Fraternity' made the British government wary of liberating the enslaved people and admitting the basic right of equality among men. So for years the motions introduced in the House of Commons seeking the end of the slave trade were all defeated and it appeared that the revolts had served no purpose.

DID YOU KNOW?

Grenville Sharp helped many enslaved people in distress. He worked as a civil servant, but studied law and was determined to prove that under British law one man could not own another.

EXAM TIP

Remember that the ending of enslavement resulted from the combined effects of the resistance effort of the enslaved, the humanitarian campaign and political and economic change in Britain.

ACTIVITY

Imagine you are a humanitarian; write a speech using enslaved revolts as evidence to support your position.

KEY POINTS

- There was an increase in enslaved rebellions during the first third of the 1800s.
- These rebellions generated positive and negative outcomes.
- The brutal punishment inflicted on the resistors won public support for the abolition movement in Britain.
- This support helped to make the humanitarian campaign successful.

SUMMARY QUESTIONS

1. What factors cause an increase in rebellions in the British Caribbean during the years 1800–1833?
2. What were the consequences of these revolts?
3. In what ways did these revolts contribute to the humanitarian campaign in Britain?

4.2 Attitudes towards slavery

LEARNING OUTCOMES

At the end of this topic you should be able to:

- Describe the attitudes of planters and their supporters to slavery.
- Explain the arguments advanced by interest groups for and against slavery.
- Classify these arguments into, economic, humanitarian and religious.

DID YOU KNOW?

The Reign of Terror was a period in the French Revolution between 1793–4 caused by extreme violence between political groups. Thousands of people were executed by guillotine.

KEY TERMS

Paternalistic: behaving like a father, in a way that is well meant but that limits a person's freedom.

Arguments of interest groups for slavery

Economic

Supporters of the system pointed out that the crops would rot in the fields and bring economic ruin if there were no slave labour to work on the plantations. Caribbean pro-slavery groups stated that Britain's prosperity would be at risk. If Britain did not make use of the system of slavery, its commercial rivals France and Holland would fill the gap and develop stronger economies than Britain.

Another argument was that liberating enslaved workers would lead to unemployment, unrest and destruction of property. People remembered the mob rule during the French Revolution, with its Reign of Terror, and the Haitian revolution, and were afraid to have a repeat of the economic losses they entailed.

Planters claimed that enslavement was essential to control the Africans and make the plantations profitable. Without enslavement there would be no profit: expensive security arrangements would be needed to maintain law and order and put financial burdens on British taxpayers.

Figure 4.2.1 An economic argument was put forward that unharvested crops would rot if there was no enslaved labour on the plantations.

Humanitarian

English people who protested against West Indian slavery were told that slaves were not as badly treated as English farm or factory workers. While enslaved Africans were provided with food, clothing and shelter, by law, the English workers were not. Enslaved Africans enjoyed a better life than they would have in their homeland, and the tropical climate and agricultural work was familiar to them. Slavery was a natural state, from ancient times in Greece and Rome as well as Africa. Without slavery, Caribbean societies would degenerate into barbarity. Europeans were fulfilling a **paternalistic** duty by exposing the African to the uplifting civilising influences of the plantation.

Religious

The Christian churches in the Caribbean supported enslavement on the grounds that God had ordained a person's position in life. The Anglican church owned enslaved Africans whom they used to build churches. The Moravian church taught their enslaved converts to be obedient and accept their position in life.

Arguments of interest groups against slavery

The basic desire for freedom was at the root of all slave revolts. Treatment was harsh, unreasonable demands were made on them and punishment was often violent. At times they were not given enough food as the law demanded and planters or attorneys would break the slave laws and codes regarding clothing, housing and medical care.

Economic

The anti-slavery group argued that if the cause of revolts was removed, the financial and human costs would be avoided.

Economists argued that the slave system retarded British business. Since cane sugar was no longer important to the British economy, the enslaved workers were no longer essential to British business. Ship owners did not want to be confined to Caribbean trade and supported emancipation because they were engaged in more profitable trade elsewhere.

Free labour was a cheaper alternative and planters could make a profit without the costs of maintaining an enslaved labour force. The plantation system was forced to keep workers who were inefficient and unproductive and the Caribbean sugar plantations were not producing new wealth to power the British economy.

Humanitarian

The humanitarians appealed to human conscience and morals. Slavery was inhuman and unjust. Evidence of the high mortality rate, brutal punishments and abuse of women and children was used to supported their position.

Religious

Slavery was wrong in the eyes of God. It was contrary to the teaching of The Bible that all men were children of God, brothers in Christ and equal. Some enslaved workers were not allowed to attend church on Sunday. Some planters refused to allow missionaries to spread the gospel on their estates.

SUMMARY QUESTIONS

1. What were the economic arguments used by pro-slavery groups to justify enslavement?
2. What other arguments did the pro-slavery groups use to justify enslavement?
3. On what grounds did the humanitarians oppose enslavement?
4. Why did the religious groups oppose enslavement?

DID YOU KNOW?

The religious view of a person's position is reflected in the lines (rarely heard today) of the famous hymn 'All things bright and beautiful':

The rich man in his castle,
The poor man at his gate:
God made them high and lowly,
And ordered their estate.

EXAM TIP

Remember that the arguments used by pro- and anti-slavery groups could be grouped under broad headings.

ACTIVITY

Imagine you are a planter or a humanitarian: prepare a speech to convince a group of Parliamentarians to support your group on the proposal to end enslavement in the Caribbean.

KEY POINTS

- Planters felt they had the right to dispose of their enslaved property as they wished.
- Pro- and anti-slavery supporters considered the economic, social and humanitarian arguments of enslavement as it affected owners, investors and the British economy.
- Missionaries viewed slavery from the religious angle, based on the teachings of the Bible.

4.3 Anti-slavery movements

LEARNING OUTCOMES

At the end of this topic you should be able to:

- Explain the factors which led to the development of anti-slavery ideas in Europe.
- Describe the anti slavery campaigns in Britain, France and Spain.

KEY TERMS

Age of Enlightenment: a term describing the period in which people began to think that democratic values were more likely to achieve a fairer society than systems based on power and privilege. People began to place more value on the individual as a human being.

DID YOU KNOW?

The Religious Society of Friends, the more formal title of the Quaker movement, was founded in the 1650s. The group believes strongly in the cause of peace and equality. During the 18th century they were an active pressure group heavily involved in the movement to end slavery. They organised lecture tours by fiery speakers and missionaries who had returned from the Caribbean and exerted a great influence on the British public.

The Age of Enlightenment

During the eighteenth century ideas from the **Age of Enlightenment** led to a growing dislike for slavery, and concern about the welfare of enslaved Africans across the Atlantic world. Events such as the American war of Independence, the French and Haitian Revolutions and the abolitionist movement for emancipation helped to merge ideas and action.

British anti-slavery movements

Thomas Clarkson initiated the movement to abolish the slave trade. John Wesley, founder of the Methodist Church, campaigned vigorously against it. The Clapham Sect formed the Society for Effecting the Abolition of the Slave Trade. Josiah Wedgwood produced supporting china cameos (Figure 4.3.2). The Act to Abolish the Slave Trade was passed in 1807, to take effect in 1808.

Granville Sharp was the first Englishman to agitate publicly against slavery (see 4.1). He was joined by Thomas Clarkson, James Ramsay and William Wilberforce. The Society of Friends (the Quakers) sought to eliminate enslavement. In 1823 the Anti-Slavery Society was founded. With the support of free traders, industrialists and new business interests, the reformed parliament and the impact of a series of revolts in the Caribbean, the British parliament passed the law to abolish slavery in 1833, to take effect on 1 August 1834.

French anti-slavery movements

The French abolition movement developed slowly. The National Revolutionary government abolished slavery in 1794, but it was restored by Napoleon in 1803. The *Société pour L'Abolition de L'Esclavage* put pressure on the French government which, by 1840,

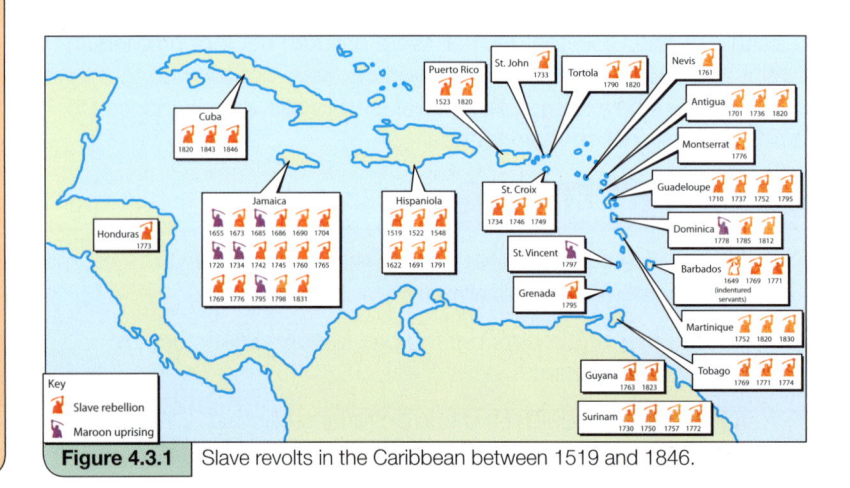

Figure 4.3.1 Slave revolts in the Caribbean between 1519 and 1846.

had taken the first steps towards abolition. Declining returns from cane sugar producers in the French colonies and the 1848 revolution led to the success of the motion which ended slavery in the French colonies in 1848.

Spanish anti-slavery movements

In the Spanish colonies civil war, rebellion and industrial technology encouraged the abolition movement, and other forms of labour became important: contract workers, Chinese indentured workers and free white wage-earners. In Puerto Rico slavery was abolished in 1873. Civil war in Cuba 1868-78 led to a government plan for gradual emancipation in 1880. In 1886 the remaining enslaved were freed.

Abolition of the slave trade 1807

The most determined spokesman for the abolition of slavery was William Wilberforce. The Bill was eventually passed in 1807. The law came into operation on 1 January 1808.

The first bill to abolish the trade in captured Africans on moral grounds was debated in the House of Commons in 1783. It was defeated because the slave system was considered important to the British economy. The abolition came in 1808 when Parliament was satisfied that this was in the best interest of the national economy.

Figure 4.3.2 The Wedgwood Medallion, named after the famous pottery that produced it, worn by supporters of the abolitionist movement.

DID YOU KNOW?

Before the Abolition of the slave trade, the Limitation Act of 1805 restricted the trade in the new colonies of Tobago, Trinidad, St. Lucia and British Guiana.

EXAM TIP

Note that the Act of 1807 put a legal end to the trading and shipping of slave but and illegal trade continued, but the use of slave labour as such was allowed to continue.

ACTIVITY

Create a chart showing the course of the emancipation movement in the British, French and Spanish colonies.

SUMMARY QUESTIONS

1. What was the Enlightenment and how did it affect the anti-slavery movement?
2. In what ways was the British anti-slavery movement different from those of France and Spain?
3. What role did enslaved Africans play in the emancipation process?
4. What factors assisted the French and Spanish emancipation process? Give three factors for each country.

KEY POINTS

- The Enlightenment facilitated the spread of anti-slavery ideas in Europe.
- The British anti-slavery movement was more organised than that of the French and Spanish.
- Revolts of the enslaved played an important part in the emancipation process.
- Victor Schoelcher was central to the French abolition campaign. He was assisted by the 1848 rebellion and the fall in the value of cane sugar from the French colonies.
- The Spanish movement was assisted by war technology, and slave rebellions.

4.4 Amelioration

LEARNING OUTCOMES

At the end of this topic you should be able to:

- Outline the aims of the British and French amelioration policies.
- Describe the main features of the British and French amelioration policies.
- Explain the outcomes of the British and French amelioration policies.

KEY TERMS

Amelioration: making something better; for enslaved people it meant improving living and working conditions.

Manumission: the act of setting an enslaved person free.

The concept of amelioration

The idea behind **amelioration** was to improve the living and working conditions of the enslaved, and so appease the opponents of slavery. It sought to convince planters that brutality was not necessary and enslavers could respond to the growing criticisms of the practice to silence their opponents. Planter resistance to the ending of the slave trade and continued brutality made it clear to the anti-slavery group that more definite action was necessary. This led to the amelioration proposals of 1823.

British amelioration policy

The policy aimed to:

- Reduce the harshness of Caribbean slavery.
- Improve the living and working conditions of enslaved workers.
- Respond to some of the demands of the enslaved.
- Encourage planters to be more flexible in their dealing with the enslaved workers.
- Demonstrate to planters that they could operate profitably with less coercion of their workers.

The amelioration proposal (1823)

- Women were not to be flogged.
- Overseers and drivers should not carry whips.
- Enslaved males were to be punished 24 hours after the offence occurred.
- A record of all punishments of enslaved males must be kept.
- Pregnant women and children should have a better diet.
- Religious instruction was to be provided to all enslaved Africans (Figure 4.4.1).
- Church marriage between enslaved men and women was to be encouraged.
- Families were not to be separated.
- Sunday market was to be abolished and another market day allocated. Sunday was reserved for worship.
- Evidence of slaves was to be admitted in court.
- Enslaved Africans would be allowed to purchase their freedom if they could pay the **manumission** fees.
- Protectors of slaves were to be appointed

Results

The proposals were proclaimed in the new colonies, Trinidad, Guyana and St Lucia, which did not have Assemblies. The colonial legislatures in the other colonies were encouraged to implement the measures, but they objected to the proposals because they saw

Figure 4.4.1 Under the policy of amelioration, slaves were to have the opportunity to receive religious instruction.

them as imperial interference and claimed that the measures would make the enslaved population unruly and insubordinate.

Planters became hostile to the imperial government, the anti-slavery groups and especially to missionaries, who were targeted with violent actions. Their hostility convinced the enslaved men and women that they were being denied the freedom that had been granted to them. This stimulated further revolts.

French amelioration policies

The French government passed laws to ameliorate slavery which were similar to the British laws. The laws encouraged education and Christian marriage for the enslaved and sought to reduce brutal punishment. Arrangements were made for supervising and recording punishments, and magistrates were authorised to inspect plantations and report cruelties and activities which did not comply with the law.

The French did not develop a specific amelioration policy, but like the entire emancipation process, individual amelioration proposals were heavily debated. In 1840 a Commission established to inquire into slavery recommended two paths to emancipation:

- general emancipation after 10 years with compensation to owners.
- phased emancipation for children, skilled workers, domestics and, finally, field hands.

Spanish amelioration policies

In response to the Cuban Civil War the Moret Law immediately freed all enslaved persons born after September 1868 and all enslaved persons over 60. Blacks participated in the war on the promise of freedom from Spanish colonialism.

ACTIVITY

Trace the steps to French Emancipation, noting the difference from the British process.

SUMMARY QUESTIONS

1. Why wasn't there a smooth transition to freedom after the ending of the slave trade?
2. What were the amelioration proposals?
3. What were the aims of the amelioration proposals and how successful were they?
4. Why was there an increase in revolts between 1808 and 1833?
5. Why was the British anti-slavery campaign stepped up after 1823?
6. Why did the French choose to give immediate emancipation in 1838?

DID YOU KNOW?

The Cubans expanded their slave system between 1830 and 1869, the era of emancipation in the rest of the region, using African captives supplied by American and European traders.

EXAM TIP

Familiarise yourself with the Amelioration proposals and the reasons why planters objected to them.

KEY POINTS

- The end of the slave trade did not lead to a smooth transition to freedom
- Amelioration proposals suggested ways to improve living and working conditions for the enslaved.
- Planters were hostile to the amelioration measures and they targeted the resident missionaries.
- Their responses made the enslaved population agitated.
- Slave revolts increased between 1808 and 1833.
- The anti-slavery campaign was stepped up after 1823.
- The French debated the issue and opted for immediate emancipation in 1848.

4.5 The British Emancipation Act 1833

LEARNING OUTCOMES

At the end of this topic you should be able to:

- Identify the factors which contributed to the successful passage of the 1833 Emancipation Act.
- State the main clauses of the Emancipation Act.
- Describe the apprenticeship system.
- Explain the ways in which clauses of the Act served or worked against the interests of planter and enslaved.

The steps toward the Act

Leading economist Adam Smith declared that slavery was a wasteful system that produced expensive commodities and that free labour would be cheaper. His views were supported by the new industrial class and the free traders in Britain. The mounting anti-slavery campaign needed support in Parliament to get the required legislation approved. This was provided after the Reform Act of 1832 which had brought into Parliament a new breed of representatives who supported emancipation.

The passage of the Act

Leading abolitionists William Wilberforce and Thomas Fowell Buxton (Figure 4.5.1), both became ill before the Act was passed. The bill went through three readings before it was passed on 29 August 1833, to take effect 1 August 1834.

Figure 4.5.1 Thomas Fowell Buxton.

KEY TERMS

Stipendiary magistrates: officials who supervised the apprentices. A stipend is a salary.

Freedom

Contrary to the gloomy predictions of planters, August 1 1834 passed without trouble as a day of religious celebration and cultural activity in the British Caribbean. The 668,000 enslaved Africans looked forward to a better day after the Act was passed.

The Act stated that:

- Children under 6 years of age were to be freed immediately.
- All children over 6 were to serve a period of apprenticeship.
- 100 **stipendiary magistrates** were allocated to supervise the operations of the Apprenticeship system (see 4.6).
- Planters would be paid £20,000,000 compensation for their loss of property.
- Workers would be classified.

Local assemblies made some alterations to the Act in their territories, but generally field slaves had to serve 40½ hours each week, until 1 August 1840. House slaves had to serve full-time, but only until 1 August 1838.

Apprenticeship

At emancipation, slavery was abolished, so unfree Africans in the Caribbean were called apprentices. They were required to serve, in what was supposed to be preparation for freedom.

While some slaves were legally free, they had to work part-time as 'apprentices' for their former masters. Between 1834 and 1838 plantation workers in the British West Indies, except for Antigua, lived under an unsettled system whereby they were neither slaves nor fully free citizens. They were called apprentices, but they were not training for a new job as the term implies today. For the ex-slave there was nothing new about working on a plantation. The system was a means of safeguarding the planters, the answer to the problem of granting full freedom while still ensuring that the plantations would have the necessary labour to keep them going. In a way it was part of the compensation granted to the planters on emancipation.

The supporters of apprenticeship claimed that it would help to introduce the slaves gradually into total self-sufficiency. The Abolition Act required the 'apprentice' to work 40½ hours a week without wages; any extra hours would be paid for. As before, the masters had to provide the 'apprentices' with shelter, clothing, medical care and food, or with land and time to tend their own gardens. There is more information about the apprentice system in 4.6.

Compensation

Under the Act, £20 million was to be paid to former slave owners as compensation for the loss of their slaves, but the money would only be issued after each colony had passed a proper local Act of Emancipation. This measure was intended to pacify the pro-slavery element and convince planters that they should accept the emancipation package. The politicians respected the planters' defence of their investment, and so they were compensated. There was to be no compensation paid to the enslaved Africans for their long years of unpaid labour.

EXAM TIP

Ensure that you can identify clauses of the Emancipation Act which favoured planters and those which provided benefits to enslaved Africans.

ACTIVITY

Make a chart with two columns, showing the ways in which the provisions of emancipation favoured planters on the one hand, and enslaved Africans on the other.

SUMMARY QUESTIONS

1. What four sets of factors combined to produce emancipation?
2. What contributions did economists and philosophers make to the emancipation process?
3. Why was emancipation a gradual process?

KEY POINTS

- Emancipation was the result of the combined input of economists, philosophers, religious leaders and the resistance efforts of enslaved Africans.
- Emancipation was a gradual process.
- Emancipation was not intended to bring a radical change to Caribbean society.

4.6 Apprenticeship

LEARNING OUTCOMES

At the end of this topic you should be able to:

- State the provisions of the apprenticeship clauses.
- Identify the role and difficulties encountered by the stipendiary magistrates.
- Describe the workings of the apprenticeship system.
- Assess its impact to 1838.

Figure 4.6.1 A special magistrate on tour in the West Indies in the 1830s.

DID YOU KNOW?

There were some stipendiary magistrates with good reputations, such as John Bowen Colthurst of Barbados and St Vincent, James Grady of Guyana, William Orderly and William Ramsey of Jamaica.

Features and conditions

The apprenticeship clauses stated that:

- Children under six were to be free immediately unless their mothers could not care for them, in which case they would be apprenticed to the estate until they were 21.
- All apprentices were classified as praedial or non-praedial workers.
- Non-praedials, or skilled, workers would serve a 4-year apprenticeship and praedials, agricultural workers, six years.
- Employers would continue to provide traditional food and clothing allowances and shelter to the apprentices and they continued to be responsible for the sick and aged.
- Apprentices would work for 40½ hours without pay and had to be paid for any additional labour that they provided.
- 100 stipendiary magistrates would supervise the operations of the system
- The local legislatures were required to pass the supporting laws.

In 4.5 a brief outline was given of the apprenticeship system which would tie the ex-slave to the cane field for a few more years after the passing of the Emancipation Act. Rules were set out: if apprentices worked nine hours a day they would have Friday afternoons off to work in their own grounds and prepare vegetables for the Saturday market. If they worked eight hours a day for five days a week, as the planters wanted them to do, there was no afternoon free.

Conditions varied according to the amount of land: Jamaica, Trinidad, Guyana and the Windward Islands had forested areas where smallholdings could be cultivated. In Barbados and the Leeward Islands, land was scarcer and the people were compelled to work the extra hours on estates to earn enough to supplement plantation rations.

During this period 'apprentices' could buy their full freedom, whether their masters were in favour of it or not.

Stipendiary magistrates

Stipendiary magistrates, usually retired military officers, were sent out as impartial officers to supervise apprenticeship. They were paid a stipend of £300 per year. There were problems from the start as only 150 were sent out, 60 of whom were stationed in Jamaica. Their numbers were supplemented by local Justices of the Peace (JPs) or magistrates.

The job was very demanding, requiring long journeys, mainly on horseback, across very poor roads and hilly terrain, to deal with a large number of time-consuming matters. The system was conflict-ridden over basic matters like punishments, complaints, wages, rents and customary allowances. The remuneration proved inadequate to the heavy transportation costs which included maintaining the horses, as well as supporting themselves. Some stipendiary magistrates suffered and died from tropical diseases, overwork and the effects of exposure to all types of weather. Some became reliant on planters with whom they socialised. In addition, the locals were either planters, their relatives or planter supporters and could not be impartial.

Since the master no longer had any right to punish the people working for him, decisions on these matters were in the hands of the special magistrate. He had the power to sentence an 'apprentice' to a certain number of days in the workhouse, a building set aside for punishment. This dreadful place housed a treadmill and frames upon which offenders were flogged if they were insolent (see 4.1). The workhouse and prison in each district were run by a superintendent and soon there were scandalous stories about the cruelty of these men and the brutality of their administration. Special magistrates often refrained from sentencing people guilty of mild offences because they knew what the conditions in the workhouses were like.

Responses

Many of the former enslaved men and women did not understand the new system, and in every colony there were arguments over how the hours of work each day should be divided. The confusion arose because the Act of Parliament gave no indication how the hours were to be divided. Each employer made his own arrangement which was usually not in the best interests of the apprentices. There were conflicts based on the expectations and aspirations of the apprentices which clashed with the planters' fixation on enslavement and possession of human property. Planters continued to operate as they did during enslavement, and apprentices sought freedom.

Results

Apprenticeship was a period of tension in the colonies. The system did not meet with the expectations of either farmers, planters or apprentices. While planters used the opportunity to extend the system of enslavement, there were signs of impending crisis which the stipendiary magistrates were not able to contain.

In 1836 Joseph Sturge and three colleagues visited the West Indies to assess the apprenticeship system. They visited plantations and talked to planters, magistrates and members of the Assemblies and reported that apprenticeship had not benefited the apprentices and was the cause of escalating conflicts in the region. Fearing that societies would explode if one group of apprentices was freed before the other, the British government terminated the system. On 1 August 1838 all apprentices were legally fully free.

EXAM TIP

Remember that the main cause of conflict during apprenticeship was the opposing aims of planters and apprentices.

ACTIVITY

Make a table showing the difficulties, and achievements, of apprentices, planters and stipendiary magistrates during the apprenticeship period.

SUMMARY QUESTIONS

1. What were the aims of the apprenticeship system?
2. What were the terms of apprenticeship system?
3. What difficulties were faced by the stipendiary magistrates during the apprenticeship period?
4. Why did the apprenticeship system end early?

KEY POINTS

- Apprenticeship was a part of the compensation package for planters.
- Apprenticeship was declared to be a time to prepare the enslaved and their masters for freedom under the supervision of the Stipendiary magistrates.
- The colonial assemblies still had law-making powers during the apprenticeship period.
- The system was conflict-ridden and did not work smoothly.
- It was terminated to prevent rebellion and disorder.

4.7 Emancipation in British Caribbean territories

LEARNING OUTCOMES

At the end of this topic you should be able to:

- Describe the attitudes of planters and free African men and women to freedom after 1838.
- Comment on the difficulties the free African people encountered in their bid to make themselves independent.
- Explain the strategies they employed to overcome the obstacles they faced.

Figure 4.7.1 An engraving of the time showing emancipation being celebrated in Barbados. There were parades and dancing in the street, but none of the disorder that the planters had expected.

DID YOU KNOW?

By 1837 the British anti-slavery societies were reactivated to pursue an anti-apprenticeship campaign.

Attitude of planters to emancipation

Many planters could not accept that the labourers whom they had 'owned' for so many years were no longer their property. Society was still overshadowed by the patterns of slavery in the previous century, especially since the planter-controlled assemblies still held decision-making power. Planters objected to the premature termination of apprenticeship. They were mainly concerned with maintaining a cheap, controllable labour force to service their plantations and were determined to prevent any alternative activity which would make the freed men and women independent of the estates.

Their attitude was displayed in the many obstructive tactics they used against their workers. These included laws to hinder and frustrate, such as anti-squatting and vagrancy laws, costly licences for dogs, cutting wood and boats, taxes on land that was not used to cultivate sugar, high land prices, sales of land only in large parcels, refusal to sell at all in some instances, and very low wages. Planters refused to see the Africans as anything other than a labour force because their thought processes had not been emancipated.

Attitude of freed Africans to emancipation

The freed African men and women were anxious to establish their independence during the era of full freedom. They recognised the importance of land in this process and sought to acquire it by purchase, rent or squatting. Their first act was to establish their homes in independent villages away from plantation control and remove their wives and children from plantation labour. They engaged in alternative labour where possible: fishing, hunting, farming their own plots of land, skilled occupations, business ventures, such as higgling, making and selling coals, market vending, shop-keeping and animal rearing. In many cases workers were forced to remain as estate labourers because of the limited employment opportunities available, but they made maximum use of opportunities to generate their own employment. Those who continued to work on the estates faced continuing conflicts over wages and terms of employment and sought to supplement their incomes in a variety of ways. Free African men and women saw emancipation as the opportunity to become truly liberated and move up from the lowest rung of the social ladder. In the quest for upward mobility high value was placed on the skilled trades, business ventures and education, for which their connection with the Christian churches was important.

The era of full freedom

We have seen that full emancipation took many years to achieve. The Abolition of Slavery Bill had been passed in 1807, putting an end to trading and shipping slaves, but did not prohibit the use of slave labour. In 1811 another act was passed to punish any British subject who traded in slaves by 'transportation', with the offender forcefully transported to a colony in need of labour. The British Navy was put on the lookout for British slavers in the Atlantic, and naval officers were offered rewards for recovering such ships.

Africans liberated in this way were under the protection of the Crown. In 1827, slave trading was declared to be piracy and punishable by death. It was not until the stroke of midnight on 31 July 1838, however, that the British West Indies gained almost 700,000 new citizens—men and women who, though not yet entitled to vote, were otherwise free to order the course of their lives and those of their children. As we have seen, however, there were still many limitations on their liberty.

The experience of freedom

Antigua and Bermuda opted for immediate emancipation. In Antigua, planters were convinced that the freed African men and women would remain dependent on the plantations for employment and for water, which was critically short on the island. With labour guaranteed, planters could avoid both the expense of apprenticeship and the interference of stipendiary magistrates.

In Antigua the governors reminded the freed men and women of their responsibilities to work to support themselves. While emancipation did not prepare them for freedom, it did show them the challenges that the quest for real freedom would bring.

In the remaining territories free villages developed, the work force was reduced as women and children were removed from estate labour, cultivation of small plots of land took place and there were other forms of independent employment, much to the anger of plantation owners. The free Africans still faced planter hostility.

Mobility of labour

Extensive acres of unused land were available in Guyana, Jamaica, and Trinidad where freed African men and women could purchase or squat to establish homes, communities and small farms. This was not possible in the smaller territories. In Barbados and Antigua, where the sugar estates occupied most of the land space, mobility was more difficult.

There were opportunities in the more mountainous islands: in Dominica, Tobago, Grenada and St Vincent hilly terrain inhibited plantation expansion. While some freed slaves worked on newly acquired plots of land, others moved into the towns and became tradesmen, boatmen, messengers and stevedores working at the harbours here.

In Barbados, Antigua and St Kitts, however, the estates could still rely on the labour force, since the large landowners still dominated the economy and all the land and labourers had few other sources of livelihood.

EXAM TIP

Remember that in post-emancipation society planters used their influence to direct policy to support their interest. The laws replaced the whip.

ACTIVITY

Imagine you are a freed African in any Caribbean territory. Write a journal describing your experiences during your first five years of freedom.

KEY POINTS

- Aspirations of the freed African men and women clashed with desires of plantation owners.
- Developments in Antigua signalled the pattern for the rest of the Caribbean.
- The physical environment of the colonies affected opportunities available for establishing an independent existence.
- Freed Africans used several ways to reduce their dependence on plantation labour.
- Planters used military, economic, social and legal means to preserve many aspects of slavery.

SUMMARY QUESTIONS

1. Why were there so many conflicts in society after 1838?
2. What factors assisted freed Africans to establish independence from plantations after 1838?
3. What measures did planters use to maintain aspects of enslavement in the years after 1838?
4. What strategies did freed Africans use to establish their independence from plantations after 1838?

4.8 Emancipation in other Caribbean territories

LEARNING OUTCOMES

At the end of this topic you should be able to:

- Describe the course of emancipation in the French, Dutch, Danish and Spanish Caribbean
- Identify their differences and similarities.
- Explain the nature of British impact on emancipation in the other Caribbean territories.

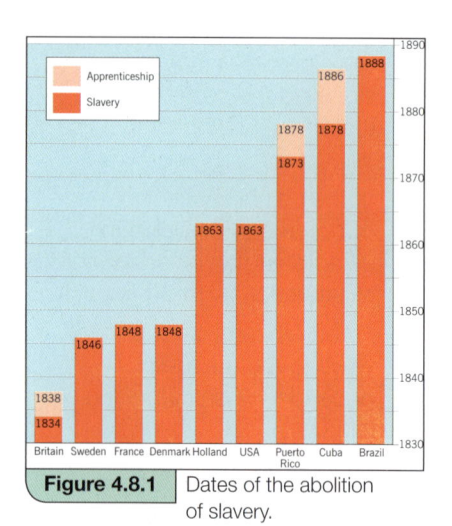

Nearly 50 years after emancipation in the British colonies enslavement was eliminated from the remaining slave-holding colonies and the descendants of freed Africans were employed in the professions and administrative positions. These developments influenced the course of emancipation in the non-British Caribbean.

Emancipation in French territories

The introduction of the amelioration policy in the French territories was followed by considerable debate. A commission of enquiry reported on measures to bring about emancipation and recommended two approaches which reflected the existing divisions in French society on the issue:

- general emancipation after ten years
- partial phased emancipation starting with children, skilled slaves, domestics and finally field hands.

The report sparked a debate to determine the better approach but beet and cane sugar producers were arguing over the home market. Initially the government sided with the cane growers and imposed a tax on beet sugar in 1837.

In spite of this the beet sugar producers offered stiff competition to the cane producers and in 1838 a number of planters in Martinique and Guadeloupe went bankrupt. Victor Schoelcher, sometimes called 'The Wilberforce of France', supported immediate emancipation and campaigned using speeches, pamphlets and articles. The 1848 revolution stimulated a contest between those supporting immediate and those favouring gradual emancipation. Schoelcher wanted to avoid the British apprenticeship experience and argued successfully for immediate emancipation with limited compensation and no apprenticeship period.

Figure 4.8.1 Dates of the abolition of slavery.

Emancipation in Dutch territories

The Dutch showed little interest in the anti-slavery movement until the 1840s, when they were influenced by other developments both in the Caribbean and South and Central America. The Society for the Advancement of the Abolition was formed in 1842 and campaigned for emancipation, to which both king and government were opposed. Publications helped win support for the movement, and in the 1850s emancipation dominated the government's agenda.

In 1857 an emancipation plan was submitted, but rejected because of dissatisfaction with the compensation arrangement, particularly among Surinamese planters. Parliament had to approve emancipation as the sugar cane industry declined in the face of competition from beet sugar, and rebellions occurred in St Eustatius and St Maarten.

DID YOU KNOW?

France was the first nation to abolish the slave trade and slavery in 1794, only to have it reinstated by Napoleon in 1802. Haiti was the first country permanently to end enslavement.

July 1 1863 was emancipation day in the Dutch colonies, but the enslaved African men and women were required to contribute to the compensation to be paid to planters. They were placed under state authority to continue giving their labour for a minimum wage, a system which lasted until 1873.

Emancipation in Danish territories

Emancipation in the Danish Caribbean was primarily the result of the efforts of the enslaved Africans. The Danish offered a policy of gradual amelioration called the Free Birth system, in which children born from 28 July 1847 were to be free and adults were to serve a 12-year apprenticeship until 1859. Enslaved Africans in St Croix rejected this plan, protested demanding freedom and revolted in July 1848.

The Governor General gave in to their demands and granted immediate freedom in St Croix and then to the rest of the Danish territories, but the ring leaders were punished with imprisonment and deportation.

Planters were compensated and the freed people were allowed to occupy their homes and grounds on the estate for 3 months, but were later forced by law to enter into labour contracts with their employers.

Emancipation in Spanish territories

The Spanish authorities sought to take advantage of the market conditions stimulated by the decline in the British colonies and the confusion in the French colonies, by developing the sugar industry in Cuba. They lost their slave suppliers at the end of the American Civil war in 1865, and in 1868 the Spanish monarchy that had supported the slave trade was overthrown.

There were many officials in the new Spanish government who supported the movements for emancipation in Cuba (where civil war helped the cause) and Puerto Rico. Freedoms were granted in Cuba in 1870 and Puerto Rico in 1873 and compensation was paid to planters. The freed were required to enter into contracts with their employers with any plantation they wished, but rules stipulated wages and conditions.

At this time other forms of labour began to be important to the Cuban sugar industry: indentured Chinese, free white and workers trained to operate modern technological improvement were preferred.

ACTIVITY

Copy and complete the following table. Circle any similarities that you notice in blue, and differences in red.

Territory	System of apprenticeship	Terms of each system
French		
Spanish		
Dutch		

EXAM TIP

Make sure that you are familiar with the similarities and differences between the course and terms of emancipation in the non-British Caribbean territories.

SUMMARY QUESTIONS

1. How did economic and political matters stimulate the emancipation process in the French colonies?
2. What role did the enslaved Africans play in the emancipation process in the French colonies?
3. How did enslaved Africans affect the emancipation process in the Danish colonies?
4. What impact did the ten years war have on emancipation in the Spanish colonies?
5. Why did it take so long for the Dutch emancipation movement to be organised?

KEY POINTS

- Emancipation in the French territories was stimulated by economic, political factors, and by the enslaved themselves.
- In the Dutch colonies, organisation of an emancipation movement was slow.
- In the Danish colonies the enslaved dictated matters.
- In the Spanish colonies the Ten Years' War was crucial.

Section B, Theme 5: Adjustments to emancipation (1838–76)

5.1 Problems of the sugar industry

LEARNING OUTCOMES

At the end of this topic you should be able to:
- Identify the problems which affected the sugar industry in the British Caribbean (1838–54).
- Explain the causes of the problems.
- Describe the mechanisms implemented to correct them.

Labour

After 1838, a major problem of labour relations developed in the British Caribbean. Planters still wanted to keep the freed men and women as a cheap controllable labour force with poor working conditions.

Negotiations began in the sugar industry, but planters found it difficult to negotiate with what they had regarded as their property. The freed people wanted to assert their independence, living away from plantation control in villages and engaging in independent economic activity.

Planters complained about the labour shortage crisis which threatened their plantations. In many cases these claims were exaggerated.

Capital

Plantation society had been built on a credit system where all major expenditure was charged to plantation produce and paid after the crop was sold. In the era of freedom wages and services had to be paid for in cash, which was in short supply.

In addition, many plantations were heavily in debt. Plantation operations needed to be modernised to be competitive. In some islands the plantation works remained exactly as they were initially established. These were no longer efficient, and other problems such as loss of soil fertility, natural disasters, pestilence and disease meant large capital outlays.

Many British Caribbean planters, except those in Trinidad and Guyana found it difficult to attract investors, so were unable to modernise their operations and were operating at a loss. Some plantations changed hands or were abandoned.

This currency crisis was a fatal blow for the British West Indies. Under slavery a person's wealth was judged by the number of slaves he or she owned. Suddenly position was judged in terms of money and for years many planters had been deeply in debt. Although they had been paid £20 million in compensation, most of this money went to pay off the debts to merchants in England. There was little money left to invest in the plantations, and already some of the planters could not even raise the cash to pay labourers.

Free trade

The Free Trade Law of 1846 was a serious blow to British Caribbean planters. It removed one important prop on which plantations depended: protection from competition. It exposed the weakness of the plantation system which, because it enjoyed a guaranteed market, its operators had not tried to make efficient and competitive.

Figure 5.1.1 Working in a boiling house.

DID YOU KNOW?

The West Indies had no specified currency: Spanish dollars, doubloons, pistoles, escudos and United States dollars were all permitted as legal tender.

As economists pointed out, the slave system was expensive, wasteful, underproductive and old-fashioned.

The Act equalised the duties on all sugar entering Britain, making Caribbean sugar face competition from the Spanish Caribbean, Brazil, Florida, Louisiana, Java, Mauritius, Natal, Queensland and Fiji. There was a 30 per cent reduction in British Caribbean exports to Britain between 1847 and 1852 and a significant fall in the price of sugar.

Producers also faced rising production and shipping costs and some estates experienced low productivity. The planters complained that they were disadvantaged. They found it difficult to obtain loans and credit because banks and credit institutions were closing. The value of estates fell sharply. Colonial governments found it difficult to collect taxes, so there was less money for administration and they could not pay salaries and wages.

The British government established the Encumbered Estates Court Act in 1854 to facilitate the sale of indebted estates. The court was authorised to arrange for the sale of properties and divide the proceeds so that new owners did not inherit the debts of the property. St Vincent and Tobago made use of this facility in the 1850s. Continuing distress cries from planters about the ill effects of free trade led the British government to set up the 1848 Select Committee to investigate the state of the colonies. Its report confirmed that there was distress in the colonies and the government postponed full equalisation to 1854.

Technology

The industrial revolution produced new industrial implements that had been in use in many countries since the 1800s. In the Caribbean the main innovation had been the three-roller mill and the Jamaica train. By the middle of the 1900s increased scientific knowledge and new technology meant that modern equipment and processes were available to planters.

Generally, however, these new technologies were too expensive for planters so were not commonly used. Railways were used in Guyana and Trinidad, and planters in Barbados, St Kitts and Nevis and Antigua attempted to make changes in their methods of production; in most of the remaining territories planters kept their traditional outmoded practices.

SUMMARY QUESTIONS

1. What were the problems of the sugar industry after 1838?
2. What evidence is there to support the view that a shortage of credit was the main problem of the sugar industry during the years of freedom?
3. What did the Sugar Duties Act of 1846 state?
4. How did the Sugar Duties Act affect sugar production in the Caribbean?
5. What caused the labour problems in the British Caribbean during the years of freedom?

DID YOU KNOW?

Ploughs, new crop varieties and fertilisers could increase yield; central factories, steam-driven mills, double-crushing juice extractors and the vacuum pan could increase efficiency and maximise output. Railways could significantly reduce transportation costs.

EXAM TIP

Remember that post-emancipation labour problems were not simply shortages of labour. They involved the conflicting ambitions of planter and worker, the nature of their relationship, attitudes and terms of employment.

ACTIVITY

Make a list of the problems faced by both planters and workers during the period 1838–54.

KEY POINTS

- The major challenge faced by the sugar industry in free society was a shortage of credit.
- Many planters were unable to take advantage of new technology to improve their operations
- Free trade aggravated the problems of Caribbean planters.
- Acute labour problems were caused by poor planter/worker relations.

5.2 Attitudes to labour

LEARNING OUTCOMES

At the end of this topic you should be able to:

- describe the attitudes to labour of landowners/employers and free persons in the English-speaking Caribbean after 1838.

KEY TERMS

Coercive: applied by force or with the use of threats

DID YOU KNOW?

Sierra Leone was created as a country to house liberated Africans who were rescued from slave traders after British Abolition.

Landowners/employers

Landowners were concerned about the effects of freedom: they were afraid that they would lose their labour and that plantation operations would be crippled. They continued to see the free workers as a labour force to which they had a right, and they favoured strong **coercive** policies to keep workers on the estates. They believed the rightful place of the freed Africans was on the estates and tried to prevent them from developing alternative means of support. They described the free Africans as lazy and having a 'distaste' for agriculture, despite the fact that there was ample evidence of cultivation of a variety of crops across the countryside by the freed people.

In Trinidad planters were opposed to the task system which they felt made workers too rich. They too accused their workers of laziness, ignoring the fact that many used the system to their advantage and completed several tasks in one day to give them more free time for alternative pursuits. Planters felt that labourers should be kept poor and dependent on the plantations.

Free persons

Freed people sought alternatives to estate labour because they wanted to be free of the burdens of estate labour and the planter controls that came with it. Where land was available they established their own smallholdings. They saw labour as essential to self-improvement and they worked hard, but demanded adequate compensation for their efforts. They were not prepared to accept the low wages and unfair practices of planters, and these, along with the planter-influenced **coercive** laws, contributed to the conflicts which characterised the era of freedom.

The attitude to labour by different groups of people is reflected in the writings of administrators and government officials, visitors, missionaries and plantation owners and managers. These people had the opportunity to record their sentiments and the laws and plantation practices. There are some writers, however, particularly missionaries, who were sympathetic to the workers and their accounts contradict those of the pro-plantation group.

As they tried to put workers in a bad light, planters and their supporters contradicted themselves. They argued that the sugar industry suffered from a shortage of labour because of the unwillingness of workers to work, but then they wrote about the extensive areas brought under cultivation by the hard work of the freed men and women who produced a wide range of crops.

The free workers showed their attitude to labour by their commitment to their own cultivation. Their attitude to work was different on the plantations because of the frustrations they faced in their dealings with planters.

> **EXAM TIP**
>
> Remember that the emancipation laws did not emancipate planters from the practices of enslavement. During the era of freedom planters tried to manipulate the system and continue enslavement practices.

Figure 5.2.1 Working the land today: contrary to planter claims, freed men and women worked hard on their own plots of land.

> **ACTIVITY**
>
> Using the text *Caribbean Generations* or any other source book, examine reports on labour and economics in the post-emancipation period. Identify statements which are pro-labour, pro-planter and contradictory.

> **KEY POINTS**
>
> - The attitude to labour was primarily shaped by the old racist view that Africans were best suited to agricultural labour.
> - Planters and their supporters blamed the workers for the problems which faced the sugar industry.
> - The attitude of workers to labour is best represented by the way they handled their own plots of land.

> **SUMMARY QUESTIONS**
>
> 1. What factors were responsible for the way planters viewed and treated their workers after Emancipation?
> 2. Why did planters claim that the freed Africans were lazy and did not want to work?
> 3. What evidence is there to show that the planter claim of the lazy African was untrue?

79

5.3 Schemes of migration

LEARNING OUTCOMES

At the end of this topic you should be able to:

- Identify the various schemes of migration that occurred in the Caribbean.
- Locate the source and receiving countries on a blank map of the world.
- Explain the reasons why migrants left their home countries to come to the Caribbean.

Immigration schemes

Immigration schemes were intended to provide the labour needed for the sugar industry, to provide models of hard work, create a surplus of workers to drive wages down and reduce planter operating costs. White migrants were needed to improve the black/white ratio.

Immigration occurred before and after emancipation. Since abolition, planters had sought alternative sources of labour. For some the most practical method was to encourage family life to generate a local supply of workers. They tried to attract migrants from within the Caribbean, but later, in Trinidad, the Abolition and Immigration Society was formed to support immigration.

Planters complained about a shortage of labour, the laziness of the freed Africans who abandoned the estates and the imminent economic disaster this was causing. The British government established a committee which recommended immigration schemes.

White immigration

In the post-emancipation era white immigrants from European countries and the Atlantic Islands came to Caribbean from several territories: the Azores, Madeira, Canary Islands, Britain, France, Germany and Malta.

The Portuguese from Madeira (an island off the north coast of Africa) were the most significant white immigrants in the Caribbean. There was a better gender balance among the Madeirans than other immigrant groups because family migration was encouraged. While the Madeirans provided valuable service to the Grenada cocoa industry, white immigration failed to satisfy planter needs. Some immigrants broke their contracts and left the plantations to engage in other economic activity, or they migrated to the US.

The Portuguese preferred the **retail** trades and were the majority of shopkeepers in Guyana in 1882. In Grenada some became peasant farmers. Generally they were not satisfied with working conditions and health arrangements and felt that employers broke the contract agreements.

The death rate among white immigrants was very high as they fell victim to diseases such as malaria and yellow fever.

African

The first waves of West African immigration into the British Caribbean went to the Bahamas, Guyana, Trinidad and Grenada. In the 1840s Africans rescued from slave ships by British naval patrols in the Atlantic were brought and other migrants were brought from Gambia, St Helena and Sierra Leone.

ACTIVITY

On a world map locate the home countries of the various groups of immigrants who came to the Caribbean.

Figure 5.3.1 Portuguese from Madeira were encouraged to migrate in family groups.

These African contract workers helped to support the sugar industry before the importation of Asian immigrants. They were employed on sugar and cocoa estates in Trinidad and the Windward islands. Terms of employment included free housing, medical care and plots of land for food cultivation.

Indians

After an initial failed experiment in 1838 that led to a ban on importing Indian workers, in 1844 Guyana, Trinidad and Jamaica began importing Indians. Indians looking for higher earnings and a better life were mainly recruited (some were kidnapped) from the north-west provinces of India. They were **indentured** under 5-year contracts as field labourers. Conditions stated wages, benefits, punishments for breaches of the contract and return passages to India. There were provisions for re-indenture at the end of the contract.

The system ended in 1917 after opposition from India, groups within the colonies, the anti-slavery societies, missionaries and resistance by the indentured workers themselves.

Between 1838 and 1917 half of those arriving from India went to Guyana, about a third to Trinidad and just under 10 per cent to Jamaica.

Chinese

Chinese immigration to the British-colonised Caribbean began in the 1850s. People were willing to leave a country which had experienced a population explosion, heavy competition for land, high taxes, a cruel administration and a rebellion.

Between 1853 and 1884, most Chinese immigrants went to Guyana, with a small percentage to Trinidad, and fewer still to Jamaica.

Chinese immigration ended because it was considered expensive, and planters and the Chinese authorities were dissatisfied. The Chinese left plantation labour as soon as they could. Employers preferred Indian workers and there were anti-immigration protests in China. The last ships arrived in Jamaica in 1884.

Cuba was one of the largest importers of Chinese labourers between 1853 and 1874. Their contribution to the sugar industry was more significant than in the British colonies.

KEY TERMS

Indentured: bound by a written and signed contractual arrangement, applied to workers to provide labour on estates for a stipulated time under specific terms.

Retail: selling goods in small quantities, usually in shops.

DID YOU KNOW?

Grenada received 50 percent of their liberated African migrants before the end of Apprenticeship.

EXAM TIP

Remember to revise the reasons why immigrants left their home countries and the difficulties they faced in their host countries.

KEY POINTS

- Immigrants to the Caribbean came from different parts of the world.
- Some immigration schemes were more successful than others.
- Both employers, immigrants and their home governments were dissatisfied with the schemes.
- The largest scheme brought Indian indentured workers.

SUMMARY QUESTIONS

1. Which countries provided immigrant labour to the Caribbean after Emancipation?
2. Which was the most successful immigration scheme and why?
3. Which schemes were unsuccessful and why?
4. What caused employers, immigrants and their home governments to be dissatisfied with the immigration schemes?

5.4 Economic, social and cultural effects of migration

LEARNING OUTCOMES

At the end of this topic you should be able to:

- Describe the ways immigrants have impacted on Caribbean culture.
- Assess the impact of immigration on the host societies.
- Explain their impact on the economies of the host colony.

Supply

Migration was more likely to be successful in populous regions, and for the British in places where they exercised some controls, as in their colonies such as India and West Africa, or where they had military, naval and/or political influence through anti-slave trading activity, such as China and the Atlantic.

Social conditions, such as poverty and unemployment also encouraged migration: people grasped the opportunities to migrate to attain a better life.

Migrants were as also encouraged by the agents who presented rosy pictures of the colonies. In some instances indentured workers were kidnapped or lured to the immigration centres by trickery.

News about the real conditions of the colonies also affected the supply of migrants.

Production

The success of a particular migration scheme depended on how far it met the aims of the planters to maintain operations and increase production. Indian immigration was considered the most successful and both Trinidad and Guyana increased sugar production. In 1838 production had fallen, but by 1876 had surpassed earlier levels.

Other migration schemes were less successful: neither white nor Chinese immigrants liked working on the estates.

Viability

Success of an immigration scheme also depended on viability, that is whether it could be maintained. The sources of white migrants were not populous areas and could not supply migrants in the numbers needed. In times of distress, temporary interest in migration would develop but would not be maintained in the long term. Whites still felt that their superiority prevented them from working alongside black workers. The high costs of white and Chinese immigration made them both unviable.

Impact of migrants on society

The introduction of Asians changed the size and racial composition of the population. The foundations were laid for later mixing of these groups to produce new mixed race populations. Tensions increased, however, between Indian and Africans, who were hostile and suspicious of each other. Each felt superior. African workers felt that Indians had taken away their jobs and prevented them from earning higher wages. Resident Europeans scorned the Portuguese immigrants who were considered 'lesser' whites. Within the Indian

Figure 5.4.1 Many migrant workers did not like agricultural work on the estates.

DID YOU KNOW?

To encourage female immigration, recruiters in India were paid more for females than for males.

community, the shortage of Indian women created rivalry, often violent, for spouses. In Trinidad this led to wife murders.

The increased population placed heavy stresses on services such as health, which was already inadequate. There was an increase in vagrants—indentured workers who ran away, or were expelled from the estates because of illness or old age. They lived on the streets or crowded the hospitals. The prison population also increased as indentured workers were punished for breaking the terms of their contracts. The costs of maintaining both the hospitals and prisons increased.

Impact on culture

Indian and Chinese immigrants introduced, for example new foods, cooking implements, plants, medical knowledge, skills, crafts, religions, styles of dress, architecture and musical instruments.

The Chinese introduced the game since incorporated into the national lottery system in Trinidad as Play Wey. African immigrants strengthened African traditions and language and the African-based faith groups developed in some territories. In Trinidad the traditional planting and reaping rites of hill rice cultivation introduced by immigrants still take place.

Impact on the economy

Indian immigrants provided the labour force needed for the sugar industries of Trinidad and Guyana, allowing the planters to pay low wages, expand cultivation, increase production and maintain their social and political status.

The outlook for these industries was very positive. Nevertheless, immigration consumed 50 per cent of the revenue of the colonies. A large portion of the medical costs of the system had to be borne by the state.

Indians

Indian immigrants were classified as agricultural workers, but were in fact skilled craftsmen. They contributed their skills as jewellers, crafting leather, rearing cattle and growing and selling rice. Their religious temples and mosques changed the architectural landscape and their celebrations diversified the culture of the region. They introduced popular foods such as roti (and the tarwa pan for making it) and curried dishes.

Chinese

Chinese immigrants were very dissatisfied with working conditions. They abandoned plantation agriculture and did not impact significantly on the sugar industry in the British colonies. As vegetable cultivators, however, they expanded the range of food items available for purchase. They also set up shops in rural communities. In Trinidad they added now familiar food items to the culture.

Madeirans

The migrants from Madeira were not successful as labourers. They did not readily acclimatise and were unhappy with the housing, medical care and low wages. Many left the estates and some left the Caribbean. Those who remained contributed to the economy by their activities as shopkeepers, especially in Guyana where they dominated the shop-keeping business.

> **EXAM TIP**
>
> You must be able to distinguish between the social, economic and political impact of the immigrants.

> **ACTIVITY**
>
> Make a list of new foods, plants and ways of preparing food that were introduced by the different immigrant groups in the Caribbean.

> **SUMMARY QUESTIONS**
>
> 1. In what ways did immigrants impact on Caribbean culture?
> 2. What is the nature of the impact of immigrants on the population and race relations in the Caribbean?
> 3. How did immigration affect the Caribbean sugar industry?
> 4. In what ways did the immigrants put pressure on the infrastructure and treasury of the British Caribbean colonies?

> **KEY POINTS**
>
> - Immigrants diversified food and culture in the region.
> - They facilitated the survival and expansion of the sugar industry.
> - They put a heavy strain on the infrastructure and treasury.
> - They changed racial relations.

5.5 Emergence of free villages

LEARNING OUTCOMES

At the end of this topic students should be able to:

- Identify the factors which assisted the development of free villages.
- State the views of main individuals on village development.
- Explain the strategies which were used by planters to overcome their difficulties.

DID YOU KNOW?

Baptist missionaries, Reverend Phillippo, William Knibb, John Clark and the Baptist Western Union, led the development of peasant settlement in Jamaica.

Figure 5.5.1 Sturge Town, St Ann Jamaica, one of the first free villages.

Enabling factors

The most powerful enabling factor was the determination of the freed Africans to attain real freedom. This meant they had to establish their independence from plantation control. They recognised the importance of land-owning. Some had saved their earnings during apprenticeship and were able to purchase land despite the high prices that owners demanded.

The physical features of the colonies influenced the ability of the freed people to obtain land. In territories with unused land or abandoned estates free communities developed rapidly because it was possible to buy, rent or squat on available land. In territories where the sugar industry encountered particular difficulties, desperate planters were forced to sell land. In some instances groups of free people pooled their resources to buy properties to establish free villages; in other instances missionaries assisted the establishment of free communities.

The pace of village development was slower in islands like, Antigua, Barbados and St Kitts where a viable sugar industry existed and sugar cane occupied most of the land. The missionaries and the anti-slavery society provided significant assistance to peasant development. Missionaries acted as mediators between owner and purchaser to acquire land. Where planters were unwilling to sell land, missionaries bought it, subdivided it and resold it to the peasants.

Views of outstanding personalities

Some individuals made outstanding contributions to the development of free villages. They were missionaries, the anti-slavery society and some planters who recognised that the peasants needed assistance to establish themselves as free people. They were all convinced that the free men and women should live in villages and farm, and provided assistance to create farming communities. Baptist ministers in Jamaica wanted to establish farming villages so they helped to negotiate sales and provided financial assistance to peasants to get themselves established. Sligoville was the first such village, established in 1835.

William Knibb hoped to create a society of small farmers in Jamaica after Emancipation. He purchased land, divided it among 70 families and with assistance from Joseph Sturge established Sturge Town, a village with a school, church and community centre. It became the model for other villages such as Wilberforce, Clarksonville and Buxton. In Antigua, Moravian missionaries sponsored a free village. Reynold Elcock of Mt Wilton estate in Barbados, who died in 1821, left money in his will for enslaved people to buy land. They bought parts of Rock Hall Estate which formed the basis of Rock Hall Village.

Responses

The peasants were anxious to own land and they responded favourably to the assistance they received. Many joined the congregations of the churches which assisted them. The villages grew in numbers. Historical records show increases in Antigua between 1842 and 1858 of free village residents, and in Trinidad an increase in numbers of small farmers. Similar increases are recorded for Demerara, Berbice and Jamaica. Increasingly, peasants bought land from the estates; in Guyana records show sales to freed Africans of **proprietary** and communal villages.

Labour supply on plantations

There were various ways planters tried to maintain labour supply.

In reaction to the rapid village movement some planters founded villages on lands close to or on estate lands to create a pool of labour to which they could have easy access.

The 'located labour system' was an annual arrangement which included a money wage and payment in kind for the house and ground which the workers were allowed to occupy with medical benefits. This system was usually found on territories with low population density. Some workers were tenants on the estates on a labour/rent arrangement by which rent was paid in estate labour for a specified period.

Some were tenants under lease arrangement, usually for, say, 2–3 years. Some were part time labourers, sugar cane farmers and **metayers**. The metayage (Metairie) system became widely used in St Lucia, Tobago, Montserrat, Grenada and Nevis. The costs of production and profits were shared by planter and metayer on an agreed basis. To planters it was a last resort to keep their estates operational when cash was not available. To the metayers, it was a better alternative to estate labour and they tried to use the system to their advantage. Planters engaged in many unfair practices which caused conflicts wherever the system was used.

The task system was another device used by planters, especially in Trinidad. Specific tasks were identified as a day's work. It was popular with workers who were able to complete more than one task in a day, but not by planters, who felt it was disadvantageous to them.

> **KEY TERMS**
>
> **Proprietary**: held in private ownership.
>
> **Metayers**: French term for workers on the land who received a share of the produce.

> **EXAM TIP**
>
> Ensure that you are familiar with the systems, other than immigration, that were used by planters to deal with their labour problems.

> **ACTIVITY**
>
> Make a chart showing, on one side, a list of the reasons why planters opposed the village movement, and on the other side why freed African men and women favoured it.

> **KEY POINTS**
>
> - Several factors assisted the development of free villages.
> - Planters viewed village movement as a negative development.
> - Planters used a number of strategies to keep workers on the estates.
> - Many conflicts occurred in the day-to-day operations of these strategies.

> **SUMMARY QUESTIONS**
>
> 1. What factors assisted the development of free villages in the years after Emancipation?
> 2. Why were planters opposed to the development of free villages?
> 3. What strategies did planters use to prevent the development of free villages in the Caribbean after Emancipation?
> 4. What were the outcomes of these efforts?

5.6 Creation of a new society

LEARNING OUTCOMES

At the end of this topic you should be able to:

- Outline the challenges which faced the new societies formed after 1838.
- Describe the methods used to provide education in free society.
- Explain the methods of control which were used in the era of freedom.

Conditions in the new communities

Services and facilities in the new communities were not considered a priority of the colonial governments. Houses such as the chattel houses of Barbados were temporary structures which could be easily removed if conflicts developed with the land owner. Houses had no sanitary provisions and there were no garbage collection systems in the villages. Villagers depended on rivers and streams, ponds or pools of stagnant and often polluted water, which they shared with their animals. Water had to be collected and stored and was often scarce during the dry season. The stagnant water bred mosquitoes.

Epidemics of yellow fever, dysentery and diarrhoea, smallpox and measles were common. There were no accessible health services for villagers: after apprenticeship, there were fewer doctors in the colonies. They were mainly located in the urban areas and villagers could not afford them. Barbados, Antigua and Jamaica were the only colonies with public hospitals in 1838. A cholera epidemic raged through the colonies in the 1850s.

Schools

The need to provide education for the children of freed Africans was recognised by the provision of the Negro Education Grant, but in 1845 colonial governments became responsible for education. Grants were given mainly to the established churches and were never adequate. The Mico Charity was set up by Lady Mico, widow of a prominent businessman. It became the main source of funding for Caribbean education through day schools and 'normal', or teacher training, schools. The emphasis in the day schools was on the basic skills of reading, writing and arithmetic, and moral education and industrial education for the destitute and orphaned children.

The established churches became more involved in primary schools but schools were short of trained teachers, school buildings were not always properly maintained. The language of instruction was English, which was not the native language in colonies which had been colonised by France. Parents were dissatisfied with the curriculum content and attendance dropped.

The churches dominated secondary education in the colonies.

DID YOU KNOW?

Antigua and Jamaica were the only colonies with public hospitals in 1838.

Figure 5.6.1 Mico University College: Kingston, Jamaica.

Social control

In free society laws, prison and policing became the means used by the colonial elite to maintain control over the working population. More money was allocated to this than to education. Police services were instituted to preserve law and order and protect the state.

In Trinidad, police officers were recruited from law-abiding individuals from Barbados and other territories. Colonial governments used legislation to force workers to continue working on the plantations. There were laws to deal with property crimes, vagrancy, vending and other alternative forms of employment and to impose heavy taxes on the freed people. Prisons or 'Houses of Correction' still inflicted brutal punishments, such as the treadmill, to force people to obey the oppressive laws and to suppress protest and unrest.

Health services

The first steps to provide public health services were taken after the cholera epidemic of the 1850s. Boards of health were established and laws were passed to prevent pollution of rivers and streams by bathing and washing, but the freed population had to use these for domestic purposes. Waste water from households flowed onto the streets in the absence of proper drainage and piles of rubbish were common sights. Steps were taken to provide pipe-borne water and rubbish collection to urban areas in the late 1850s.

In the 1870s medical services were organised in the larger territories and district medical officers were appointed. There were no significant improvements for the mass of the population until the mid-1900s.

The emergence of new political voices

Missionaries, particularly from the Baptist church, advocated better treatment for the free black population. Members of the educated coloured middle class believed that political change was necessary and called for **representation**. They included:

- Paul Bogle, George William Gordon and Edward Jordan in Jamaica, and Samuel Jackson Prescod and William Conrad Reeves in Barbados.

EXAM TIP

Remember that school, church, laws, police and prison were used as agencies of social control of the freed Africans.

KEY TERMS

Representation: having a chosen person to speak on one's behalf in a court or assembly.

ACTIVITY

Write pen portraits of five men who spoke up against white ruling class domination and argued for political change.

SUMMARY QUESTIONS

1. What problems did the residents of the free villages face?
2. Why were the freed Africans dissatisfied with the education that was provided for them?
3. By what methods did the planters attempt to control the free Africans after Emancipation?
4. Why did educated coloured people seek to obtain political representation?

KEY POINTS

- The free villages faced many problems
- Education was provided for the freed Africans but it did not meet with their expectations.
- In the era of freedom, law, police and prison assumed importance in controlling the population.
- Educated coloureds argued for political representation.

5.7 Contribution of the peasantry

LEARNING OUTCOMES

At the end of this topic you should be able to:

- Classify the contributions of the Caribbean peasantry into social, economic and political.
- State examples of peasant political action.
- Assess the overall contribution to Caribbean society.

DID YOU KNOW?

Crops for export produced by peasant farmers included coconuts, ginger, pimento, copra, cotton, honey, beeswax, coffee, cocoa, arrowroot, limes, rice and spices.

Social

The development of peasant communities in the Caribbean after 1838 led to free expression of African culture and a resurgence of African traditions. Later a similar development occurred with Indian peasants who contributed to the cultural diversity now so typical of Caribbean society. In the new free villages they formed communities which promoted self-help and co-operation and became the centres of social, cultural and economic activities. Peasants used their earnings to educate their children, some of whom rose in time to positions in administration and became strong supporters of change.

Economic

Peasants proved that other crops could be successfully grown along with the major export crops. They diversified the economy, removing dependence on one or two export crops and produced additional crops for export. Peasants in Trinidad pioneered the cocoa industry which became a major export crop between 1870 and 1922.

Peasants cultivated food crops which reduced the dependence on imported food. They established local markets and developed the internal marketing system which provided foodstuff to workers and planters and generated incomes for vendors.

The sale produce was an important trade for both vendors and purchasers, for those in St Vincent and Grenada, who sold food items to Trinidad, those from St Lucia who sold to Barbados, and from Nevis to St Kitts and Antigua.

In addition to creating employment for the cultivator and vendors, there was employment for boat-builders, boatmen and their crews.

Political

Peasants did not have representation in the political administration of the colonies, but were politically active through their reactions to discriminatory and oppressive policies imposed on them by the colonial assemblies, and the demanding and unfair labour practices of their employers. Riots, strikes, marches to the governors' house, fires, disruption of court proceedings and petitions were some of the strategies used to communicate feelings to the authorities.

The 1865 Morant Bay Rebellion (see 5.8) in Jamaica is famous, but there were equally important protests in other territories. In 1842, there were strikes in Guyana against the 'Rules and Regulations' which planters sought to impose in Demerara and Essequibo.

Also in Guyana, a strike in Leguan resulted from the attempt to reduce wages in 1846. In 1848 there was a colony-wide strike against wage reduction. Cane fields were set on fire and plantation property destroyed.

Reduced wages also led to strikes in Grenada, at the end of 1847.

In 1862 a riot occurred in Barbados against rising prices, wage reduction and retrenchment. Said to be the longest labour riot in the history of Barbados, all parishes except Michael, St Joseph and St Andrew were affected.

Discontent over the excessive dog tax caused the 1867 Mason Hall Dog Tax Riot in Tobago. 100 villagers refused to pay the tax and petitioned the Governor. His unsympathetic response led to the riot. In 1876 low wages, costly medical services, overcharging and indebtedness to estate shops and the desire for land caused the Belmanna Riots there.

Changing landscape

The spread of cultivation and settlements into new areas developed into modern towns and villages with expanding road networks. A new class of landowners emerged with cultivation practices that changed the landscape from the plantation style of one crop over extensive areas to crop variety on smaller parcels of land. Hitherto useless land was brought under rice cultivation in Trinidad and Guyana (Figure 5.7.1).

Figure 5.7.1 Land that had been unproductive was used for rice production.

SUMMARY QUESTIONS

1. In what ways did peasants change Caribbean society?
2. What did the peasants contribute to the development of modern Caribbean society?
3. What areas of social and economic activity were considered of primary importance to the peasants and why?

DID YOU KNOW?

In 1845 Maria Coulter of St Vincent bought 18 acres of land in St Andrew for £420 which she resold as house plots of 1/10 acre to labourers at £30 or £40.

EXAM TIP

Remember that the contribution of the peasantry includes job creation in a society which focussed on estate labour.

ACTIVITY

Make a ship's log for a vessel plying intercolonial trade between 1839 and 1900. Describe preparations for the voyage, how items for trade were obtained. List the items carried, the destinations, how business was conducted on your arrival and items acquired for the homeward voyage.

KEY POINTS

- Peasants changed Caribbean society in several ways.
- They demonstrated that economic development was possible outside sugar plantations.
- Peasant villages laid the foundation for the development of modern Caribbean communities.
- Peasants used their earnings to educate their children, some of whom rose to positions in administration and became advocates of change.

5.8 Crown Colony government

LEARNING OUTCOMES

At the end of this topic you should be able to:

- Describe the old representative system.
- Define Crown Colony government.
- Explain the reasons for its introduction in the British Caribbean colonies.
- Describe the response in the colonies to its introduction.

KEY TERMS

Bicameral: a parliament with two law-making parts, an elected 'lower' house, and non-elected 'upper house'.

DID YOU KNOW?

The Executive Council members who advised the Governor were nominated from the largest planters in the colony.

Figure 5.8.1 Paul Bogle: this statue stands outside the courthouse in Morant Bay, St Thomas, Jamaica.

Old representative government

The old representative system was a **bicameral** system, with an Upper House, the Council, and an elected Lower House, or Assembly, for which there was a property qualification. The Governor presided, with advice from an executive council.

The assemblies, which controlled colonial finances, often disagreed with imperial policies. When the sugar industry slumped, the assemblies pleaded for assistance from the **imperial** government which was considering ways to reduce costs and avoid conflicts. There were many signs that colonial governments were unsatisfactory.

Popular disaffection

The assemblies pursued policies that were intended to preserve aspects of slave society. Signs of popular discontent increased when the problems of the sugar industry made the ruling class more oppressive. Unfavourable reports on the state of health, prisons and education in the colonies, and frequent protests, convinced the British government that change was necessary.

Changing colonial office policy

The first changes occurred in Trinidad, St Lucia and Guyana, which were not given assemblies. As 'crown colonies' they were ruled under the system of Crown Colony government. Justification was that the colonies were previously the possessions of other powers and that foreign systems, cultures and peoples had to be brought in line with those of the British.

Introducing the system to the older colonies would cause conflict unless the assemblies could be convinced to surrender their powers. The Morant Bay rebellion provided an ideal opportunity.

Morant Bay

The Morant Bay rebellion was caused by oppressive economic problems, an uncaring and unrepresentative government, lack of access to land, increasing evictions of tenants and squatters and popular disgust with the court system.

The rebellion, led by Paul Bogle (Figure 5.8.1), occurred in St Thomas, Jamaica, on 11 October 1865. About 600 people were killed, as many wounded and Bogle and George William Gordon were hanged. This provided the opportunity for change in colonial administration.

Confederation riots in Barbados

In Barbados the planters were alarmed at the prospect of black labourers migrating for better conditions. They were also concerned about the move to Crown Colony government in neighbouring territories and staunchly guarded the rights of their Assembly (see also 8.1).

The black poor believed that the planters were blocking the governor's efforts to assist them. Riots broke out. Plantations and property were destroyed. Finally Barbados kept its Assembly and was no longer included in the federal plan.

Adoption of Crown Colony government

The British government established a Commission of Enquiry which reported that the system of government was not workable. The Jamaican Assembly was given the choice either to extend voting rights or surrender its powers to the Crown. It chose the latter and voted its own abolition. In 1866 the Crown Colony was established. The Governor ruled with the assistance of the nominated Legislative Council. While Council had the right to introduce legislation, ultimate power lay with the Colonial Office.

Assemblies surrendered their powers through fear of the political interests of the increasing number of black and coloured land owners qualified to vote. The coloureds in the Jamaican Assembly did not support planter policy, causing fear that a black-controlled Assembly would not seek the interest of sugar planters. Rather than face that possibility, they preferred to abolish the assembly.

Reaction to Crown Colony government

Planters, prominent coloureds and educated blacks felt that the agents of Crown Colony government answered to a distant ruler and had no sympathy for local people. The most important posts were reserved for members of the British colonial service and there were no means for considering public views. There were many complaints about inefficient and corrupt officials and the many foreign white officials in the top posts. Nominated elites were unrepresentative and possessed wide powers.

SUMMARY QUESTIONS

1. Why did the British government want to remove the Assemblies in the Caribbean?
2. What were the causes and consequences of the Morant Bay rebellion?
3. In what ways was Crown Colony government different from the old representative system?
4. How did the British government justify the implementation of Crown Colony government?

EXAM TIP

Remember that Morant Bay stimulated the general application of Crown Colony government, but the real cause of its introduction was to prevent black landowners from gaining control of the Assemblies.

ACTIVITY

Do some research and make a list of the events which occurred during the Morant Bay rebellion.

KEY POINTS

- The Old representative System presented obstacles to effective imperial control of the colonies.
- The desire of the British government to remove colonial Assemblies was evident since the early 1800s.
- Morant Bay was the catalyst to wider application of the policy.
- The political ambitions of the black and coloured landowners concerned planters and the British administration.
- The British government justified the system but there was much opposition to its implementation.
- The Confederation riots assisted Barbados to negotiate the preservation of its Assembly.

Section B, Theme 6: Caribbean economy (1875–1985)

6.1 The Caribbean and the world economy

LEARNING OUTCOMES

At the end of this topic you should be able to:

- Explain how world events impacted upon the economies of the West Indies, with special emphasis on the British colonised Caribbean.

DID YOU KNOW?

The Theory of Free trade was introduced by Adam Smith in his book *The Wealth of Nations*, published in 1776.

EXAM TIP

Pay attention to the reasons Britain opened her West Indian islands to free trade.

KEY TERMS

Royal Commission: a formal public enquiry set up by a government into a specific issue.

Britain opens up her markets

The 1846 Sugar Equalization Act allowed cane sugar produced in other countries on to the British market on the same terms as sugar from the British-colonised Caribbean. By the 1870s sugar produced in Brazil, Cuba, the Dominican Republic and Puerto Rico, which sold at cheaper prices, began to displace British Caribbean sugar. In the 1880s European-produced subsidised beet sugar flooded the British market and caused a fall in prices. Caribbean planters looked to North America and trade agreements with Canada and the United States.

The British Empire expands

British capitalists wanted new markets for the large volumes of items produced as a result of the industrial revolution. The older colonies offered very limited markets because of their small size and the poverty of their populations. Intense rivalry between countries for new territory led to the 'scramble for Africa' and Asia.

World depression bites

Between 1870 and the 1930s were depression years in the British Caribbean (Figure 6.1.1). Caribbean producers except Cuba and Puerto Rico found it difficult to make a profit. Many trading houses on which British Caribbean planters depended went bankrupt and planters were unable to attract investors. The value of estates dropped sharply and colonial governments found it difficult to collect taxes and pay wages on time. Reducing wages created conflict and tension.

Many planters went out of business. The sugar industry remained viable in Antigua, Barbados and St Kitts and Nevis, but of 2,200 estates in the region in 1838 there were 800 in 1900. The British government established the 1897 **Royal Commission** which recommended economic diversification. Post-war conditions stimulated further global depression in 1929.

Post war developments

During World Wars I and II West Indian people suffered economic hardships including shortages and rationing. The British followed a policy of preferential treatment for products like sugar.

By 1950 world production of sugar had recovered and Britain stopped preferential treatment and took a fixed quota. Sugar growers complained that this was not enough. In 1953 an International Sugar Agreement allowed British Caribbean sugar to compete in a free market. In 1958 the United States stopped importing Cuban Sugar and gave preference to sugar produced in the British Caribbean.

After 1945 Caribbean islands were encouraged to prevent reliance on imports and establish new industries by exploiting their natural resources. Loans were given as well as land grants. Special concessions were given to cement, textile and petro-chemical industries.

Move towards self-government

From 1865 most Caribbean islands had a Crown Colony government, except Barbados which still had representative government. Since the Governor had all the power under Crown Colony the white representatives were elected by him but had no say.

After 1875 Crown Colony government was attacked by mixed race people who called for proper representation. Before 1900 the British Government did permit governors to allow a few mixed race planters and men of means to sit in the Assembly.

Limited **franchise** was allowed in 1921. After the social unrest in 1936–37 the Moyne Commission of 1938 (see 8.3) suggested its extension and a move towards self-rule. During World War II the United States put pressure on the British to grant some form of self-government. In 1943–4 women were allowed to vote in some territories.

Between 1945 and 1947 Crown Colony was ended and territories were being prepared for self-government. The Westminster model was introduced: a parliament consisting of two houses. A primer, later known as a Prime Minister, was chosen by the governor to run the internal affairs of the island. The Crown still had control over defence and foreign policy and the primer consulted with the governor. There were political parties and people had the right to vote.

Between 1959–61 an attempt at federation failed. In 1962 most British West Indian territories opted for full independence.

SUMMARY QUESTIONS

1. Why did Britain introduce free trade policy in the 1840s?
2. How were people in the British Caribbean affected by the Great Depression of 1929?
3. Why did the British government support economic diversification for the Caribbean colonies from the end of the 1900s?
4. What factors stimulated the drive for self- government in the British-colonised Caribbean?

Figure 6.1.1 Between 1870 and the 1930s were depression years in the British Caribbean.

KEY TERMS

Franchise: the right to vote.

ACTIVITY

Design a timeline using images and maps to show the chronological stages in the movement towards independence in the British West Indies.

KEY POINTS

- Due to economic hardships Britain introduced a free trade policy.
- The British Caribbean colonies were exposed to competition on the British market and Britain sought expanding markets.
- The great depression had serious economic consequences for British Caribbean people.
- The demand for political change increased in the region.
- After World War II the process to self-government occurred gradually.

93

6.2 Decline of the sugar industry

LEARNING OUTCOMES

At the end of this topic you should be able to:

- Explain the factors that created the crisis in the British-colonised Caribbean sugar industry in the late 19th century.

Environmental factors

Sugar planters were adversely affected by natural disasters. A hurricane destroyed plantation works in Tobago in 1848. Drought was a seasonal feature of Antigua and Jamaica. In 1902 St Vincent's Soufriere volcano erupted, followed by Mt Pelee on Martinique (Figure 6.2.1). Earthquake and fire killed 5,800 in Jamaica in 1907.

Many islands were too mountainous to grow sugar cane. Tropical soils are only fertile for short periods and are quickly exhausted.

Figure 6.2.1 The eruption of Mt Pelée on Martinique in 1902 followed that of La Soufrière the day before.

DID YOU KNOW?

La Soufriere erupted on 7 May 1902, followed by the eruption of Mt Pelee in Martinique on the following day, killing 30,000. This destroyed the town of Saint-Pierre and the crops around it.

Trade regulations

The 1846 Sugar Equalization Act which opened British Caribbean sugar to free trade had a negative impact on the sugar industry. With the removal of preferential treatment Caribbean producers sugar faced competition from other producers who used enslaved labour and whose costs of production were lower than their own. The influx of subsidised beet sugar on the British market drove prices down to levels that were unprofitable for the British Caribbean planters, causing the failure of estates and economic instability in the region. Bounties were removed in 1920 but British Caribbean sugar planters, were unable to regain control of the sugar market and continued to plead for **imperial** assistance.

Technological backwardness

The sugar industry in the British Caribbean, especially in the smaller territories, remained very traditional in its operations. For some planters, indebtedness and inability to obtain credit and attract

EXAM TIP

Remember the impact of environmental factors on the Caribbean sugar industry, and the ecological factors that played havoc with sugar production.

investors prevented them from modernising their operations. Many never attempted to adjust their labour systems to suit a free society. They sought to resolve all the industry's problems through labour arrangements and remained dependent on an outdated labour-intensive system. By contrast their competitors took full advantage of new technology.

Factors of production

Capital

The sugar industry was established on a system of capital investment to establish the plantations, and credit advances, based on expected crop returns, to maintain operations. By 1875 Caribbean sugar was not attracting many investors, falling prices caused many of their credit houses to go out of business and crop returns were unable to clear debts. The indebted planters were unable to pay wages and meet everyday operating expenses. Estates were **foreclosed**, abandoned or sold at low prices. The 1854 the Encumbered Estates Act was established to manage the process.

Land

Land prices, which were very high in the 1700s, fell in the 1800s with the fall in sugar prices. Many estates changed hands. Soil fertility loss after years of continued cultivation was evident on some plantations. It was not possible to expand into new areas because suitable land was limited in some of the smaller territories and planters were unable to afford fertilisers and new cane varieties to boost production.

Labour

Planters continued to attempt to maintain a large labour force. From 1838 discontent over wages was evident but planters sought to reduce these as a way of dealing with the problems faced by the industry. The period was marked by escalating conflicts over wages, hours and terms of work. As we saw in 5.3 planters resolved the problem by indentured immigration but labourers were unhappy with working conditions. Workers migrated to the larger territories where rates of pay were higher. The fall in land prices released planter control of land in the British colonies, permitting African men and women to have increased access either as owners or squatters.

SUMMARY QUESTIONS

1. In what ways did natural disasters affect the Sugar industry in the 1800s?
2. What factors prevented Caribbean sugar planters from making use of new methods and technologies?
3. In what ways did beet sugar production affect the British Caribbean sugar industry?
4. What role did the factors of production play in the decline of the British Caribbean sugar industry?

KEY TERMS

Foreclosed: foreclosure is seizure of property by owners or financial authorities when contractual payments have not been made.

EXAM TIP

Make sure that you understand the connection between the factors of production (land, labour and capital) that caused the decline of the British Caribbean sugar industry.

ACTIVITY

Draw up a table listing, in one column, the inventions that could have been used to save the sugar industry. In the opposite column write a short note to explain why they were not implemented.

KEY POINTS

- Natural disasters and declining soil fertility negatively impacted on sugar cane production.
- Free Trade caused distress in the British Caribbean sugar industry.
- Planters were unable to afford new technologies to improve production and increase competiveness.

6.3 Resolving the crisis

LEARNING OUTCOMES

At the end of this topic you should be able to:

- Identify the measures used to deal with the crisis in the Caribbean sugar industry in the late 1800s and early 1900s.
- Assess the impact of these measures on the industry.

DID YOU KNOW?

Barbados, Trinidad and, Guyana and St Lucia did not adopt the Encumbered Estates Court Act.

EXAM TIP

Pay attention to the measures used by Britain to relieve distress in the colonies.

Imperial policies

In spite of complaints from planters, the British government could not change its policy because of pressure from the industrial and commercial sectors and the downturn in the British economy. However, they did take measures to ease the burdens on the Caribbean economies. They supported immigration in some territories and established several committees to examine the state of the colonies, identify problems and recommend solutions.

1847–8

A Select Committee of Enquiry to investigate the condition of the sugar and coffee industries in the British colonies resulted in a postponement of equalisation to 1854. The postponement was a result of pressure from planters to keep existing conditions.

1882

A Royal Commission sent to Jamaica and the Windward and Leeward Islands made several recommendations, although few were implemented:

- a reduction of the size of the Jamaica public service, to cut costs
- a single government for the Leeward and Windward Islands
- reduction in officers and salaries of the public service
- a standardised tax system for all the territories
- a reduction of import duties on basic foods, and an increase on luxury items
- removal of export taxes
- immigration
- encouragement of agricultural diversification by small farmers.

1896–7

The Royal Commission (Norman Commission) stated that foreign beet sugar was the cause of distress in the sugar industry and recommended:

- agricultural diversification
- expansion of the peasantry to increase food production
- agricultural education
- establishment of a Department of Botany to help small farmers
- financial grants to the Leeward Islands, Dominica and St Vincent to help land settlement and road development
- land settlement policies and the application of more scientific agriculture and improvement of the efficiency of estates.

The British government approved funds for implementing the recommendations and improving shipping to help the banana industry. It also established the Imperial Department of Agriculture in Barbados to help agricultural diversification.

Markets

As they faced increasing competition on the British market, Caribbean planters sought new markets for their sugar. Between 1875 and 1898, they accessed the US market. By 1882 Americans were buying about 50 per cent of British Caribbean sugar. In 1895 they bought 50 per cent of Trinidad's sugar. After 1898 that market was dominated by Cuban, Puerto Rican and American-grown sugar. Then they turned to Canada, which offered preferential tax to British Caribbean sugar in 1897, up to the 1920s.

Science and technology

The industrial revolution produced new technology which could increase productivity and efficiency. Encouraged by the British government, larger mills and factories and new equipment were widely used in the Caribbean. Steam-driven mills replaced water or animal-drawn mills and were in common use by 1900. Amalgamation of estates and the establishment of central factories first occurred in Guyana and Trinidad. Jamaica followed in the 1880s and Barbados in the 1920s. The vacuum pan (Figure 6.3.1) and the centrifugal dryer were introduced.

Field operations were improved by the use of fertilisers, ploughs and tillers and new varieties of disease-resistant cane. Railways provided swifter transport and carried greater volume. Research and experimentation conducted at the Imperial Department of Agriculture and the Imperial College of Tropical Agriculture led to new practices.

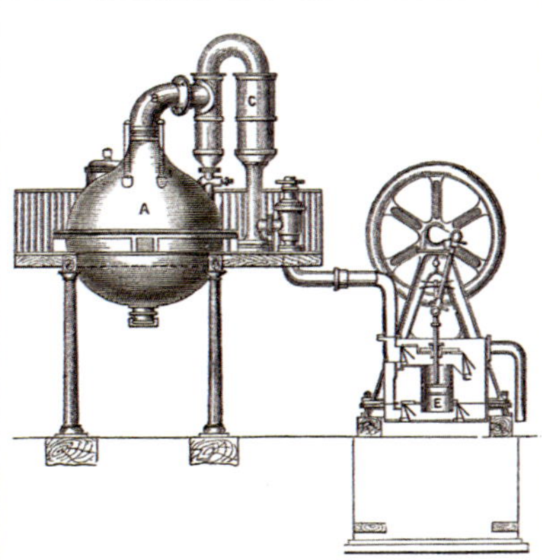

Figure 6.3.1 The vacuum pan improved efficiency in sugar production: the first to be used in the British Caribbean was in Guyana in 1832.

DID YOU KNOW?

The centrifugal dryer replaced the dripping method of the old curing house. The first vacuum pan in the British Caribbean was installed in Guyana in 1832.

The Imperial College of Tropical Agriculture in Trinidad was the forerunner of the 1960 University of the West Indies, St Augustine.

SUMMARY QUESTIONS

1. State why the 1847-48 commission was established and explain its impact on the British Caribbean sugar industry.
2. What were the main recommendations of the Norman Commission?
3. Describe the ways in which Caribbean sugar industry was modernised between 1846 and 1920.

KEY POINTS

- To assist the planters Britain delayed the period of equalisation.
- Planters were encouraged to seek new markets and practise more scientific agriculture.
- The British set up committees to investigate and report on the state of the sugar industry.
- Implementing their recommendations, especially those of the Norman Commission, was supported by the British government
- Plantations were modernised with new technology.

ACTIVITY

Draw up a timeline from 1875 to 1945 showing the chronology of British policies that were implemented to provide relief to the Caribbean sugar industry.

6.4 Growth of Cuba's sugar industry

LEARNING OUTCOMES

At the end of this topic you should be able to:
- Explain the factors that led to the growth of the Cuban sugar industry in the 1900s.

KEY TERMS

Reciprocal: in return for. A reciprocal agreement ensures benefits for both parties.

EXAM TIP

Pay attention to the significance of US investment in Cuba.

DID YOU KNOW?

The centrifuge is the equipment that separates sugar crystals from the mother liquid.

Triple crushing mills used in Cuba permitted extraction of 90 per cent of the juice from the canes.

Investments

After 1898, the most significant factor in the development of the Cuban sugar industry was the massive investment by US capitalists who came to dominate the industry within few years. The Platt Amendment (the 1903 **reciprocal** trade accord and legislation which permitted private railroads) allowed US investors free access to Cuba's land resources.

High sugar prices during World War I attracted even more US capitalists to Cuba. In 1915, US investment in Cuban sugar was estimated at $50 million and this rose by 1200 per cent in six years. In 1924, the Caribbean, mainly Cuba, received 63 per cent of US investment in world agricultural enterprise, the greatest US investment in the world. This enabled investors to purchase vast territory, build more powerful new mills and multiply private railroads for transporting cane and make the Cuban sugar industry highly mechanised.

Advanced technology

The Cuban sugar industry was characterised by gigantic mills which dominated thousands of hectares (acres) of land (Figure 6.4.1). Technology enabled rapid expansion of the industry. The *centrales* (sugar factories) built after 1898 included combinations of lands that were formerly estates, cattle or hog farms and forests. Between 1900 and 1915, 27 colossal *ingenios* (mills) which could produce enormous quantities of sugar in a single day, were established. Gigantic *latifundios* (estates) developed to feed these *centrales* and the network of private railroads moved cane swiftly from field to factory, and sugar from factory to port.

In 1898 the extent of private railroads in just two provinces was greater than had existed in the whole island. Modern technology brought greater efficiency to the Cuban sugar industry, tripled yields in refining and reduced costs of production.

The production of more than 1 million metric tons of sugar by about 15 *centrales* equalled what had been produced by 400 *centrales* in the late 1900s. Skilled workers trained to operate and service the modern equipment were employed.

Entrepreneurship

Investors in the Cuban sugar industry saw the potential for profits offered by the island's huge land resources, the security offered by Cuba's relationship with the USA and the declining position of beet sugar on the world market after World War I.

Land was cheap and the extensive forested areas offered opportunities for expansion. It was easy to attract labour through immigration schemes which paid wages in line with US trade union laws.

Markets

In 1903 the Reciprocal Trade Accord, which reduced by 20 per cent the tariffs on sugar and other products entering the US, provided Cuban sugar with an assured market. This was improved by The Sugar Act of 1948 which gave preferences to Cuban sugar in return for its cooperation in providing the US with additional supplies during World War II. Cuba did not have to compete with other producers on the US market until 1959 when the United States placed an **embargo** after the Castro Revolution.

Figure 6.4.1 A 19th century view of an *ingenio* (mill) in Cuba. Cuban sugar mills covered thousands of hectares of land.

> **EXAM TIP**
>
> Focus on the significance of the US market to the development of the Cuban sugar industry.

> **KEY TERMS**
>
> **Embargo**: a ban on trade with a foreign power.

> **ACTIVITY**
>
> Using old pictures of Cuba's sugar industry in the 1800s and early 1900s, describe the differences you notice between the two periods.

> **KEY POINTS**
>
> - Americans invested heavily in the Cuban sugar industry.
> - Modern technology was central to its growth and expansion.
> - Extensive land area, cheap prices and the Cuba/US relationship facilitated the rapid expansion of the industry.
> - Cuban sugar received preferential treatment on the US market up to 1959.

> **SUMMARY QUESTIONS**
>
> 1. What role did investment play in the development of the Cuban sugar industry?
> 2. What factors contributed to the success of the Cuban sugar industry?
> 3. Describe the technological features which contributed to the expansion of the Cuban sugar industry in the 1900s.

6.5 Growth and survival of alternative agriculture

LEARNING OUTCOMES

At the end of this topic you should be able to:

- Explain the factors that led to the development of alternative agriculture in the British Caribbean.
- List the crops that were cultivated.
- Assess the success of alternative agricultural ventures in the region.
- Explain the factors that encouraged the growth and survival of alternative agricultural enterprises in the British-colonised Caribbean up to 1935.

EXAM TIP

Focus on how the imperial government helped develop alternative crops in the British Caribbean.

Figure 6.5.1 Markets were found for alternative products such as coal.

DID YOU KNOW?

Cash crops for export included bananas, ginger, pimento, nutmegs, coconuts, rice, arrowroot, citrus and cocoa.

Government policies

After 1846 the policy of the imperial government shifted from its initial support for sugar production to encourage agricultural diversification. This change occurred after the sugar industry faced difficult times, and after freed Africans had pioneered diversification. They had been excluded by law from cultivating plantation crops.

Planters were opposed to the development of alternative crops. They argued that the resources would be better put to assist the sugar industry. They were also opposed to the off-estate activity of the freed workers.

Several officials commented on the dangers of the heavy reliance on only a single crop, but in response to the report of the Norman Commission (6.3), the British government encouraged colonial governors to implement its recommendations. The planters remained opposed.

Education and training

The Norman Commission had recommended providing agricultural education to make agriculture attractive, improve the quality of labour in the colonies and promote scientific agriculture.

Training programmes were provided at Departments of Agriculture. Cambridge University created a special school certificate programme for the colonies which was examined annually.

There were programmes for some estate workers. Teacher training programmes included agriculture and school principals were given short courses. Agriculture was introduced as a secondary school subject for the sons of planters to create a class of trained managers, and also at primary school level. Gardens were established in schools and the produce displayed at annual exhibitions, with prizes awarded to the schools with the best gardens, shared between students, teachers and principals.

Some parents were opposed to the programme because they felt it was restricting their children's opportunities. Some school principals did not want their schools to participate.

Markets

Markets for alternative crops were found locally, regionally and internationally. The internal marketing system provided an important outlet for food crops, fruit, locally made candies, jams, preserves, food preparations and coals (Figure 6.5.1). These items were also sold in the inter-island trade to Barbados and Trinidad. Here the sugar industry remained the dominant agricultural activity and there was a demand for food items in the growing urban centres.

Cash crops were exported to Europe, the United States and Britain. Agricultural exhibitions were held in each colony and the best produce was displayed at the grand exhibition in London which was organised annually by the Empire Marketing Board.

Investment capital

Initial investment into alternative crop production and trade came from the small farmers themselves. They saved their earnings, used traditional financial strategies such as sou-sou, reared and sold animals to generate capital for investment.

Opportunities for cheaper land acquisition increased where the sugar industry had failed. When the business possibilities of the new crops were demonstrated merchants, businessmen and plantation owners also became involved, along with some foreign and investment. The United Fruit Company invested in the banana industry and Cadbury's invested in the cocoa industry.

Investment in the inter-island trade remained mainly in the hands of the traders who increased their fleets as business grew.

Entrepreneurship

To make freedom real, the freed African men and women continued a trend begun during enslavement: they became **entrepreneurs**. The search for alternatives to plantation labour made them respond to the needs of free society by stimulating several types of business activity.

There was no organisational structure in place to develop a truly free society: planters wanted to maintain the practices of enslavement. The freed men and women assumed responsibility for creating independent spaces and economic activities through business activities.

These ventures allowed them to dominate the internal marketing system, and expand as hucksters and higglers, street vendors, shop and parlour keepers and reduce dependence on the exploitative plantation shops. They also used their skills to establish bakeries, woodworking, carpentry and other craft shops. Some entered into labour contracts with landowners which allowed them access to land which they cultivated to earn money for future business investment.

> **KEY TERMS**
>
> **Entrepreneur**: a person who sets up a business.

> **DID YOU KNOW?**
>
> The United Fruit Company was a corporation started in 1899 whose main purpose was to buy fruit, especially bananas from Central and South America and the Caribbean, and sell it in the United States.

> **ACTIVITY**
>
> On a blank map of the Caribbean name the British colonies and insert the alternative crops produced in each colony.

> **KEY POINTS**
>
> - Alternative crops were pioneered by free African men and women without assistance from government.
> - Markets were found locally, regionally and internationally.
> - Merchant and planters became involved when these crops proved profitable.
> - Agricultural education was introduced to make agriculture acceptable to the people.
> - Entrepreneurship was an important means to independence in free society.

> **SUMMARY QUESTIONS**
>
> 1. What factors led to the cultivation of alternative crops during the second half of the 1800s?
> 2. What problems did cultivators of alternative face and how did they overcome them?
> 3. Why and with what success was agricultural education introduced in the British Caribbean?

6.6 Services and tourism

LEARNING OUTCOMES

At the end of this topic you should be able to:

- Explain the factors that led to the establishment and growth of the service industries in the Caribbean up to 1985.

DID YOU KNOW?

Trinidad introduced the telephone in 1885 after three years of putting up lines and poles.

KEY TERMS

Flora and fauna: plants and animals of a region.

The move from agriculture

In the latter half of the 1900s the focus was mainly on sugar and other export crops. Falling revenues and the difficulties faced by the major export crops stimulated the development of alternatives. Visitors were attracted to natural features of the region such as waterfalls, caves, beaches, **flora and fauna** and the warm climate and botanic gardens. These provided the nucleus for the development of a tourist industry.

In Trinidad, the tourist industry was stimulated by some organised visits to the Pitch Lake in the 1890s but the island's economy was still based on the trade in pitch, the highly profitable cocoa, and when this failed, the oil industry.

Tourism developed in the other territories in the 1900s with the need to diversify the economies and create more employment opportunities.

Service industries

The demand for service industries increased with the growth of alternative economic activity. The changing fortunes of the sugar industry caused the collapse of its bankers, the West Indian Bank in 1847. The Colonial Bank was reorganised into an international bank in the 1860s. Canadian banks entered Jamaica in 1889, Trinidad in 1901 and Guyana in 1914, all aiming to provide banking services to the expanding business sector, which until then had no access to banks.

These businesses and the growing urban centres demanded a range of services including porters, drivers, trucking and heavy goods transportation, store clerks and attendants, lower level public servants, domestic and factory workers, cleaners and public transportation services.

They needed the security of banks and insurance companies to handle and protect their finances. With the growth of the business sector, life insurance was viewed as a means of saving money and as investment. By 1912 there were a growing number of insurance companies and a number of local and foreign insurance companies operating in the region.

Improved infrastructure

Improved infrastructure was required to support the diversification drive. Previously, emphasis had been on the needs of the sugar industry but the new business stimulated urbanisation and development which required basic services. Attention was now paid to road construction, transport (including rail and sea transport), communications, water supply, housing, sanitation and health services. The administrative structure was reorganised to create departments such as public works and health departments with responsibility for these services.

The usual means of obtaining water was from wells and rivers. Pipe-borne water was not fully implemented until after emancipation. In Trinidad dams were built and pipes ran water to Port of Spain by 1851, but in the 1900s many islands still did not have piped water.

The growth of tourism

European visitors have always been fascinated by the Caribbean landscape. During the 1700s and 1800s most visitors were absentee plantation owners and their relatives, missionaries, humanitarians, military or naval officers or administrators. The Caribbean was feared as 'the white man's grave' because of the high death rate of Europeans. Towards the end of the 1800s attitudes changed and the tropical climate became favoured for health and to escape dreary European winters.

The growing demand for visitor accommodation stimulated the growth of hotels and guest houses. After 1900s the Caribbean tourist industry expanded and tourism offered increased revenue earning opportunities and was able to replace the declining sugar industry (Figure 6.6.1). Communication was made easier with improved sea transport and the development of the airline industry.

Visitor numbers increased in the 1940s and by the 1960s arrivals exceeded 300,000. Tourism had become a major revenue earner, stimulating significant foreign and government investment in the industry. Some sugar estates were converted to hotels. To support the industry governments paid more attention to infrastructural development.

Figure 6.6.1 The early 20th century saw the expansion of the tourist industry in the region.

EXAM TIP

Focus on the factors which caused the development of tourism in the Caribbean.

DID YOU KNOW?

The Royal Victoria hotel opened in the Bahamas in 1861, Crane Beach Hotel Barbados in 1887 and the Mandeville and Titchfield in Jamaica in the 1880s. Between 1890 and 1969, 106 hotels were opened in Jamaica.

SUMMARY QUESTIONS

1. Why did Caribbean administrators attempt to diversify their economies into non-agricultural industries from the late 1800s?
2. What infrastructural changes occurred in the British Caribbean during the early 1900s and why?
3. Why did tourism become an important economic activity in the Caribbean in the 1900s?

ACTIVITY

Make a list of services and infrastructural improvements that were needed for the development of tourism.

KEY POINTS

- The Caribbean islands expanded their economic base into non-agricultural areas.
- Banking, insurance, health and tourism were service industries that developed in the late 1800s.
- Infrastructure was developed to facilitate economic diversity.

6.7 Industrial development factors

> **LEARNING OUTCOMES**
>
> At the end of this topic you should be able to:
> - Explain the factors that led to the establishment and growth of the extractive industries in the Caribbean.

> **DID YOU KNOW?**
>
> Asphalt was discovered in 1595 by Sir Walter Raleigh in Trinidad and used to cover boats to protect them from leaking.

> **DID YOU KNOW?**
>
> 'Industrialisation by Invitation' was an idea put forward in the 1950s by Sir Arthur Lewis, a Caribbean economist. His aim was to spur on production.

> **EXAM TIP**
>
> Remember that governments made concerted efforts to encourage the growth of industry in the Caribbean.

Natural resources

Industrialisation involved exploitation of the natural resources of the Caribbean: asphalt and petroleum in Trinidad; bauxite in Jamaica; gold, diamonds, manganese and bauxite in Guyana; lumber in Belize, Guyana and Trinidad and fisheries across the region. Commercial development of asphalt began in Trinidad in 1860, for street-paving in the USA and Britain.

Oil was discovered in Aripero, Trinidad in 1866 but the industry was not developed until the 1900s. The fuel demands of the British navy, when it changed from coal to steam, and the growth of the air industry provided important markets for Trinidad's oil. Many British and American companies became involved in the industry.

Gold was the first non-agricultural resource to be developed in the region.

Deposits of bauxite, which is used for aviation and automobile parts, pots, pans and roofing, were discovered in Jamaica in 1869 but production began only after World War II. Jamaica became the world's largest producer. Bauxite was discovered in Guyana in 1898; production began in Guyana in 1916. US and Canadian companies Alcan and Alcoa were the main investors.

Lumber from Belize, Guyana and Trinidad was used to make paper products. Marine resources led to the development of large commercial fishing enterprises.

Government policies

Fearing loss of income from sugar and alternative crops, colonial governments focused on industrialisation. They also wanted the Caribbean to become less dependent on imports, so legislation was passed in favour of foreign firms, and incentives were given in the form of land grants, protection from foreign competition, tax holidays and reduced taxes and tariffs.

In the 1950s governments invited foreign firms to enter the islands under favourable terms, and make use of local labour and resources. Under this policy many automobile, refrigerator and television firms opened in the Caribbean. Governments provided finance, advice and expertise to advance new industries.

Investment capital

Considerable capital was needed to extract and develop resources in the Caribbean. Foreign investment was needed and the colonial government gave incentives for foreign investors, as well as investing money itself. Most were large corporations, from England, the United States and Canada. They poured millions of dollars into the colonies for extraction manufacturing.

Technology

Until the early 20th century most industries depended on manual labour. New technology revolutionised the new industries and materials once dug out by manual labour were now extracted using excavators. Rigs, drills and refining equipment were brought in. Railways transported pitch to the ports and tankers and huge containers stored the oil.

The need for infrastructure to support the new industries led to new forms of transportation as cars, trucks, tankers, planes and ships were introduced, along with new forms of communication including the telegraph, telephone and television. Over time new forms of energy including electricity were used in industry.

Methods of communication

By 1850 there were a few private postal services, but a local system was not set up until the 1870s. Well into the 1980s most postal services were partly government controlled.

Steam ships also brought mail. Other forms of communication introduced included the telegraph in the 1880s, followed by the telephone. With the introduction of the plane, airmail began to be used in the late 1920s.

The cinema was introduced to Trinidad in 1911 (Figure 6.7.1), the radio in the 1930s and television in the 1950s. Although the initial stimulus for these communication technologies came from industry, they had an important effect on Caribbean society.

Human resources

After 1838 people moved to urban areas where the new industries offered higher wages. Many sugar and agricultural companies complained that their workers had abandoned them. Since much of the labour was unskilled employers offered training. Towns grew up where labourers from the peasantry and former **indentured** workers settled.

The surplus of cheap labour was also attractive to investors. Working conditions were often dangerous and dismissal instant. There were protests when wages did not rise in line with **inflation** and the cost of living. In spite of this, a labourer's income was higher than that of an agricultural worker.

Figure 6.7.1 The cinema was introduced to Trinidad in 1911.

ACTIVITY

Draw up a table with 3 headings: Asphalt, Petroleum and Bauxite. In each column put in two manufacturing industries that developed from each, and the dates they started.

KEY TERMS

Inflation: a general increase in prices.

KEY POINTS

- Natural resources (gold, asphalt, petroleum, bauxite) were developed.
- Colonial governments depended on foreign investment.
- Capital investment came mainly from big corporations.
- New equipment and machinery transformed production.
- There were advances in communication.
- Agricultural workers migrated to industry.

SUMMARY QUESTIONS

1. List the natural resources which were exploited in the Caribbean, the territory in which they were found and state what they were used for.
2. What strategies were used by Caribbean governments to encourage the development of non-agricultural industries?
3. In what ways did industrialisation affect the people of the Caribbean?

6.8 The effects of industrialisation

LEARNING OUTCOMES

At the end of this topic you should be able to:

- Assess the effects of industrialisation on the English-speaking Caribbean

EXAM TIP

Look at the different heavy and light industries associated with industrialisation and how these changed Caribbean economic patterns.

Urbanisation

We have seen how movement into towns and cities increased with industrialisation after 1890. Urban areas soon became overcrowded with poorly constructed wooden and adobe houses. Sanitary conditions were poor and the air and water were polluted.

By the middle of the 20th century brick, iron and steel were replacing the wooden structures, joined in the 1980s by high-rise buildings.

Occupations

Jobs could be obtained in the primary (extractive) industries, secondary (manufacturing) and tertiary (service) industries. Hauling and transportation were needed as well as extraction. The by-products from these industries led to jobs in the petro-chemical industries, involving plastics, synthetic oils and lubricants. From the aluminium industry evolved jobs in the automobile industry, refrigeration and roofing.

In manufacturing there were jobs in the garment industry as seamstresses, ironers, washers. In the food industry there were jobs in confectionery, milk and beer production. Other occupations included match-making, cigarettes, bricks, furniture and cement production.

Impact on women—social, economic, political

Before industrialisation women worked in agriculture and in markets. Since the asphalt, petroleum and bauxite industries mainly hired men, women tended to be employed in light manufacturing jobs. There was an increase in the number of women in employment because:

- Many factories preferred to employ women, who were paid less than men.
- The garment manufacturing and textile industries employed dressmakers and seamstresses.
- There was increased demand for domestic launderesses.
- Expanded educational opportunities allowed some women to qualify for entry into the public service.
- Hotels and tourist businesses employed women as waitresses.
- Female labour was demanded in steam laundries, food processing, agro-industries, paper factories and glass trades, match-making, cigar making, soap production, canning and tanning.
- The demand for male labour during World Wars I and II created openings for women in areas which had been reserved for men.
- Women moved into urban areas and worked as carriers, on the wharfs and as higglers (Figure 6.8.1).

Figure 6.8.1 Women worked as carriers, on the wharfs and as higglers.

There were negative outcomes. The development of garment factories reduced the demand for the services of skilled seamstresses and dressmakers who had to give up their independent operations and depend on paid labour from the factories. Women were not offered training and worked long hours for low pay without learning new skills.

Many women joined protest groups demanding change and compensation. They joined with men to protest working conditions in the 1930s and joined trade unions.

Standard of living

Higher wages meant that workers could move from mere subsistence. With many different goods and services people had more choice. The new inventions in communication and transportation improved people's lives and brought changes.

At the same time, people were oppressed by **inflation**, high prices, depression and slumps. Early working conditions were poor; there was no compensation for accidents, pensions, protection from employers and sometimes no increase in wages. This development of trade unions in the 1930s led to improvements, but even up to the later 20th century many industries had a poor record for treatment of workers.

DID YOU KNOW?

Even though women worked in many manufacturing industries, gender discrimination still continued.

ACTIVITY

Do an oral interview of people who lived during the industrialisation period. Find out how they felt about technological changes, conditions of work and the way of life at that time and how different it was from today.

KEY POINTS

- Urbanisation brought both positive and negative consequences.
- Industrialisation facilitated the employment of women.
- The impact of industrialisation varied according to social groups.

SUMMARY QUESTIONS

1. Explain the relationship between industrialisation and urbanisation.
2. How did industrialisation affect workers and employment in the Caribbean?
3. Explain the impact of industrialisation on women.

Section B Practice exam questions

SECTION B: Multiple-choice questions

1. Caribbean slave revolts contributed to the movement for Emancipation because they caused people in Britain to:
   i. question whether the laws of England permitted enslavement.
   ii. focus on the moral issue of enslavement.
   iii. show more humanitarian concern for enslaved people.

   a. i and ii only
   b. i only
   c. i and iii only
   d. i, ii and iii

2. Which of the following did NOT result from the Amelioration Proposals?
   a. Planters were opposed to the British government.
   b. There was an increase in enslaved resistance.
   c. The Assemblies refused to pass the laws.
   d. Many churchmen worked on the plantations.

3. Which of the Following was NOT a French slave-holding territory?
   a. Martinique
   b. Guadeloupe
   c. Dominica
   d. Haitii

4. Chinese immigration was terminated because:
   i. It was too expensive.
   ii. There were anti-Chinese immigration protests in China.
   iii. Planters preferred Indian immigrants.

   a. i only
   b. ii only
   c. iii only
   d. i, ii and iii

5. Peasants contributed to the economic development of Caribbean society in the following ways, EXCEPT:
   a. diversification of the economy
   b. increased food production
   c. development of inter-colonial trade
   d. starting manufacturing industries

6. Which of the following statements is NOT true of the Morant Bay Rebellion?
   a. The rebellion occurred in St Thomas, Jamaica, on 11 October 1865.
   b. The people revolted because the government did not pay attention to their complaints.
   c. A large number of white people were killed.
   d. About 600 black people were put to death and many were flogged.

7. The British government justified the introduction of Crown Colony government on the following grounds EXCEPT:
   a. to be impartial and serve the interests of all classes.
   b. to help the freed African attain political office.
   c. to reduce planter control of the colonies.
   d. to avoid the obstruction of the old Assemblies.

8. Which of the following countries provided markets for the new crops which were produced in the British Caribbean?
   i. Europe
   ii. The United States
   iii. Britain

   a. i only
   b. ii only
   c. iii only
   d. i, ii and iii.

9. Identify the MAIN reason why some parents were opposed to agricultural education.
   a. There were too many conflicts in the agricultural sector.
   b. They thought it would make their children dependent on estate labour.
   c. Agriculture was not seen as a desirable occupation.
   d. The wages paid in agriculture were too low.

10. All of the following are negative impacts of industrialisation on women EXCEPT:
    a. The development of garment factories reduced the demand for the services of skilled seamstresses.
    b. There was a demand for female labour in the light manufacturing industries.
    c. Many dressmakers had to give up their independent operations and depend on paid labour from the factories.
    d. The number of seamstresses fell from 13,000 in 1911 to 900 in 1931.

SECTION B: Additional practice questions

1. a In which three territories did major revolts occur during the 1800s?
   b What impacts, both positive and negative, did these revolts have on the emancipation process?

2. a State any THREE economic activities of the peasantry in the British Caribbean 1838–76.
   b Explain why the peasants of Jamaica felt that the colonial government and institutions up to 1866 were uncaring and insensitive.

3. What was responsible for the state of the British Caribbean sugar industry during the second half of the 1800s?

> Further practice questions and examples can be found on the online support website.

Section C, Theme 7: The United States in the Caribbean (1776–1985)

7.1 Reasons for the US interest in the Caribbean

> **LEARNING OUTCOMES**
>
> At the end of this topic you should be able to:
> - Explain the reasons for the United States' interest in the Caribbean between 1776–1870.

British North America and the Caribbean

Trade with the British North American colonies supplied Caribbean colonies with flour, beef, cornflour, oil and salted fish, and, for the plantations, livestock, staves and building materials. The trade provided a market in turn for Caribbean sugar, rum, molasses, hides, indigo and mahogany.

When the American War of independence began in 1776 Britain enforced the Navigation Acts and banned the British Caribbean colonies from trading with the USA until 1822 (except for 1783 when the policy was relaxed). US trade with the Spanish, French and Dutch colonies was not interrupted.

Defence

The United States believed that the security of its borders was related to the security of its neighbouring territory. This meant protecting the independent democracies in Central and South America, keeping foreign countries out of the Caribbean and keeping the region safe for democracy.

This policy was based on the Monroe Doctrine of 1823 which established the Western Hemisphere as the American responsibility and banned foreign nations from interfering in any of the territories. Interference would be viewed as an attack on the US.

This was the justification for US intervention in the Guyana/Venezuela border dispute in 1895, in Cuba 1898–9, Haiti 1905–20 and the Dominican Republic in 1916. It was also the reason for intervention in Cuba in 1959 and Grenada in 1983.

> **DID YOU KNOW?**
>
> The Monroe Doctrine was created by US President James Munroe in 1823.
>
> Journalist John O'Sullivan coined the term Manifest Destiny in 1839.

Expansionism

The idea that the US should expand was based on the belief in 'Manifest Destiny', the right to expand into new regions, have control of territory from coast to coast and become a great power. Once the national borders were secure, in the late 19th century Americans aimed to acquire overseas possessions to increase their supply of natural resources and ensure access to overseas markets. This led to influence in Cuba, Puerto Rico, Central and South America.

Trade and investments

Trade with the West Indies already existed in the 18th century. This increased with industrialisation to provide a market for mass-produced goods and to provide raw materials and other resources in turn.

> **EXAM TIP**
>
> Make sure that you understand how Manifest Destiny drove the United States to expand.

After 1865 the United States invested heavily in the Caribbean. From 1849 attempts were made to buy Cuba, since she was rich in land, to grow tropical crops. With the Gold Rush in California in 1849 attempts to find a shorter passage to the Pacific led to United States investment in the project to construct the Panama Canal. US private and government investment was pumped into railways, construction, mining, and plantations in Cuba, Puerto Rico, Haiti, the Dominican Republic and Honduras (Figure 7.1.1). Many United States companies quickly became rich.

Figure 7.1.1 The US invested heavily in the Caribbean, including the railway in Haiti.

US ideology

The Monroe Doctrine and Manifest Destiny were two of the ideologies, or beliefs, that led to US involvement in the Caribbean. Justification for this came from several policies:

- The Platt Amendment, 1903. The US forced the Cuban government to agree to terms that resulted in Cuba's loss of sovereignty. US jurisdiction was extended over Cuba and the US was allowed to establish naval bases on Cuban territory. Cuba could sign no treaties without US permission.
- Roosevelt Corollary, 1904. This strengthened the Monroe Doctrine. President Roosevelt announced the right of the US to oppose European intervention in the Western Hemisphere and to intervene in the domestic affairs of its neighbours who were unable to maintain law and order and democracy.
- Dollar Diplomacy, 1909–13. American business would be promoted in the hemisphere, and diplomacy would be used to promote US foreign policy goals. Security and protection for investments in the Caribbean would be provided and the US would intervene if anything went wrong.
- Gunboat Diplomacy was a basic policy by which the US was always prepared to apply economic pressure and use its military strength to control the Caribbean countries.
- Big Stick Policy 1916–33. This was a policy by which the United States used diplomacy and/or military force to intervene in Caribbean and Latin American countries.
- Good Neighbour Policy 1933. President Franklyn D. Roosevelt realised that previous policies had caused animosity to the US so he supported a new approach which promoted respect and goodwill and gave the impression that armed intervention would end.

DID YOU KNOW?

The proverb used by Roosevelt to support the use of American power in the world was 'Speak softly but carry a big stick.'

ACTIVITY

Make a list of the Caribbean territories in which the US intervened. For each territory, state the year of intervention and the policy which guided its operation.

KEY POINTS

- Before 1776 the relationship between the American colonies and the Caribbean was based on trade.
- After 1783 US relations with the Caribbean was based on expansion, investment and intervention.
- These approaches resulted from the central ideology of Manifest Destiny, the Monroe Doctrine and its supporting policies used to justify US actions.

SUMMARY QUESTIONS

1. Describe the nature of the relationship between the 13 American colonies and the Caribbean before 1776.
2. Why and how did this relationship change after 1776?
3. What policies justified and supported US activity in the Caribbean after 1776?

7.2 Factors and conditions of US relations in the Caribbean

LEARNING OUTCOMES

At the end of this topic you should be able to:

- explain the factors responsible for United States' involvement in selected Caribbean territories between 1898 and 1985.

DID YOU KNOW?

The United States bought the Danish islands for US$25 million and renamed it the US Virgin Islands.

KEY TERMS

Depression: a long-term downturn in economic activity.

Imperialism

Having completing its internal expansion in the 1860s, and after the end of the American Civil War, the US was ready for external expansion. Several factors influenced this shift:

- **depression** which began in 1893
- a fear that natural resources would be exhausted
- awareness of the new imperialism among the European powers
- concern that the US would be left out of the benefits of empire and new markets if it did not become involved.

To become a great nation, the US needed to build up its sea power and acquire colonies and defensive bases. This led to a focus on shipbuilding. By 1900 the US was the third largest naval power in the world 1900. Three examples of increasing US influence in the hemisphere were:

- the Venezuela/Guyana border dispute: the US supported Venezuela and forced Britain to agree to arbitration
- the Spanish/Cuban/American War of 1898, which gave the US control over Cuba
- the purchase of the Danish islands in 1917.

Trade routes

As we have seen, American ships had been plying trade between the West Indies and the mainland since the 18th century. By the 1800s the waters of the Caribbean were major shipping routes. With American investment in Cuba, Puerto Rico, Haiti and the Dominican Republic political stability was essential in the region to protect the trade route. The annexation of Hawaii and the growth of its Pacific trade stimulated interest in the construction of the Panama Canal and the urgent need to maintain peace in the region.

With the opening of the Pacific coast to trade since 1849, the United States saw the important potential for a canal near Panama. Since there was considerable investment in islands like Cuba, Haiti, the Dominican Republic and Puerto Rico there was a constant flow of goods from these territories to the United States. It was important to keep these routes free from trouble.

National security

For Americans, national security extended beyond their geographical boundaries. It meant protecting their independence, maintaining peace and stability in the region, excluding foreign intervention in the hemisphere, securing their trade and investment and keeping the world safe for democracy. A threat in any of these areas was seen as a threat to US national interest which necessitated military intervention from the US as the self-appointed regional police force.

Political instability

Americans believed that for the United States to be fully secure and stable there must be peace and political stability in their sphere of influence. This meant rulers who were favoured by the US, who supported US policies, who were considered democratic and who administered their countries along the lines determined by the US.

Rulers who failed to comply with the wishes of the US were classified as undemocratic. The occurrence of political tension in their countries would make Americans regard them as unstable and provide legitimate reasons to intervene. Administrative, social and political reforms which often empowered unpopular rulers would then be implemented.

Foreign interferences

The US saw the wider Caribbean region as the American hemisphere which had to be protected from foreign interference. We have seen how The Monroe Doctrine and The Roosevelt Corollary (7.1) made it clear that America would not tolerate foreign involvement in the affairs of the countries of the region and that any such involvement would be viewed as an attack on the US. We have also seen how in 1895 this resulted in a clear message to Britain regarding the Venezuela/Guyana border dispute. It also applied to German interests in the Dominican Republic 1916, and French and German interests in Haiti in 1915.

US intervention prevented the European powers from exercising any control over countries in the hemisphere.

Ideological conflict

Part of the Manifest Destiny of the US was the obligation to spread democracy across the globe. They gave financial, military and advisory support to any administration in the hemisphere that was pursuing those ideals. The US was firmly opposed to leftist or socialist governments and those which expressed anti-American sentiments and it intervened in countries where stability and US interests were threatened by opponents to democracy. Thus the US intervened in the Dominican Republic (1899, 1911), Haiti (1915), Guyana (1953), Cuba (1959) and Grenada (1983; see Figure 7.3.1).

SUMMARY QUESTIONS

1. What factors led the US to pursue imperialist policies from the 1890s?
2. How did the US define national security?
3. Why did the US intervene in Caribbean countries between 1890 and 1983?

EXAM TIP

Focus on the reasons why the US wanted to exclude foreign involvement from the Caribbean region.

Figure 7.2.1 The US intervened in countries where it believed its interests were threatened.

ACTIVITY

Draw up a table that lists all the Caribbean territories in which the United States intervened, up to 1985. Give the year of the intervention, include the reason for it and the result.

KEY POINTS

- Overseas expansion established the US as a great power.
- US overseas expansion was caused by several factors.
- US security and national interest were closely linked to regional peace and security.
- Trade, ideology and politics stimulated US intervention in the region.

7.3 US foreign policy 1: Cuba, Puerto Rico and Panama

LEARNING OUTCOMES

At the end of this topic you should be able to:

- Explain the causes of the United States' involvement in Cuba, Puerto Rico and Panama
- Explain the consequences of this involvement.

DID YOU KNOW?

Puerto Rican peasants had to seek employment in the US controlled sugar industry to be able to pay the heavy taxes imposed on them by the US authorities.

Cuba 1898

The war with Spain provided the US with the opportunity to put its expansionist policy into practice.

The Cuban struggle for independence from Spain, the explosion of the battleship Maine in the harbour of Havana and stories of Spanish brutality to the nationalist fighters caused US to join the war in April 1895. Already weakened by the nationalist troops, Spain was easily defeated by the American troops and on 12 August signed the treaty giving Cuba independence.

American military forces remained in Cuba until 1902, improved infrastructure, reformed medical and sanitation services and reorganised the island's administrative system. Disappointed that the new Cuban constitution made no reference to the US, Congress passed the Platt Amendment which took away Cuban sovereignty, giving the US the right to intervene in Cuba to preserve life, property and independence and to establish naval stations on the island.

American investors flocked to Cuba and invested heavily in the sugar industry buying up plantations, factories, refineries and railroads, causing sugar to dominate the economy. Revolts against American imperialism led to US troops occupying the island in 1906–9 and in 1912.

Puerto Rico 1898

Puerto Rican resistance to Spanish rule began in the 1820s and increased in the 1890s. Spain agreed to partial independence when control of the island fell to the US. American troops occupied the island in 1898 and remained there until 1900.

In the 1890s the Puerto Rican crisis in the sugar industry caused land prices to fall dramatically. Lands were eagerly bought up by Americans, who invested in the industry, created large plantations on the island and transformed farmers into paid labourers dependent on imported food.

During the first year of the occupation transfer of land was common and large companies owned by a small group of American investors were formed, but there were also some independent English, French, German, Corsican and Spanish investors.

In 1900 the Foraker Act established a civilian government and defined Puerto Rico as an 'incorporated territory' of the US.

High sugar prices during World War I favoured Puerto Rico whose sugar was sold on the protected US market. Poor Puerto Ricans were subject to political, economic and cultural domination, as the US controlled all spheres of life, and they did not benefit from the prosperity.

In 1917 the Jones Act declared Puerto Rico American territory and all Puerto Ricans to be American citizens.

Panama 1903

The US sought a canal to link the Atlantic to the Pacific to facilitate trade and defence. Nicaragua was the first site considered, then the shorter route through Panama, then part of Colombia, was favoured. Treaty arrangements which gave Colombia $10 million and an annual rent of $250,000.00, and perpetual rights to a six-mile radius canal zone to the US, caused outrage in Colombia where the Senate refused to approve it.

President Roosevelt was angry. He supported an organised revolt in Panama in November 1903 and the US landed troops to maintain order and prevent the government of Colombia from putting down the revolt. Within three days the independence of Panama was recognised, the Panamanian government agreed to the terms which Colombia had rejected and work began on the canal (Figure 7.3.1). It was opened in 1914.

Figure 7.3.1 Many Caribbean labourers worked on the construction of the Panama Canal.

ACTIVITY

Create a cartoon or poster representation of US intervention in Cuba, Puerto Rico and Panama.

SUMMARY QUESTIONS

1. Why did the US join the Spanish /Cuban war in 1898?
2. How did American control affect the political life of Puerto Rican people?
3. Explain how the US gained control of the land area around the Panama Canal in 1903.

EXAM TIP

Remember how the US obtained a favourable agreement to construct the Panama Canal.

DID YOU KNOW?

Jamaicans provided labour for the Caribbean Railroad Company in Panama (1850–5). Caribbean workers worked on the Panama Canal under Ferdinand de Lesseps (1881–9). More than 150,000 Caribbean workers built the Panama Canal (1904–14).

KEY POINTS

- US intervened in Cuba to further its interests in the region.
- US possession of Puerto Rico caused the loss of its independence.
- The desire for a canal to facilitate movement of goods and people led to soured relations between the US and Colombia and resulted in the independence of Panama.

7.4 US foreign policy 2: Haiti, Dominican Republic and Grenada

LEARNING OUTCOMES

At the end of this topic you should be able to:
- Explain the factors responsible for United States' involvement in Haiti, Dominican Republic and Grenada 1898–1985.

KEY TERMS

Puppet administration: a government that appears to be independent but is in fact controlled by an outside power.

DID YOU KNOW?

Cacos, Haitian guerrillas, put up a strong resistance against the US occupation.

KEY TERMS

Guerrilla: from the Spanish 'little war', a fighter in a small independent group.

EXAM TIP

Concentrate on the impact of World War I (and the need to protect the Panama Canal) on the United States' decision to intervene in Haiti and the Dominican Republic.

Haiti 1915

The overthrow of President Guillaume Sam, killed by a mob, led to a US invasion of Haiti in 1915. Political and strategic reasons given for the invasion were the need for reforms to end political instability, suspicion of German intent to establish a naval base in Môle St Nicholas, and continual revolutionary activity in northern Haiti.

There were, however, other explanations. The frequent change of government was of concern to American businessmen who had investents in banking, railway and agriculture. US financial investments in the country had increased significantly by 1910 and loans had been made to the Haitians. In addition, the likely successor to President Sam was an anti-American nationalist, President Arias, whom the US opposed.

US troops landed in Haiti on 28 July, and with support from troops from Cuba, defeated the Haitians and occupied the country. They installed a **puppet administration** and:

- permitted whites to own land
- reintroduced forced labour and taxes on peasants
- re-established economic and political control by a coloured elite, so reducing black political influence
- restored white elitism (white US officials controlled the top administrative positions)
- decreased the size of the Haitian army.

US marines arrested guerrilla leaders, disarmed the population and trained a national police force to fight the **guerrillas** and impose order.

Many Haitians hated the US presence, seeing it as a reversal of the gains they had made in 1804. The US occupation lasted for 19 years, but US marines remained in Haiti until 1934. The US controlled the Haitian national budget until 1941.

Dominican Republic 1916

Political instability in the Dominican Republic after the assassination of President Rámon Cáceres caused violent confrontation and civil war. Political and military leaders fought for power. US attempts to end the civil war failed and they threatened to intervene if a solution was not found. In 1916, when Dominicans refused a treaty which would have made them a protectorate of the US, the government collapsed and the US invaded the country (Figure 7.4.1).

Peasant guerrillas resisted the US military and sugar company security forces in a war that lasted from 1917 to 1921. The US used members of the US-marine-trained Dominican National Guard to put down the rebellion and punish the **guerrillas**.

Figure 7.4.1 In 1916 political instability in the Dominican Republic led to a US invasion.

Grenada 1983

On 13 March 1979 the New Jewel Movement run by Maurice Bishop overthrew Eric Gairy's United Labour Party government. Bishop established the People's Revolutionary Government. The United States feared that many of Bishop's economic reforms seemed communist in nature and that, like Cuba, the island was favouring **communism**. Bishop himself accused the United States of bullying and destabilising tactics.

Fears grew when it was discovered that Cuban engineers were helping in the construction of the National Airport.

In October 1983, with civil unrest and violence increasing, President Ronald Reagan sanctioned 'Operation Urgent' and the United States invaded with 6000 troops. An interim government was set up and United States troops withdrew in phases.

The United States claimed that it had invaded at the request of the Members of the OECS (the Organisation of Eastern Caribbean States, led by the Prime Minister of Dominica, Eugenia Charles), and the Governor General of Grenada, Sir Paul Scoon, and to protect US citizens at St George University. But the US was uncomfortable with a communist government in the Caribbean and used the opportunity to send a strong warning to the region.

SUMMARY QUESTIONS

1. Describe the actions taken by the US occupation government in Haiti between 1915 and 1934.
2. What were the consequences for the people of the Dominican Republic of the US occupation in 1916?
3. Why did the US invade Grenada in 1983?

DID YOU KNOW?

Trinidad and Tobago and Guyana were the only two Caribbean nations which opposed the US invasion of Grenada.

ACTIVITY

Prepare a table to compare US actions in Haiti, Dominican Republic and Grenada. On one side list similarities and on the other state differences. Draw conclusions about US actions in these territories.

KEY TERMS

Communism: political system that supports common ownership and sharing of wealth. There is a history of US opposition to communist movements in the Caribbean.

KEY POINTS

- US intervention in Haiti, the Dominican Republic and Grenada illustrate the application of the Monroe Doctrine and the Platt Amendment.
- Facilitating and protecting US business interests were its main concerns.
- The US supported unpopular and corrupt regimes in the interests of 'democracy'.
- US intervention did not increase political rights of the ordinary citizens nor reduce political instability in Haiti.
- US determination to advance democracy and prevent the spread of communism in the region led to the invasion of Grenada.

7.5 US involvement: economic, political and cultural consequences

LEARNING OUTCOMES

At the end of this topic you should be able to:

- Assess the consequences of the United States' involvement in Caribbean territories 1898–1985.

DID YOU KNOW?

Territories giving concern to the US in 1983 were Cuba, Grenada and Nicaragua under the Sandinistas, Jamaica under Michael Manley and Suriname under Bouterse.

EXAM TIP

Pay attention to the importance of the politics of the time in the US decision to invade Grenada. The era was known as the Cold War (see 7.7).

KEY TERMS

Prohibition: a ban imposed in the US on producing, importing, transporting or selling alcoholic drinks. The ban lasted from 1920 until 1933.

Cuba after 1898

After the war of 1898 (see 7.3), Cuba was free of Spanish rule but came under US control. The Platt Amendment of 1901 dominated political life and took away Cuban sovereignty by preventing Cuba from engaging in any diplomatic and financial dealings with foreign governments. The US now had the right to intervene to preserve law and order. This they did in 1917, 1933 and 1959.

By 1905 US businesses controlled more than 60 per cent of rural property in Cuba. American investors also controlled industries in tobacco, mining, railroads and power production, although British, German and French investments were still allowed. High prices during World War I caused speculation and generated huge profits for American investors. In 1920 the beet sugar industry recovered, the price of cane sugar fell, investors went bankrupt and many Cuban banks collapsed. This allowed American and Canadian banks to dominate the Cuban economy. American investors bought up prime land to establish and expand sugar estates. Cuba became the major supplier of sugar to the US which consumed all the sugar exports between 1903 and 1910. By 1920 the sugar industry was dominated by the US. Over 75,000 acres of Cuban land was in the hands of a small group of American individuals and corporations.

US tourists flocked to Cuba to escape **Prohibition** while US investors built many hotels and resorts where drinking and gambling were common forms of entertainment for the visitors. The US forged strong links with Cuban President Fulgencio Batista who protected their interests, but at the expense of the Cuban people.

The oppressed Cubans joined with Fidel Castro to liberate Cuba from American imperial control and American-installed puppet governments.

Puerto Rico after 1898

Puerto Rico was ceded to Spain by treaty in 1898, after which US troops occupied the island and brought it under US control. The island was ruled by a US military government for two years until, by the Foraker Act of 1902, the US established a civilian government which was controlled by US-appointed officials. The Act was intended to restrict foreign business.

By the 1920s US corporations dominated commercial agriculture, with US investors and companies owning large estates and sugar dominating the economy. Most Puerto Ricans depended on the sugar industry for their livelihood. Sugar production doubled, tobacco and coffee industries expanded. Peasants, however, became landless and dependent on paid employment. Labourers were forced to accept unfavourable terms and low wages. Many became unemployed (Figure 7.5.1).

Puerto Rico became fully integrated into the US economy and was dependent on the US for economic survival. It was made an incorporated territory of the US in 1907, but the US still exercised political control of the island, appointing governors and the main officials.

The US still maintains political and legal control as Congress controls immigration and other critical policies and is able to support American economic exploitation of the island. There is more information about the status of the territory and its citizens in 8.10.

Panama 1903

The French company that had been working on the Panama Canal collapsed in 1889, causing the US to abandon its rival venture to build a canal through Nicaragua, and take over construction. In 1903 the United States and Colombia (the proposed canal was in Colombian territory) signed a treaty that enabled the US to take over the construction, but the Congress of Colombia rejected the measure. The US then supported the separatist movement in Panama and hindered Columbian efforts to crush a rebellion which broke out in Panama.

The Revolutionary Junta declared the independence of the Republic of Panama in November 1903 and the new republic was immediately recognised by the US. The new Panamanian government signed a treaty for the creation of the proposed canal. In exchange for US control, Panama would receive assistance in attaining its independence from Columbia.

The US flag was hoisted on the Canal Zone on 4 May 1903, beginning American influence in the area. Many Caribbean workers migrated to Panama in search of work, but US firms dominated business. Local Panamanians enjoyed few of the business opportunities and resented the US influence. Workers in the Canal Zone benefitted from better health, but there were social, racial and industrial divisions.

In the 1940s the US invested in the country's defences and after the war they provided technical and financial aid. Increased opposition to US control led to a decision in 1967 to share administration of the Canal and grant more rights.

Haiti 1915

The US intervened in Haiti in 1915, to protect investments in banking, railway, and agriculture amid the political confusion. Haiti also had an outstanding loan. The US was also suspicious of German activity in the region and used the entire island as a base during World War I.

The Haitian constitution was amended to permit foreign land ownership and several firms received concessions to establish plantations. They paid low wages while receiving huge profits. Privileges and top positions were given to whites and coloureds, who had long been

Figure 7.5.1 While some industries expanded in Puerto Rico, many poorer people were unemployed or working for very low wages.

DID YOU KNOW?

On 15 August 1914, the Panama Canal was inaugurated with the passage of the USS *Ancon,* a cargo and passenger ship, two weeks after the outbreak of World War I. After decades of protest and negotiations, The Panama Canal passed to Panamanian control in December 1999.

7.5 (continued)

in conflict with blacks for dominance. Haitians reacted with three rebellions between 1915 and 1920, all suppressed by US forces.

US policies protected their investments and increased their interests. There were improvements in health and education, water and sanitation, electrification, railway construction, banking, and social services—but only in some urban areas. The intervention aggravated Haiti's social, political and economic problems, with most Haitians remaining poor, exploited, unemployed and landless, problems that were still evident in 1985.

US political decisions were offensive to many Haitians who saw them as a reversal of the strides made since independence in 1804. People felt oppressed by forced labour, destruction of democratic institutions and the racism of the troops. The US reduced black political influence, decreased the size of the Haitian army and sent the disbanded soldiers to work in agriculture and other areas. Male peasants worked without pay on projects such as road construction.

Meanwhile the US re-established white rule and coloured control of politics and business and so increased racial and class tensions between black and whites and coloureds in Haiti.

Haitians who lived or worked in or near the US barracks did develop a taste for American consumer goods, but the more lasting impact is reflected in music, clothes and language.

Dominican Republic 1916

On 16 May 1916, after more than four years of civil war which followed the assassination of President Cáceres, the US intervened in the Dominican Republic. The occupation was extended across the country for two main reasons:

- The US claimed that the Dominican Republic had incurred unauthorised debts with foreign countries and had contravened the 1907 agreement
- the occupation was necessary to prevent a perceived German threat during the war.

A puppet regime directed by the US military governor was installed. In spite of increased opposition, the occupation lasted until 1924.

The US made some improvements to infrastructure, communication, health and education but their main policy was to make the Dominican Republic a safe haven for US business, with US sugar companies encroaching on peasant properties.

Uprisings by *gavileros* (guerrillas) were unsuccessful and American companies received concessions for lumber, cotton plantations, flour mills and oil exploration. They displaced the German companies who had controlled the foreign market before the war.

American firms opened new businesses; tax incentives encouraged US imports, which displaced local **artisans**. By 1919 two-thirds of

Figure 7.5.2 The Dominican Republic today: US involvement aimed to make a safe haven for US business.

KEY TERMS

Artisan: a skilled, often manual, worker.

the country's trade came from the US and its foreign trade favoured the US. As elsewhere, Dominicans received low-paid jobs in prosperous industries. Income flowed uncontrollably to the US.

Grenada 1983

In 1983 the US was concerned at communist influence in the region. A political crisis in Grenada led to discussions between President Ronald Reagan, Prime Minister Eugenia Charles of Dominica (Chairman of the OECS) and the Prime Ministers of the OECS countries, and intervention took place on 25 October 1983, with support from military and policemen from Barbados and the OECS. The motive was to protect US citizens in Grenada, to respond to an official request for assistance from the OECS, and an appeal from other regional states.

After a four-day battle between the US forces and the People's Revolutionary Army and Cuban soldiers, restoration of order was supervised by the US forces and policemen from the OECS and Barbados. A US embassy was established, and a US Information Service, to oversee political and economic rehabilitation.

Rehabilitation included completion of Port Salines Airport, construction projects, road, infrastructure and school repair and rebuilding of the destroyed hospital. Compensation was to be paid for damaged property. Grenadian students in Cuba were offered scholarships in the US and injured Grenadians were offered health care. US experts advised on every aspect of life, there were special advisers on security and international relations and US businessmen were encouraged to invest in Grenada.

The US supported an interim government and an Advisory Council was established to until elections could be held. Once this process for restoring democratic government had begun, the US provided significant financial assistance to government programmes in Grenada, and aid to other Caribbean countries.

> **ACTIVITY**
>
> Research the Cold War and how it affected developments in Grenada in 1983. List the key points, as if you were making a presentation to a group.

> **KEY POINTS**
>
> - US corporations dominated the Cuban sugar industry after 1898.
> - Puerto Rico became a colony of the US.
> - Infrastructural and social improvements were made there, but for most people welfare was not improved.
> - The US created an American zone in Panama.
> - US intervention in Grenada was largely determined by political concerns, especially the Cold War with the USSR.

> **SUMMARY QUESTIONS**
>
> 1. In what ways did the Platt Amendment affect the development of Cuba?
> 2. What benefits did the people of Panama gain form the construction of the Panama Canal?
> 3. What were the long-term consequences of the US intervention for Haiti?
> 4. Explain the nature of the economic relationship that developed between the USA and the Dominican Republic.
> 5. Explain the factors which led to the US invasion of Grenada in 1983.

7.6 Policies of the Castro revolution

LEARNING OUTCOMES

At the end of this topic you should be able to:
- Define the Castro Revolution.
- Describe the policies of the Castro revolution.

Figure 7.6.1 Fidel Castro wanted to transform Cuba into a developed independent nation.

KEY TERMS

Tertiary: third. Tertiary education refers to colleges and universities for students who have completed secondary schooling.

EXAM TIP

Emphasis should be placed on how Castro used nationalism and communism to support the Revolution.

DID YOU KNOW?

The US government recognised the Castro Government on 7 January 1959.

Castro's rise to power

After two failed attempts in 1953 and 1955 to remove the corrupt, oppressive regime of Fulgencio Batista, Fidel Castro formed the 26 July Movement, launched a long guerrilla war which finally removed Batista at the end of 1958. Castro aimed to transform Cuba to a developed independent nation and members of his movement formed the core the new government (Figure 7.6.1).

Political, economic and social reforms

Castro established a provisional government which he controlled, and legalised the Communist party. The government took control of all aspects of the economy and owned all sugar mills and factories. Under the Agrarian Reform Law of 1959 Castro confiscated and redistributed large land holdings and banned foreign land ownership. He nationalised US-owned businesses which brought conflict with the US. This led to closer relations with the then USSR: on 16 April 1961 Castro declared the revolution socialist and made the Communist party Cuba's only party. In 1972 Cuba became a member of the Soviet bloc, Council for Mutual Economic Assistance.

Social reform was very important to Castro. His education, health and housing system became the best in Latin America. He built and staffed hospitals and clinics across the island. Education was also key to the success of Cuba. Castro built primary, secondary and **tertiary** institutions and technical schools and reduced illiteracy. By 1970 Cuban doctors, nurses, technicians and agriculturalists were being sent to Latin America, Africa and Asia as advisers and experts. In housing he reduced rentals and instituted a housing scheme that led to 80,000 homes being built in 1963.

Consolidation of the revolution

To consolidate his revolution, Castro centralised his government and removed all opposition. Land owners, industrialists, businessmen, rich and middle-class people, playwrights and intellectuals were imprisoned or deported. He permitted prison inmates to migrate to the US. Through nationalisation the government controlled all aspects of Cuban life.

Castro offered Cubans a complete change from the experiences of the Batista era. He gained popular support by his land, housing and health care policies which were supported by a pro-Cuba education programme and a policy of slogans advertised across the country to create a loyal population.

Castro used long public speeches to attack his opponents. He encouraged the Cuban people to develop the virtues of austerity, discipline, selflessness and comradeship on which to build a new Cuba. Castro accelerated the programme of centralisation in response to US aggression and in anticipation of a US attack.

Then Castro sought external support through assistance to revolutionary struggles in Angola, Mozambique and Ethiopia and the spread of revolutionary ideas around the world.

Nationalism and communism

The Cuban revolution began as a nationalist struggle rooted in the long anti-colonial struggle to make Cuba free. *Cuba Libre* (Free Cuba) was a nationalist slogan which was used to develop popular support for the revolution. Castro stimulated nationalism by explaining to his followers what was necessary to liberate Cuba.

It meant freeing Cuba from oppression and oppressors, from local and foreign exploiters and from countries which sought to impose their will on the people of Cuba. It also meant keeping the resources of Cuba to benefit the people of Cuba. He showed through his social policies how the communist approach would benefit the population. US responses to his policies caused Castro to forge closer ties with the USSR. The US was identified as the enemy of the Revolution and people of Cuba. Communism and the Communist Party of Cuba would help Cuba preserve its sovereignty against US aggression.

Opposition to the US

Castro had seen first-hand the corruption and abuse by the US in Cuba and sought to free Cuba from US influence. In 1960 he warned the Cuban people of the danger of an invasion by the enemies of the Cuban Revolution and urged them not to give up the fight. His famous slogan was *Patria o muerte, venceremos* (Country or death, we will conquer). Then came a tit-for-tat series of measures. In 1960 he confiscated US-owned plantations and industries and nationalised others. In retaliation the US cut sugar quotas and put political pressure on Castro.

In response Castro signed a treaty with the USSR to sell sugar in return for oil. The USSR also gave them a loan to industrialise the nation. Castro then cancelled all United States mining leases. The United States cancelled all sugar exports, but the USSR bought all Cuba's sugar. In November 1960 the US imposed a trade **embargo** on Cuba. Castro then fully embraced communist USSR which gave Cuba economic, political and social assistance.

SUMMARY QUESTIONS

1. What caused the Cuban Revolution?
2. What strategies did Castro use to consolidate the Revolution?
3. Describe the social policies Castro implemented in Cuba.

DID YOU KNOW?

Heroes of the Cuban Revolution were Jose Martí, Ernesto 'Che' Guevara and Antonio Macéo.

ACTIVITY

You are a solider in Castro's revolutionary army stationed in the mountains. Write a letter to your parents in Havana telling them why you joined the movement and how you see the nation changing in the future.

KEY POINTS

- The Cuban Revolution was a part of the Cuban anti-colonial struggle.
- Corruption of the Batista administration and US interference sparked the Cuban revolution.
- Castro aimed to create a new, developed and free Cuba.
- Castro used political, economic and social policies to consolidate the revolution.
- Castro used a variety of measures to unite his people to fight against enemies of the Revolution.
- His policies affected relations with the USA and the USSR.

7.7 The US response

LEARNING OUTCOMES

At the end of this topic you should be able to:

- Describe US responses to the policies of the Castro revolution.

Figure 7.7.1 Anti-Castro rebel prisoners. The failure of the Bay of Pigs invasion in 1961 enhanced Castro's image.

KEY TERMS

Ideological: relating to the ideas and ideals of a political theory.

DID YOU KNOW?

The United States launched the Alliance for Progress, which gave economic, cultural and social assistance to nation states in the western hemisphere which remained democratic.

The Cold War

After World War II tensions between communist USSR and the democratic US resulted in the Cold War, which lasted from 1945 to the fall of communism in 1989. This was a state of hostility between the two superpowers when they sought to influence world events and dominate by winning support for their **ideological** position without coming into open warfare with each other.

As they competed for global influence, both countries were engaged in an arms race in preparation for open conflict and to provide assistance to their supporters. Cuba became involved in cold war politics because it was viewed by US politicians as an important part of the defence of the southern US, key to maintaining control of the Caribbean and the shipping lanes to and from the Panama Canal. The US was also concerned with the menace of **communism**.

Political and economic embargo

In response to Cuban's National and Centralisation policy, the US aimed to cripple Cuba's trade. It cancelled Cuban sugar quotas and discouraged citizens from travelling to Cuba. In 1962 the United States imposed an economic **embargo** and a naval blockade of the island, allowing in only limited supplies of food and medication.

President Eisenhower ended political relations with Cuba in January 1961, branded Cuba a rogue state and banned all Cuban politicians from entering the United States. Americans arranged for Cuba to be expelled from the Organisation of American States (OAS) and supported Castro's opponents in several attempts to overthrow him.

Ideological warfare

To prevent communist influence from spreading, the United States followed a policy of assistance to fragile states and aggression towards the countries which did not comply with its wishes. At the OAS conference in 1962 the US declared that any country adopting communist ideology would be considered unfriendly and hostile to the United States and subject to US retaliation. When Guyana, under Cheddi Jagan, showed signs of communist leanings the US sent CIA agents to destabilise the country.

Military intervention

Bay of Pigs

Cuba's nationalisation of foreign-owned and larger Cuban-owned businesses created local tension which led to the first big wave of angry anti-Castro migrants to the US. They organised a plan with support from President Kennedy, for 13,000 Cuban exiles to invade

Cuba, stir up a rebellion and overthrow Castro. Using US bombers piloted by Cuban exiles, the plan was to make an air strike followed by two landings in the Bay of Pigs area to launch the attack. The attack was a miserable failure. The exiles were defeated by Castro's forces. Over 1,250 were killed and the remainder were captured and bartered in 1963 for medical supplies. Cubans saw it as a victory over the meddlesome USA. It earned support for the Revolution and enhanced Castro's image (Figure 7.7.1).

Cuban missile crisis

After the Bay of Pigs disaster Castro concluded a commercial and military pact with the USSR. He wanted to prevent a repeat of the Bay of Pigs attempt and to quell internal rumblings in Cuba, while the USSR wanted to reduce Chinese influence in the Third World and enhance its own as well as counter the US. By October 1962 the USSR had provided missile warheads and troops to Cuba.

President Kennedy demanded their withdrawal and surrounded the island. A Russian ship armed with more war heads on its way to Cuba approached the US fleet. It was stopped and searched, bringing the world to the brink of a war. Kennedy demanded the removal of the Russian missiles and blockaded Cuba. The ship turned back and a US plane was shot down but President Kennedy and Premier Khrushchev negotiated, without Castro's knowledge. Khrushchev agreed to withdraw troops and warheads in return for a US pledge that it would not attempt to invade Cuba. Cuba received more economic aid from the USSR which tied it more closely to the USSR.

International pressure

The US used its position to influence decisions and actions in international bodies that favoured US policies against communist countries. It dominated the OAS and sought European, African and Asian support for a total isolation of Cuba in all international organisations (the UN and its agencies, the World Bank and the IMF), in order to defeat the Castro regime. While many European countries supported the American position, many newly independent countries in Africa and Asia, with negative colonial experiences under European imperialists, did not.

DID YOU KNOW?
The Cuban Missile crisis began as a dispute over the right of Cuba to possess offensive weapons and ended in a superpower confrontation in which Cuba was a mere pawn.

EXAM TIP
Make sure that you understand the reasons for US involvement in The Bay of Pigs and Cuban Missile Crisis.

ACTIVITY
Using your dictionary, define the following terms: socialism, capitalism, communism, democracy, ideology, embargo, imperialism.

KEY POINTS
- The Cold War resulted from ideological differences between the United States and the USSR.
- The United States used several mechanisms to try to cripple communist Cuba.
- US pressured countries in the region to remain democratic.

SUMMARY QUESTIONS
1. What was the Cold War?
2. Explain the aims and consequences of the Bay of Pigs.
3. What was the Missile Crisis and what were its outcomes?
4. Assess the success of US attempts to isolate Cuba from the international community.

7.8 The impact of the Castro revolution

LEARNING OUTCOMES

At the end of this topic you should be able to:

- Explain the impact on the Caribbean of the Castro revolution between 1959 and 1985.

DID YOU KNOW?

The United States sent CIA agents into countries like Guyana and Nicaragua to help prevent communist forces from taking over their governments.

EXAM TIP

Make sure you understand the ways in which the United States exercised influence over Caribbean countries.

DID YOU KNOW?

NATO (the North Atlantic Treaty Organisation) was set up to be a buffer against the influence of communist countries.

Creation of US economic and political spheres of influence

As the cold war progressed, countries that aligned themselves to the United States fell under their influence. The US took on the role of a regional police force to ensure that these countries continued to uphold democratic principles. Americans kept a close watch on Caribbean politics and politicians to stamp out communist leanings wherever they appeared.

To support their political influence, the US invested heavenly in economic, political and social programmes in countries which were considered friendly. Thus they created an economic sphere of influence in the region. These spheres of influence were further strengthened by supporting local security forces through training programmes for the military and police forces and providing arms.

Anti-communist campaign

To counter the spread of communism the US blocked anyone with communist leanings from entering their country and passed laws to prosecute anyone who publicly supported communism. After 1959 the country aggressively pursued a defence system to counter the spread of Cuba's communist influences by giving generous financial, logistical and other aid to anti-communist movements and governments. It also became involved in anti-communist activities in Nicaragua, Guyana and Grenada.

During the 1980s the United States changed tactics. To discredit Cuba, China and the USSR they highlighted the human rights abuses of communist countries, while they continued to impose sanctions against Cuba and support democratic governments.

Cubans in the United States

Thousands of Cuban refugees poured into Florida after 1958. In 1960 the United States passed the Cuban Adjustment Act which allowed Cuban refugees financial and other forms of assistance to settle in the US. The Cuban American population has a great influence over political developments in the US as both the republican and democratic parties seek their vote and many participate in the political administration of Florida and the Federal government. They continued to support the continuation of sanctions against Cuba and all anti-Castro measures which lasted throughout the 20th century.

Cubans have established businesses which provide large amounts of revenue to Florida. They have introduced Cuban food, language and culture to the US.

Spread of socialism

In spite of American attempts to restrict the influence of the Cuban revolution, after 1960 Castro used assistance to liberation movements around the world as a means to defy the US and build up a following of supporters and spread socialist ideas.

He provided military assistance and technical and professional expertise to former colonies in Latin American, African and Asian countries. Cuban nurses, doctors, teachers and technicians were sent to assist developing countries around the world.

Che Guevara, Castro's second-in-command and ambassador of the Cuban revolution, personally fought in the Congo and Mozambique between 1964 and 1966 (Figure 7.8.1). In November 1966 Guevara took the revolution to Bolivia, where he was killed giving support to revolutionaries.

Other areas in the world supported by Castro in the 1970s were:

- Angola, where Castro sent over 60,000 troops to help the nationalists fight for independence against Portugal and its ally, South Africa
- Mozambique, where he gave support to the liberation movement
- Libya, then under the rule of Colonel Gadhafi
- Ethiopia, where in 1977–8 Castro supported the Ethiopian Marxist government against the Somalians
- Nicaragua, where in 1979 he sent 15,000 Cuban soldiers to help the communist Sandinista National Liberation Front against the Nicaraguan government.
- Grenada, where in 1982–3 Cuban technicians were sent to help construct the island's airport.

> **EXAM TIP**
>
> Focus on the economic, social and political impact of the Cuban-American community on the United States

Figure 7.8.1 Che Guevara was Castro's famous second-in-command and became an inspirational leader for many revolutionary movements.

> **ACTIVITY**
>
> On a blank map of the world name the countries which have been influenced by the Castro Revolution.

> **SUMMARY QUESTIONS**
>
> 1. What was a 'sphere of influence' and why was it considered important to both the US and the USSR?
> 2. What strategies were used by the US to prevent the spread of communist influences in the Caribbean?
> 3. Describe the role played by Cuban exiles in US policies against Cuba.
> 4. What factors influenced Castro's decision to get involved in activities in African and Asian countries?

> **KEY POINTS**
>
> - Countries that aligned with the United States were under its influence.
> - US policy was to stop the spread of communism to countries within its sphere of influence and prevent the growth of communism elsewhere.
> - Cuban exiles in America were used in US anti-Castro policies.
> - Castro's plan was to take his revolution to the rest of the world.

7.9 US involvement in the English-speaking Caribbean

LEARNING OUTCOMES

At the end of this topic you should be able to:

- Assess the impact of the United States' involvement in the English-speaking Caribbean from 1939 to 1985.

DID YOU KNOW?

Cuba is one of the last countries in the world to maintain its communist ideology and celebrate its revolution.

EXAM TIP

Pay attention to why the United States wanted to keep Caribbean states democratic.

Economic effects

The US has played an important role in Caribbean life since the 1600s when its supplies of food and essential items were critical to plantation economies. Economic links to the Caribbean became closer after 1939. Its economic impact increased during World War II when military bases were established in Trinidad and Tobago, Guyana, Antigua, St Lucia, Jamaica and the Bahamas. These provided much needed employment, increased the circulation of money and provided relief in an era when the region was plagued by high unemployment, low wages and social and economic distress.

US multinational companies also invested in the Trinidad oil industry (Texaco), the bauxite industries in Guyana (Kaiser) and Jamaica (Alcoa and Reynolds) and developed hotels and casinos across the region. There are also American banks, insurance companies, airlines and cruise ships. The US offered migration opportunities for many individuals whose remittances form important revenue for some territories. During the 1960s the US recruited skilled and domestic workers, teachers, nurses and other professionals from the region. These migrants provide markets for Caribbean foods and cultural products.

The US also offered business opportunities. Some tradesmen and women purchased items in the US to stock their businesses in the Caribbean. The country also provides aid through the 1982 Caribbean Basin Initiative to develop tourism and other areas.

Political effects

US policy in the region was centred on the preservation of democracy. It used financial aid to encourage the spread of democratic institutions, and put political pressure on countries which supported socialist or communist policies. The US intervened in British-Caribbean territories which were under communist or socialist influence: Guyana (1955, 1960s), Grenada (1983) and Jamaica under Michael Manley (1970s). The US sponsored the formation of the Organisation of American states of which the Caribbean countries are members and which provides various forms of support to its members.

Cultural effects

US troops occupied six bases in the Caribbean during World War II and US cultural influence has grown since with the development of mass media (cable TV, radio, cinema, newspapers, magazines). The impact is visible in sports, technology, music, dance, dress, film, news and food. Although many territories still reflect the influence of the former 'mother country' in education syllabuses,

US influence can be seen as people go to the US to study and bring back ideas. Basketball is a popular sport from the US (Figure 7.9.1), Americanisms are common in Caribbean language and the many fast food chains have changed eating habits.

US Currency is accepted in all the territories and American living and leisure practices are **emulated** in the region.

KEY TERMS

Emulate: to copy with the aim of excelling.

Figure 7.9.1 The impact of US influence is seen in many areas of life in the Caribbean.

ACTIVITY

Create a table with headings Economic, Social and Political Effects. Under each heading list negative and positive influences. Two works that could give you some ideas are Sparrow's calypso *Jean and Dinah* and the poems *Praises* and *Solja Work* (in *Jamaica Labrish* by Louise Bennett Coverly).

SUMMARY QUESTIONS

1. How did US investment in the region affect Caribbean countries?
2. Why did Americans seek to exercise political influence over Caribbean nations?
3. Explain the nature of the US cultural impact on the Caribbean.

KEY POINTS

- US investment in the Caribbean has been significant.
- US political influence has been used to further its interests in the region.
- The US has had a significant impact on Caribbean culture.

Section C, Theme 8: Caribbean political development up to 1985

8.1 Early attempts at unification

LEARNING OUTCOMES

At the end of this topic you should be able to:
- List the attempts at unification in the British-colonised Caribbean before 1939.
- State the different types of unions that were attempted.

KEY TERMS

Federation: a group of states that form a unity but remain independent in internal affairs.

DID YOU KNOW?

In 1831 the territories of Berbice, Demerara and Essequibo were merged to create British Guiana (now Guyana).

Leeward Islands Federation (1674)

One of the earliest attempts to unify British colonies in the Caribbean occurred in the Leeward Islands. The islands were first administered from Barbados by Lord Willoughby, but after complaints of neglect, Sir Charles Wheeler was appointed Governor in 1671. His replacement, Sir William Stapleton, instituted the first Leeward Islands **Federation**. This aimed to reduce the costs of administering the islands which were spread over 150 miles and had not yet proved to be profitable.

Each island in the **federation** was represented at an elected assembly located in St Kitts. The islands represented were Antigua, Anguilla, Barbuda, the British Virgin Islands, Montserrat, Nevis and St Kitts. The Assembly met regularly until 1711 when the islands called for self-rule and expressed dissatisfaction with a system which did not attend to their concerns.

Leeward Islands Federation (1871)

The 1871 Leeward Island Act established the Federal Colony of the Leeward Islands: Antigua, Barbuda, Dominica, Montserrat, Nevis-St Kitts, Anguilla and the Virgin Islands. There was one governor for the islands and an administrator for each presidency, as the island units were called. The islands found this federation unsatisfactory as well. Complaints continued until the federation was absorbed into the 1958 West Indies Federation.

Windward Islands Federation (1874–6)

The British government had wanted to replace the old representative system with crown rule since emancipation, but faced resistance from the assemblies. The Morant Bay Rebellion provided the opportunity to introduce crown colony government to Jamaica in 1865. Since the Windward Islands had previously been administered from Barbados, British policy was to federate Barbados and the Windward Islands under crown colony rule.

In 1875 John Pope-Hennessy was sent to Barbados to implement the confederation policy. He met stiff opposition from a section of the planting community which was divided on the issue. The anti-confederates formed the Barbados Defence Association to defend their Assembly and protect the social order and they campaigned against Pope-Hennessy and the Confederates, who also mounted public campaigns. In April 1876 tensions in the island stimulated oppressed blacks to riot. Eight blacks were killed, hundreds were wounded and plantations destroyed. Pope-Hennessy was replaced, Barbados retained its assembly and the Windward Islands Federation united Grenada, Dominica, St Lucia, St Vincent and Tobago.

Other colonial unions

The British government was always concerned about the cost of administering its Caribbean colonies, particularly the smaller island units which were not very profitable. For administrative ease they created unified colonies by joining smaller units with larger ones, or joining colonies located close to each other. Key dates relating to these unions are:

- From 1799 to 1848 the Turks and Caicos Islands were administered from the Bahamas. In 1873 they were administered from Jamaica until they were included in the 1958 federation.
- In 1833 the Leeward Islands, including Dominica, were placed under one governor. In the same year Tobago was incorporated in the Windward Islands with Barbados, Grenada and St Vincent under a governor-in-chief who resided in Barbados.
- In 1863 the Cayman Islands were administered from Jamaica with a resident chief magistrate, called a **custos**, to run the island.
- After the Federation failed in 1961 the islands of St Kitts, Nevis and Anguilla were joined in 1967. Dissatisfaction with central administration amid claims of neglect led to Anguilla's secession and declaration of independence in 1969.
- In 1980 Anguilla was officially separated from St Kitts-Nevis and given a new constitution in 1982.

Figure 8.1.1 In spite of tensions, Barbados managed to retain its assembly.

SUMMARY QUESTIONS

1. Why did the early attempts at a federation of the Leeward Islands fail?
2. Give reasons for Barbados' opposition to the Windward Islands federation.
3. Describe the other types of union of British Caribbean islands.

DID YOU KNOW?

Barbados has the oldest Assembly and the only unbroken system of government in the British Caribbean.

EXAM TIP

Focus on reasons why Barbados was not included in the Windward Islands Federation.

KEY TERMS

Custos: from the Latin, meaning a guard, a magistrate appointed by the governor of a territory. Today the post is mainly ceremonial.

ACTIVITY

Using a blank map of the Caribbean, mark and name the islands which were unified. Colour-code and date the different island unions.

KEY POINTS

- Unification of Caribbean territories was British policy since the early colonial period.
- Several attempts were made to federate the Leeward Islands between 1674 and 1958.
- The attempt failed to include Barbados in the Windward Islands federation.
- Other colonial unions existed involving the smaller territories.

8.2 The roots of nationalism

LEARNING OUTCOMES

At the end of this topic you should be able to:

- Explain the impact of World War I on the Caribbean.
- Explain the rapid spread of the UNIA in the Caribbean.
- Assess the factors which contributed to the growth of nationalism between 1900 and 1935.
- Describe Caribbean reaction to the Italian invasion of Ethiopia.

EXAM TIP

Note how the war stimulated anti-colonialism and nationalism in the region.

Figure 8.2.1 Marcus Garvey set up The Black Star Shipping Line, with the aim of helping Africans to return to the land of their ancestors.

The effect of the war on black consciousness

Caribbean soldiers who had fought in the First World War returned home disillusioned after their negative experiences. They became more conscious of the problems of the poor in their homeland and they agitated for political and social change.

Members of the educated middle class asserted their right to participation in the administration by drawing attention to the weaknesses of the colonial government.

Marcus Garvey and the UNIA movement

Marcus Garvey was a Jamaican political leader who wanted to end the suffering of black people. He saw race consciousness and organisation as the means to bring about positive change. He advocated equal rights and economic independence.

In 1914 he founded the Universal Negro Improvement Association (UNIA) in Jamaica. By 1919 there were branches in New York and in Canada. The Association spread rapidly into countries with large migrant Caribbean populations: Panama, Costa Rica, Honduras, Guatemala and Nicaragua, as well as South Africa, England and Nigeria.

The UNIA believed that Africans should write their own history, control their own media and worship according to their own belief systems. It published a newspaper, The Negro World. Garvey also set up a shipping service (Figure 8.1.1).

There was opposition, however: Garvey and his agents were feared in the Caribbean, The Negro World was banned, and Garveyites were not allowed to enter some countries and prevented from holding public meetings. The UNIA did stir up black consciousness, the fight against discrimination, the right to have political representation and the anti-colonial struggle. Garvey successfully linked racial consciousness with anti-colonial ideology. There is information about the labour relations work of the UNIA in 9.4.

Newspapers and their editors

In the second half of the 19th century several newspapers were owned and edited by black, coloured and Indian people. Focus was on the injustices and poor living conditions. There were criticisms of the colonial administration and calls for social and political reform.

The ruling elite was afraid of the growing number of educated blacks challenging them for political control. They also feared that the newspapers would stir up popular resistance. In spite of these efforts to suppress them, publication continued, assisting the growth of nationalism and black and Indian consciousness.

The Dominica conference (1932)

The possibility of closer cooperation between the Windward and Leeward Islands resulted in the 'Closer Union Commission'. When local politicians were excluded from discussions, they held their own conference in Dominica with delegates representing Trinidad and Tobago and the Windward and Leeward Islands. Delegates urged the Secretary of State to include self-government in the terms of reference of the Commission, but without success. The Conference agreed to promote cooperation in the region for the common good and supported the establishment of a federal government.

Delegates were critical of the delay in granting the adult vote in the region and the exclusion of most people by the high property and income qualification. They passed a resolution calling for a reduction in the property qualification, or for granting the vote to anyone who paid direct taxes.

Nationalism elsewhere in the British Empire

The exposure of Caribbean soldiers to people from other parts of the British Empire made them aware that the struggle against colonialism and discrimination was not confined to the Caribbean colonies. The growth of nationalism and Black consciousness, the activities of UNIA groups in the region and the publication of The Negro World and other radical newspapers all helped to increase awareness.

The struggle for Indian independence gave great encouragement to Caribbean nationalists. They also followed the resistance movements in South Africa, in particular the founding of the first modern African nationalist party, the South African Native National Congress, in 1912.

West Africans were influenced by the UNIA and its newspaper. There were calls for independence in Egypt.

The Italian invasion of Ethiopia (1935)

In October 1935 the Italian leader Benito Mussolini invaded Ethiopia, in response to an earlier humiliating defeat, in 1896.

European countries supported the Italian forces because they did not like the idea of a European defeat at the hands of an African country. With this support the Italians defeated the Ethiopians. Africans worldwide were outraged; there were protests against Italian business and the Catholic Church.

Many in the Caribbean sympathised with the Ethiopians. Prayers were said, petitions sent for West Indians to be sent to Ethiopia to fight for the Emperor and donations were made to the Ethiopian Red Cross.

Marcus Garvey and the UNIA came out in strong support for Ethiopia. The invasion unified Caribbean people against European oppression and stimulated black consciousness and nationalism. Religious nationalism developed with the Rastafarian movement in Jamaica and the establishment of the Ethiopian Orthodox Church.

DID YOU KNOW?

In 1935 Ethiopia was the only remaining independent country in Africa. It had fought successfully against Italian colonising attempts in 1896, the only African country to defeat a European power.

ACTIVITY

Locate Ethiopia on a world map.

SUMMARY QUESTIONS

1. How did World War I impact the Caribbean?
2. What was the League of Nations and when and why was it formed?
3. Assess the significance of Marcus Garvey and the UNIA to Caribbean workers in the early 1900s.
4. In what ways did the Italian invasion of Ethiopia affect the Caribbean?

KEY POINTS

- War experience helped awake nationalism among Caribbean soldiers
- Marcus Garvey linked racial consciousness with nationalism
- Independence struggles in other parts of the British Empire encouraged nationalism in the Caribbean
- The invasion of Ethiopia helped to strengthen Caribbean nationalism and anti-colonialism.

8.3 The Moyne Commission

LEARNING OUTCOMES

At the end of this topic you should be able to:
- Describe social conditions in the Caribbean in the 1930s.
- State the findings of the Moyne Commission.
- Explain the outcomes of the Moyne Commission Report.

Figure 8.3.1 Poor working and living conditions meant that many people could not support their families.

DID YOU KNOW?

The first labour riots of the 1900s occurred in Guyana as early as 1905.

Conditions in the 1930s

Years of neglect by the colonial administration, the fall in prices for the major exports of sugar, cocoa and bananas, and the world-wide depression all contributed to the disturbances of the 1930s. This unrest was an extension of the protests that had occurred in the region after World War I. Widespread unemployment was aggravated by returned migrants from Cuba, Panama and the US. Wages were low, even in profitable industries, and the prices of food and essential items were high. Plant diseases, hurricanes, drought and floods reduced productivity.

Working conditions were very poor. There were no specified hours of work, no overtime pay, employers reduced wages to maintain their profits and there were no safety measures or compensation arrangements for workers injured on the job. Unemployment levels soared as the population increased. New taxes which were imposed on imported items fell heavily on the working classes which could ill afford to bear them. Many working people could not support their families and hunger and malnutrition were common (Figure 8.3.1).

Houses were poorly constructed, badly ventilated and overcrowded, especially in urban areas. Communicable and infectious diseases such as tuberculosis, measles, small pox and chicken pox spread in the poor living conditions. Reliance on polluted pools, ponds and rivers gave rise to water-borne diseases such as dysentery and diarrhoea. Childhood diseases contributed to high infant mortality rates. Hookworm disease, venereal diseases, yaws, malaria and yellow fever were also common, and, with inadequate health care facilities, were often fatal.

There was dissatisfaction with the exclusion a large section of the population from participation in government.

Protest against the conditions

Protests and strikes occurred in societies which had become militant in the post-war era. Returning soldiers and sailors who had experienced discrimination within their own ranks during World War I protested against further discrimination. Unlike their white colleagues, they had not been adequately compensated for their contributions to the war effort.

These returning servicemen found discrimination in their home territories intolerable. In Trinidad and Tobago white South Africans employed in the Trinidad oil industry were openly racist and discriminatory against the black workers. Returned migrants from Panama, Cuba and the USA swelled the numbers of the militant unemployed and increased the number of strikes and demonstrations. The establishment and growth of Marcus Garvey's UNIA also contributed to the increase in militancy. In the case of Trinidad, the 1919 strike spread to estate workers all over the colony as well as to dockworkers, railwaymen, city council workers and workers in the asphalt industry. The spread of these disturbances was of great concern to the British government and became more alarming later in the decade.

The later phase of unrest began in Belize in February 1934 and spread throughout the region in increasing intensity to the normally tranquil Barbados in 1937. The most threatening strike occurred in the oilfields of Trinidad in June 1937. Trinidad's oil industry was highly valued as the main source of oil to the British Empire and the disturbances, which also spread to Puerto Rico, Venezuela and Mexico, were considered a serious threat to **imperial** stability.

The principal labour protests and strikes over worsening conditions are summarised in Table 8.3.1.

Table 8.3.1 Protests in Caribbean territories in the 1930s

Territory	Date of protest/s
Belize	1934
St Kitts	1935
Trinidad	1934
St Vincent	1934
St Lucia	1935, 1937
Guyana	1935, 1938, 1939
Barbados	1937
Trinidad	1937
Jamaica	1938, 1940

The Moyne Commission

The immediate response of the British authorities to the protests was to:

- strengthen the police forces and send military reinforcements to restore order
- impose censorship of the press to keep out seditious material
- arrest, imprison and sometimes deport ringleaders who were considered dangerous
- make limited concessions to labour and try to control the labour movement.

The authorities established a commission of enquiry chaired by Lord Moyne, called the West India Royal Commission, but more commonly known as The Moyne Commission.

EXAM TIP

Make sure that you can state the circumstances that led to the formation of the Moyne Commission.

DID YOU KNOW?

Some women who were involved in the protests of the 1930s were: Cleopatra White of Belize, Agnes Bernard of Jamaica, Albertina Husbands (who was later deported) and Daisy Crick of Trinidad.

8.3 (continued)

> **KEY TERMS**
>
> **Propaganda**: information and opinions deliberately put about by a group or organisation to support their cause.

The Commission was given the major task of investigating social and economic conditions in Barbados, British Guiana, British Honduras, Jamaica, the Leeward Islands, Trinidad and Tobago and the Windward Islands, and making recommendations. The members of the commission visited every colony to collect evidence from individuals, groups and members of the Legislative Council. Members also visited schools, prisons hospitals, to see local conditions for themselves. The recommendations made became the basis of British policy.

Report and recommendation of the Commission

The Commission's report was completed in 1939, but was so critical of British rule that it was not published until after World War II for fear that the Germans would use it as **propaganda**. The Commission found that the social and economic state of the working class was very poor. Health and education facilities in the region were inadequate, wages were too low and housing was deplorable. They recommended that Britain should undertake measures to:

- improve social conditions
- provide acceptable sanitary facilities
- increase employment opportunities
- remove crown colony government and gradually introduce self-government
- allow more people to vote
- promote industrial stability by legalising trade unions and protecting workers' rights
- increase access to land by implementing land settlement schemes
- develop long-term health policies, unify and reorganise the medical services and increase preventive health measures
- provide adequate finance to improve education facilities and promote educational advancement.

> **DID YOU KNOW?**
>
> To deal with the problem of absenteeism, the Moyne Commission recommended that the school meals programme should offered meals late in the week to encourage parents to send their children to school in the days before pay day when money was scarce.

Consequences of the Report

The Colonial Development and Welfare Act was passed in 1940 to organise and allocate funds to the British West Indies for long-term reconstruction. As mentioned above, however, the outbreak of World War II delayed action on the Commission's recommendations. The Act provided for £1 million from the British government to **alleviate** distress and promote educational, social and economic development in the region. Money was spent on roads and bridges, new school buildings, medical centres, training for nurses and agricultural research. Universal adult suffrage was introduced. Women were allowed to vote and to join trade unions but the Moyne Commission confirmed their role in domestic-related activities.

> **KEY TERMS**
>
> **Alleviate**: to lessen or make less severe.

Plans were made for land settlement schemes in the Windward Islands, but in Trinidad there was opposition from planters. The scheme did not benefit many people in Jamaica who could not afford the 10 per cent deposit.

New labour legislation was passed. These sought to improve wages, specify working hours, end child labour, provide for safer factory conditions, implement compensation for injuries sustained at work and set up pension schemes. Trade unions were legalised as an important strategy to restore order in the colonies but they were to be controlled by Labour Departments and Advisers who would steer their development in a direction approved by the British government. Colonial governments and employers did not want to deal with the trade unions and they continued to oppose them. Despite this the number of trade unions increased from 28 unregistered in 1939 to 40 registered, representing 100,000 workers, in 1945.

Britain's acceptance of its responsibility to its colonies resulted in grants totalling £25 million to the Caribbean between 1946 and 1956. In spite of these measures, activists, labour leaders and politicians were disappointed with the report, which they felt did not address the main causes of inequality in the colonies: lack of freedom, responsible government and social reform. They became convinced that only political independence would enable their countries to achieve significant economic and social change.

ACTIVITY

Make a table of the main consequences of the Moyne Commission under the headings Health, Trade Unions and Government.

SUMMARY QUESTIONS

1. Describe working and living conditions in the British Caribbean territories in the 1930s.
2. What was the Moyne Commission and why was it established?
3. What did the Moyne Commission recommend?
4. What impact did the Commission have on the Caribbean?

KEY POINTS

- There was severe social distress in the 1930s.
- There were protests and riots across the Caribbean.
- The British Government set up the Moyne Commission which made a number of recommendations to improve the quality of life in the Caribbean.

8.4 Political parties, adult suffrage and self-government

LEARNING OUTCOMES

At the end of this topic you should be able to:

- Identify the factors which led to the development of political parties in the British Caribbean.
- Trace the development of political parties in the British Caribbean.
- Assess the relationship between popular protest and political developments in the Caribbean (1935–58).

DID YOU KNOW?

Antonio Soberalis formed the first trade union in Belize, the Labourers and Unemployed Association, in March 1934. After strikes and riots took place, legislation approving trade unions was passed.

Figure 8.4.1 Uriah Butler was an important figure in the development of trade unions and improved conditions for workers in Trinidad and Tobago.

Establishment of trade unions

The earliest trade unions which emerged in the 1880s were not recognised, and some were forced out of existence by angry employers. There was some growth of the movement after 1910 but modern trade unionism developed in the Caribbean between 1919 and 1950. The British Guiana Labour Union was formed in 1919 and the British Guiana Workers League in 1931.

The development of trade unions was one of the most important outcomes of the disturbances of the 1930s. It was a recommendation of the Moyne Commission which felt that a properly guided British type trade union was the best guarantee of industrial stability in the region. After 1940 unions were recognised and grew in number. They included the Bustamante Industrial Trade Union, The Trinidad Oilfields Workers Trade Union and the Manpower and Citizens Association in Guyana. By 1943 there were up to 48 trade unions in the Caribbean. In July 1945 The Caribbean Labour Congress was formed and helped stabilise the Trade Union organisations.

Adult suffrage

Since the plantation era the right to vote was allowed only to property owners. This meant that in the Caribbean, suffrage was restricted to wealthy white land owners over 21. In the 1900s the emerging educated black and coloured middle class protested their exclusion and agitated for change. During the 1930s the nationalists called for political reform to allow the working classes the right to vote. One of the recommendations of The Moyne Commission was to reduce the property qualification to allow a wider range of people to vote.

Universal adult suffrage was not granted in the British Caribbean until after the end of World War II. For Jamaica this happened in 1944, Trinidad and Tobago in 1945, Barbados 1950, the Windward and Leeward Islands 1951 and Guyana in 1953.

Political parties

The early political parties developed in the 1920s to lead the movement for political reform and self-government. The founders were influenced by:

- Conditions in the region: the distress faced by the mass of the population, poor infrastructure in the colonies, discrimination and exploitation, disregard of the colonial administration for the plight of the poor and their support for the white planter and business elite, all of which convinced the party founders that political change was essential.

- Ideas expressed by black conscious and nationalist groups such as the Trinidad Working Men's Association, Pan-Africanism, Garveyism and the UNIA.
- International influences: Charles Duncan O'Neal, who was influenced by socialist ideas while studying and working in Britain, the TWA while working in Trinidad and Garveyism in Barbados, founded the Democratic League in 1924 and a Working Men's Association in Barbados in 1926. Herbert Critchlow attended several Commonwealth and international workers meetings, including the 1931 International Trade Union Committee of Negro Workers Conference in Germany and the International Red Aid in Russia in 1931.
- Trade union movement. The struggle to improve working conditions and the movement for political change supported and influenced each other as they both had similar aims.

After trade unions were legalised, many formed the base for the development of political parties. Table 8.4.1 shows some of the early political parties.

Table 8.4.1 Early political parties in Jamaica, British Guiana and Trinidad

Jamaica	British Guiana	Trinidad
Political Reform Association (1921)	Young Guiana (1916)	Trinidad Labour Party (1934, converted from TWA by A A Cipriani)
Marcus Garvey's People's Political Party (1929)	British Guiana People's Political Association (1921)	British Empire Workers (formed by Uriah Butler—Figure 8.4.1)
	Popular Party (1926)	Citizens Home Rule Party (1932, formed by Uriah Butler)

The ideas of self-government

Ideas on self-government and how it could be achieved varied among the leaders and political groups in the Caribbean and reflected socialist, pan-Africanist, Garveyite and nationalist ideas.

The more conservative leaders favoured gradual and constitutional change while the radicals supported immediate change using more aggressive methods. Some, especially the leaders of the smaller islands, favoured the federal approach because they believed that it would help them to achieve self-rule faster. Others, like Bustamante of Jamaica and the leaders of Guyana and Belize, believed they should go alone. The British government took a gradual approach, based on the notion that the country had to be ready for self-rule.

EXAM TIP

Be sure that you understand the relationship between trade unions and the development of political parties

ACTIVITY

Make a list of the most controversial issues in the federal talks.

SUMMARY QUESTIONS

1. What factors contributed to the development of political parties in the Caribbean?
2. What were the main features of the early trade unions in the Caribbean?
3. Why was adult suffrage considered important to the struggle for social and political change in the Caribbean?
4. Explain the different ideas on self-rule held by groups and their leaders in the Caribbean.

KEY POINTS

- Political parties and trade unions had similar origins.
- Several influences shaped the development of the early political parties.
- Adult suffrage was an important factor in the struggle for social and political change.
- Ideas of self-government varied among Caribbean leaders and groups.

8.5 The movement to establish a federation

LEARNING OUTCOMES

At the end of this topic you should be able to:

- Trace the development of the idea of federation in the region.
- Explain the role of the British government in the establishment of a federation.
- Explain the reasons for the failure of the Federation.

DID YOU KNOW?

A regional labour organisation was created and hosted by Nathaniel Critchlow in Georgetown in 1926.

EXAM TIP

Remember that the problems faced in the region also provided a motive for unity.

Figure 8.5.1 Aime Cesaire, of Martinique was a key figure in the negritude movement, awakening black consciousness and pride.

Reasons for unity

Earliest attempts at unity in the British Caribbean came from the British government with the aim of reducing both the costs of administering the colonies and the number of units that would be seeking assistance during unfavourable economic times. In the 1950s the British believed that smaller states could be supported by the larger ones. The territories were also similar in a number of ways:

- historical experience
- populations
- geography and climate
- problems and aspirations
- economic situations
- support for federation from the emerging trade unions and politicians
- professional associations already existed.

Economic reasons for unity

All the territories shared a common agricultural past (they grew similar crops: sugar, cocoa, bananas coffee), and faced similar problems with respect to prices, markets, production costs and profits. It was felt that they would get better terms if they negotiated as one unit. Small territories could not compete on world markets by themselves, so it was economically advantageous for them to join in federation with the larger islands. All territories could benefit from trading with each other and the larger territories could assist the development of the smaller. It was also hoped that sharing the cost of common services would reduce the strain on the individual island treasuries.

Social reasons for unity

The society which had evolved from the plantation system and the composition of the populations was similar across the region. Earlier attempts at unification and the proximity of territories allowed movement of people between the Leeward and Windward islands and, since Emancipation, with the Southern Caribbean.

In addition migration to Trinidad from other Caribbean territories to seek employment in the oil industry and at the US bases during World War II meant that there were citizens of these territories across the region who had already created the foundation for federation.

Political reasons for unity

The political systems developed in the territories were based on the British system. All except Barbados were under the Crown Colony system of government, and all were united in their desire to change this. The advocates of political change held similar ideas for political reform based on adult suffrage and participation in the political process. They all believed that the administration should be in the hands of Caribbean-born people. Political leaders travelled across the region bringing news of social and political change and giving support to each other's reform movements.

Ideology

The ideology that guided the movement for change in the Caribbean was based on ideas which people could read in local papers:

- Nationalism: the notion that the land belonged to the people and they had the right to rule it
- Anti-colonial sentiment that was growing worldwide
- Socialism and radical thought which were supported by the distress in society
- Pan-Africanism and **Negritude** (Figure 8.5.1)
- Liberation movements around the world
- The success of the movement in India
- The literature of the region.

The role of the colonial government

The British Government saw federation as a way of reducing its own responsibilities to the colonies. Reports of the various commissions strongly supported this approach and were used to form the basis of British policy. The British encouraged federation by their early attempts to bring some colonies into a central administration and establishing a number of common regional institutions. Colonial governments carried out British policies and many governors supported the idea of federation, but the local ruling elite was afraid that the radical, pan-Africanist and nationalist expressions of the reformers would result in displacing them from their position of privilege and control of Caribbean society.

Local attempts to stifle the reform movement included branding reformers as communist, so making them liable to arrest, banning individuals from entering the country and giving speeches and imposing heavy fines on newspapers to force them out of business.

SUMMARY QUESTIONS

1. What were the reasons for establishing a federation of the British Caribbean colonies?
2. Explain the role of the British Government in the development of the movement for unification in the Caribbean.
3. Describe the features of Caribbean society and politics which supported the unification process.
4. How did the colonial governments respond to the policy of unification?

KEY TERMS

Negritude: a cultural movement to awaken black consciousness and pride in African heritage. It was founded in protest against French colonial rule (*nègre* is French for black).

EXAM TIP

Remember to consider the impact of colonial governments on the integration movement.

ACTIVITY

Conduct some research and make a list of the individuals who wrote books, poems or articles which supported the reform movement in the Caribbean.

KEY POINTS

- The imperial government initiated the integration movement.
- They would agree to self-rule that conformed with British political traditions.
- There were forces in the Caribbean which supported integration.
- Colonial governments were anxious to protect the social, political and economic interests of the elite classes.

8.6 The failure of the Federation (1958)

LEARNING OUTCOMES

At the end of this topic you should be able to:

- Explain the reasons for the failure of the Federation in 1958.

DID YOU KNOW?

The annual budget of the federal government was less than the budget of the Port of Spin city Council.

Economic

Relations between the federal government and local governments were weakened by conflicting interests among the states. Personality factors aggravated the internal struggle between the federal government and entrenched territorial economic interests. The larger islands protected their own interests and did not want to take on the debt burdens of the smaller islands who in turn resented their economic power.

The federal government depended on contributions from the member states. Its annual budget was too small, however, to run its programmes and there was no established framework for allocation.

Politicians of the large islands were concerned that free movement of people would lower living standards and cause competition for local jobs.

There was no uniformity of tariffs or taxes between islands, and this affected the free movement of goods. The federal structure was very costly because of the large number of officers that were employed.

Social

Federalism was based on an ideal for which the details were not carefully worked out. This led to conflict as each territory tried to do the best for itself. The main supporters of the federal idea were trade unions, and middle-class professionals who held conferences far away from the people. Discussions did not include how federation would benefit ordinary people.

As the idea of a federation was not properly explained and there was no mechanism to involve ordinary people in the federal process, they saw no direct benefits and were suspicious. They valued their nationalism and felt they would be invisible in a greater union. Without popular support and enthusiasm, local and regional jealousies caused divisions within the federation.

A further grievance was that the top administrative posts were filled by the British government with expatriates.

Political

There were several political reasons for the failure of the Federation:

- Since the British encouraged each island to develop its own constitutional systems, leaders were insular, concerned with domestic rather than federal issues. Also, leaders did not want to lose their powers to federal leaders and they feared domination by the larger territories. Able and experienced politicians such as Eric Williams in Trinidad (Figure 8.6.1) and Norman Manley in Jamaica

Figure 8.6.1 Able and experienced politicians such as Eric Williams preferred to remain a key figure in Trinidad and Tobago rather than support federalism.

preferred to remain key figures in their own territories. Some leaders also felt that the smaller units were over-represented in the Federal Parliament.
- There was controversy over the site of the federal capital and selection of the prime minister. The wide discretionary powers of the governor-general made him more powerful than the prime minister anyway - and he was paid a higher salary.
- The territories felt that they had to give up their dream of self-rule:
- The federation was founded on unresolved issues relating to freedom of movement, federal taxation and customs union.
- There was heavy dependence on British guidance in establishing the federal structure which resulted in an omission of nearly all of the items insisted on by the nationalist leaders and creating instead an enlarged crown colony institution.
- The federal body was given a narrow range of legislative powers and could neither impose taxes nor enforce laws: this made it mainly administrative.

Ideological

While there was unity on the need to remove the ruling elite and attain self-rule, there were no clearly defined aims and no agreed structure for unification. As a result there were several different and sometimes conflicting ideological influences on the integration process which caused divisions between the islands:

- Some leaders wanted self-determination to give them more political power which they were not prepared to give up to a federal body over which they had no control.
- Some were loyal to the British Empire and did not support the more radical groups who advocated socialist approaches.
- Some of the larger territories visualised a federation that would promote their economic development and provide markets for their products, while the smaller territories hoped that the larger islands would assist their economic development.

With no clear design, individual views predominated and caused disunity.

DID YOU KNOW?
It was easier to travel to London from any Caribbean colony than to go from one colony to another.

EXAM TIP
Remember that the unification process was influenced by similarities as well as differences between the units.

ACTIVITY
Using sources such as newspaper clippings, history texts and information from websites, create a scrap book of profiles of the leading personalities in the Caribbean integration movement.

KEY POINTS
- The Federation failed because the system was not properly worked out.
- There were many controversial issues that were not resolved in the discussions.
- The influence of the British government on the process was too strong.
- The people were insufficiently involved and informed about the Federation.

SUMMARY QUESTIONS
1. What were the similarities between the Caribbean colonies which favoured the integration movement?
2. Which were the differences which created obstacles to integration?
3. What role did the British government play in the integration movement? What was the result?
4. How did the UN have an impact on the integration movement in the Caribbean?

8.7 Personalities involved in integration

LEARNING OUTCOMES

At the end of this topic you should be able to:
- Have an understanding of the contributions made by key figures involved in integration.

DID YOU KNOW?

Marryshow wrote a book entitled *Cycles of Civilisation* in which he asserted the African origins of civilisation.

EXAM TIP

Note how the authorities continued to fear change and found opportunities to arrest popular leaders.

Theophilus A Marryshow (1887–1958)

Born in Grenada, T. A. Marryshow was one of the earliest advocates of universal adult suffrage. He worked as a reporter for the Federalist and Grenadian People, in 1911 was editor of the *St George's Chronicle* and in 1915 editor of the *West Indian*. His articles advocated unity and self-rule and he travelled through the region campaigning for representative government and federation. He was elected to the Grenadian legislature from 1924 to 1957 and was a senator in the Federation.

Norman Manley (1893–1969)

Born in Jamaica, Manley was educated at Jamaica College and studied law in the UK, at Oxford University. He served in World War I and after his return to Jamaica formed the Jamaica Welfare Association to help the poor in rural areas. In 1938 he formed Jamaica's first political party, The People's National Party, and was its leader until 1969.

Manley supported the Trade Union Congress and National Workers Union and fought for full adult suffrage, which was awarded in November 1944. He was Chief Minister from 1955–9 and Premier from 1959–64.

He was a strong advocate of federation but opposition stimulated by Bustamante (who was also his cousin) caused him to lose the referendum and Jamaica to leave the federation. He became Leader of the Opposition in 1962 until he retired in 1969.

Grantley Adams (1898–1971)

Born in Barbados, Adams was educated at Harrison College and then, like Norman Manley, studied law in the UK at Oxford. He was elected to the Barbados House of Assembly in 1934 and was President of the Barbados Progressive League which became the BLP (Barbados Labour Party). He was part of a commission investigating the 1930s riots and strongly recommended reform to improve the state of the poor in Barbados. He campaigned for universal adult suffrage and became Barbados' first prime minister in 1954. He instituted programmes in social reform to improve working conditions, health, housing and education. He supported federation and was elected the first and only prime minister of the West Indies Federation.

After the collapse of the Federation Adams became leader of the Opposition until 1970 when he retired. He is one of Barbados' national heroes.

William A Bustamante (1884–1977)

William Bustamante was born in Jamaica to an Irish father and a Jamaican mother. He travelled to Central America Spain, Cuba, Canada and the US. In Jamaica he worked as a money-lender but he was so concerned about the poor that he joined the 1930s protests against poor social conditions. He wrote political commentaries for the *Daily Gleaner* and *The Jamaican Standard* in which he raised the situation of the poor. In the late 1930s he became a political advocate campaigning for better pay for policemen and improving working conditions for Jamaicans in Cuba. In 1939 he founded the Bustamante Industrial Trade Union. He supported the labour movements in St Kitts and Barbados. In 1939 he was imprisoned on charges of sedition but was released through the intervention of his cousin Norman Manley. He continued his involvement with strike action and was imprisoned for 18 months under war powers.

Bustamante formed the Jamaica Labour Party which won the 1944 elections and he became Jamaica's first Chief Minister. He opposed federation and encouraged Jamaicans to vote against it in the referendum. He became the island's first Prime Minister in 1962. He retired in 1967 and was named a national hero in 1970.

Phyllis Allfrey (1909–86)

Born in Dominica to an elite planter family, Phyllis Allfrey had a privileged upbringing based on exploitation and discrimination. Her nationalism developed in reaction to this. She was influenced by socialist ideas as she worked in welfare in London in the 1930s. On her return to Dominica she became involved in the nationalist struggle for independence. In 1954 she founded the Dominica Labour Party, Dominica's first political party, and campaigned against social injustice. She was a radical nationalist and feminist who advocated the end of colonialism and discrimination in Dominica.

Allfrey was editor of the *Dominica Herald* and also wrote for the *Dominica Star*, focussing on the aspirations of blacks in Dominica. She supported federation and joined the West Indian Federal Labour Party in 1958. Her party won a landslide victory and she became the representative for Dominica and Minister of Labour and Social Affairs in the federal Government. After racial politics brought about the collapse of the federation, she was expelled from the party.

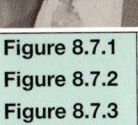

Figure 8.7.1 T. A. Marryshow.
Figure 8.7.2 Norman Manley.
Figure 8.7.3 William Bustamante.
Figure 8.7.4 Phyllis Allfrey.

DID YOU KNOW?

Phyllis Allfrey was the only woman, and the only white person, in the Federal government

ACTIVITY

Research the leading figures in the movement for political reform in the Caribbean and make a list for each Caribbean territory. Make notes on how each one contributed to the federalist cause.

SUMMARY QUESTIONS

1. Of what significance was T. A. Marryshow to the reform movement in the Caribbean?
2. Compare the contributions of Norman Manley and Grantley Adams to the movement for Caribbean integration.
3. Explain the role of Alexander Bustamante in the Federation of the West Indies.
4. What did Phyllis Allfrey contribute to the movement for change in Dominica?

KEY POINTS

- There were several important personalities in the struggle for change in the Caribbean.
- Some popular leaders were educated professionals who came from privileged backgrounds.
- They involved themselves in many activities to alleviate local poverty and distress.

8.8 Movements towards independence

LEARNING OUTCOMES

At the end of this topic you should be able to:
- Describe the steps taken by some territories to attain independence.
- Assess the reasons and process used to bring about independence.

DID YOU KNOW?

The Little Eight was attempted because the leaders of those islands felt they would not be granted self-rule individually.

KEY TERMS

Suffrage: the right to vote in political elections.

The Little Eight

Following the collapse of the federation several political leaders tried to create a federation of the smaller island units, known as The Little Eight. The eight were (1) Antigua and Barbuda, (2) Barbados, (3) Dominica, (4) Grenada, (5) Montserrat, (6) St Kitts-Nevis-Anguilla, (7) St Lucia and (8) St Vincent and the Grenadines. A framework for the constitution was drawn up in May 1962, but because of disagreement between Britain and the islands over the powers to be allocated to the federal government, the federation did not materialise and the attempt was abandoned in 1965.

Associated statehood

After the collapse of the Little Eight attempt, Barbados attained independence and six of the remaining territories (Antigua and Barbuda, Dominica, Grenada, St Kitts-Nevis-Anguilla, St Lucia and St Vincent) became Associated States with Britain under the Associated Statehood Act of 1967, with headquarters in St Lucia. Under the constitution, each island had full internal self-government but Britain retained responsibility for defence, external affairs and constitutional amendments. The British monarch, Queen Elizabeth, was the Head of State and appointed the Governor as her representative on the island. The government was administered by a premier and his cabinet and a nine-member senate.

This system lasted until each territory attained independence. Grenada was first to attain this, in 1974 (Figure 8.8.1), followed by Dominica in 1978, St Lucia and St Vincent in 1979, Antigua in 1981 and St Kitts and Nevis in 1983.

Negotiations for new constitutions

Before there could be any negotiations for the transfer of power to the colonies, the British Government wanted to ensure that political reforms, which put the territories on democratic principles in line with the Westminster system, were implemented. Each territory made constitutional amendments to introduce universal adult **suffrage** and elective systems based on political parties.

The British government was particularly concerned about ensuring that the ideology of politicians and political parties remained firmly rooted in democracy and that their investments in the region were protected.

UN decolonisation policy

Many long and bitter conflicts resulted from the process of decolonisation. Newly independent members of the UN were anxious to establish a smoother, swifter and more peaceful decolonising process. The UN recognised that the continuation of colonisation provided the basis for armed struggle and aimed to speed up the process. The 1960 UN Declaration on the Granting of Independence to Colonial Countries and Peoples (the Declaration on Decolonisation) asserted the right of all people to complete freedom, self-rule and control of their national territory and proclaimed that colonialism should be brought to a speedy and unconditional end.

In 1962 The UN General Assembly established a Special Committee on Decolonisation to monitor the implementation of the Declaration and make recommendations for its application. The UN declared three decades of decolonisation (1990–2000, 2001–11 and 2011–20), with the hope that colonial rule would end by 2020.

> **EXAM TIP**
>
> Note the importance Britain placed on ideology for the transfer of power.

> **DID YOU KNOW?**
>
> Montserrat joined WISA (West Indies Associated States) and is an associate member of CARICOM, but retains its status as a British colony.

Figure 8.8.1 Grenada was first of the Little Eight to attain independence, in 1974.

> **ACTIVITY**
>
> Find the UN website and read the UN 1960 Declaration on Decolonisation.

> **SUMMARY QUESTIONS**
>
> 1. Why did Caribbean territories have to negotiate for new constitutions?
> 2. What considerations influenced the decisions of the British government to agree to make constitutional change in the Caribbean?
> 3. Explain the significance of the UN decolonisation policy for the British Caribbean.
> 4. What were the stages utilised by the smaller Caribbean islands to attain self-government?

> **KEY POINTS**
>
> - Some Caribbean territories went through several stages in the process towards self-rule.
> - New constitutions had to be negotiated with the British government.
> - The UN decolonisation policy had an important impact on the Caribbean.

8.9 Regional integration up to 1985

LEARNING OUTCOMES
At the end of this topic you should be able to:
- List the institutions that were created to foster Caribbean integration.
- Explain why the integration process faced so many challenges.

EXAM TIP
Make sure that you understand why these territories formed another union after the recent failure of the Federation.

DID YOU KNOW?
The treaty of Chaguaramas was signed on July 4 1973 in honour of the birthday of Norman Washington Manley, a leading advocate of federation.

The Caribbean Free Trade Area (CARIFTA)

CARIFTA was formed to encourage economic development of all member states by expanding trade, permitting free movement of goods, and encouraging a diversified economy in each island. The original members Trinidad and Tobago with Antigua, Barbados and Guyana were joined by Dominica, Grenada, St Kitts-Nevis-Anguilla, St Vincent, Jamaica, Montserrat and British Honduras.

Territories were grouped into More Developed Countries (MDCs) and Less Developed Countries (LDCs). The organisation aimed to promote balanced development in the region and provide special attention to the problems and needs of the LDCs through institutions such as the Caribbean Development Bank.

The organisation was successful in increasing intra-regional trade but it was difficult to remove custom duties and tariffs to facilitate free movement of goods. Members agreed on the need for a stronger union to deepen intra-regional cooperation. This led to the founding of CARICOM.

CARICOM

In 1973 the Treaty of Chaguaramas was signed by Trinidad and Tobago, Barbados, Jamaica, Guyana and all the CARIFTA members, creating The Caribbean Common Market, or CARICOM. The Bahamas joined in 1983, Suriname in 1995/6 and Haiti in 2002.

CARICOM's objectives were to facilitate integration through a common market and common trade policies and co-ordinate foreign policies.

The Caribbean Development Bank (CDB)

The CDB was created in 1969 to promote the financial development of the region, contribute to harmonious economic growth and development and promote economic cooperation, and especially to provide urgent attention to the needs of the LDCs. The headquarters are in Barbados.

The bank finances projects which contribute to poverty reduction and assists members to make maximum use of resources, develop their economies and expand production and trade. The first president was the distinguished economist Sir Arthur Lewis.

ECCB

In 1965 the Eastern Caribbean Currency Authority was set up to manage the finances of the Eastern Caribbean territories. In 1983 the authority became the Eastern Caribbean Central Bank (ECCB). Its aim was to deepen the integration process, promote monetary stability and enhance economic planning and development. Originally based in Barbados, it was relocated to St Kitts when Barbados established its own bank.

The Organisation of Eastern Caribbean States (OECS)

The OECS was established by the Treaty of Basseterre in 1981 to develop closer relations and strengthen economic cooperation among member states. OECS members are Antigua, and Barbuda, Dominica, Grenada, Montserrat, St Kitts-Nevis, St Lucia and St Vincent and the Grenadines. The British Virgin Islands and Anguilla later became associate members. The headquarters are in St Lucia.

International representation

International organisations provide the forum for countries to deal with the challenges facing a globalised world. This is very important for small countries in a world dominated by super-powers. This approach developed from the practices of the League of Nations and the United Nations: countries work together to provide diplomatic solutions to problems, valuable to maintain international peace. Nations help others to promote their interests, and facilitate the transfer of information so very critical to modern day security.

Caribbean countries are represented in many international organisations: the UN and its agencies (Figure 8.9.1), The Commonwealth, the European Union, the Association of Caribbean and Pacific States, World Trade Organisation, IMF and other International Financial institutions, the OAS and Sporting Associations. The countries have diplomatic representatives in countries with which they have particular interests and connections.

Figure 8.9.1 It is important for Caribbean territories to be represented in international organisations.

DID YOU KNOW?
Jamaica and Trinidad and Tobago were the first Caricom members to join the UN.

ACTIVITY
Conduct some research on CARICOM to find out some of the problems encountered by the organisation.

SUMMARY QUESTIONS
1. What organisations were formed to promote regional integration in the Caribbean between 1958 and 1985?
2. Explain the difference between CARIFTA and CARICOM.
3. Why were financial institutions considered necessary in the process of Caribbean integration?
4. Why is representation on international bodies important for Caribbean states?

KEY POINTS
- The failure of federation did not end efforts to integrate the countries of the region.
- The smaller islands attached great importance to regional integration.
- Representation on International bodies was considered essential for all countries.

8.10 Alternatives to independence

LEARNING OUTCOMES

At the end of this topic you should be able to:
- Identify the alternatives to independence taken by different Caribbean territories.

KEY TERMS

Plebiscite: a vote by all eligible voters in a state on an important issue, for example a change to the country's constitution.

EXAM TIP

Note the fact that most of these islands have passed from one administrator to another.

DID YOU KNOW?

Following the 2012 vote, the Legislative Assembly of Puerto Rico enacted a resolution to request the United States president and Congress to end its current status and begin the process of admission to the union as a state, but to date there has been no response from the US government.

Plebiscite and Commonwealth of Puerto Rico

Under Spanish rule for some 400 years, Spain ceded Puerto Rico to the US in 1898. Under the 1947 Organic Act, the territory received the right to elect its governor, and in 1950 the right to prepare its constitution. Its status is *Estado Libre Asociado*, or Commonwealth.

Puerto Rico is now US territory with an unusual constitutional status and a unique relationship with the US. The country is governed by the US Congress, and its people are US citizens but they may not vote in US elections and have no representation. They have the responsibilities of American citizens, including military service, but while they may live and travel in the US, some Puerto Ricans feel like second-class citizens and still press for independence.

Constitutional changes have permitted more self-government, but the territory's political status has often been debated. Apart from the Independence Party, most people and the major political parties favour retaining commonwealth status. The most recent **plebiscite**, in 2012, showed a majority (54 per cent) in favour of a change in status, with full statehood the preferred option, but it was highly controversial and the results were criticised by several people.

US Virgin Islands (USVI)

In 1917 the US bought the Danish West Indian islands of St Thomas, St Croix and St John and renamed them the United States Virgin Islands. The islands were ruled under a naval administration until 1931. Municipal corporations and a general assembly were set up. Power was in the hands of the governor and the US president. In 1954 the population was allowed to vote for members of the legislature.

The islands remained under the direct control of the US government until 1968, when residents were first allowed to elect their own Governor.

The territories are represented in the US Congress by a resident commissioner. The UN classifies this group of islands as 'non-self-governing US territory'. Residents have US citizenship but may not vote in US presidential elections.

Tripartite kingdom: the Netherlands Antilles

The Tripartite (three parts) Kingdom of the Netherlands, created in 1954, was made up of Holland, Suriname and the Netherlands Antilles. All the units were self-governing, but defence and foreign affairs remained Holland's responsibility. All three had to agree on any constitutional change.

The Netherlands Antilles was made up of the ABC islands in the south (Aruba, Bonaire and Curaçao) and the S islands in the north (Saba, St Martin and St Eustatius). The islands received universal adult suffrage in 1948 and became self-governing in 1950. There was dissatisfaction with Dutch control, but independence was not a consideration until the outburst of protests in Curacao in 1969 and a separation movement in Aruba in the 1970s.

Suriname became independent in 1975. In 1986 Aruba became a 'status apart' as an autonomous non-independent state in the Kingdom. Curaçao and St Martin became autonomous, Saba, Bonaire and St Eustatius became 'special municipalities' of the Netherlands.

In October 2010 the Netherlands Antilles was formally dissolved. Bonaire, Saba and St Eustatius remained special municipalities, Curaçao and St Martin became constituent countries. Citizens of the Dutch islands hold Dutch passports and enjoy Dutch social benefits, but their political status is still under discussion.

Départements — French territories

In 1946 Guadeloupe (Figure 8.10.1), Martinique, French Guiana and Réunion were made *départements*, that is they were considered parts of France and their people French. This permitted France to hold on to its colonial possessions by assimilation – integrating them into French culture. Each department was administered by a prefect, responsible for external defence, internal security and regulating import and export prices. The Antilles sent representatives to the French parliament which permitted centralised imperial rule. The people were full citizens of France, could vote in French elections, elected representatives to the French parliament and were eligible for French welfare subsidies.

An independence movement developed in Martinique and Guadeloupe but France did not want to release its colonies. The Overseas departments were reformed and the local authorities received more powers, but the calls for decolonisation increased as many of the islands' problems were not resolved.

DID YOU KNOW?

The French and Dutch share colonial possession of the island of St. Martin.

Figure 8.10.1 In 1946 Guadeloupe, along with Martinique, French Guiana and Réunion were made *départements* of France. They were considered parts of France and their people French.

8.10 (continued)

British overseas territories

The Queen is the territories' head of state and is represented by a governor. Formerly the British Dependant Territories, in 1997 they became the British Overseas Territories, to remove the stigma of colonialism. While these territories are still dependent on Britain, there are groups which press for independence.

Anguilla

Anguilla was politically unified with St Kitts in 1883 when the British government sought to reduce its administrative costs by creating unified colonies. Constitutional changes were made in 1953, and in 1958 Anguilla entered the West Indies Federation and became part of the Associated State of St Kitts/Nevis/Anguilla.

In 1967 Anguilla was allocated one seat in the House of Assembly (St Kitts had seven and Nevis two). Although the islands still possessed individual island Councils, these exercised limited powers while those of the Assembly were wide. Dissatisfied Anguillans held a referendum in 1967 to break away from **associated statehood** and protest against the lack of acceptable governance.

British troops invaded the island on 19 March 1969 and ended the protest. The referendum was implemented in 1980 and provision made for the British government to administer the island which was made a crown colony. In 1980 the Commissioner's title was changed to Governor. Anguilla remains a British colony.

Bermuda

Since 1620 Bermuda has been classified as a self-governing colony. The constitution of 1968 introduced universal adult suffrage. Some Bermudians support a move for independence and although the issue has been debated it was defeated in the 1995 independence referendum. Many Bermudians feel that independence would impose unnecessary costs on the island and not be beneficial.

British Virgin Islands

The British Virgin Islands were ruled by the English from 1666. Dissatisfaction with the administration caused riots in 1853 which resulted in changed constitutional arrangements, but these only increased British control. Direct British rule was introduced in 1867. The islands formed part of the Leeward Islands federation in 1956. Crown Colony government was introduced and the BVI remains a British colony.

> **KEY TERMS**
>
> **Associated statehood**: the semi-independent stage during which states had control over internal affairs, while the colonial power was responsible for external affairs such as defence.

> **EXAM TIP**
>
> Always read exam questions very carefully and note the focus: this might be on English-speaking territories, for example.

The Cayman Islands

The British government made the Cayman Islands a dependency of Jamaica in 1863. The islands were run by an Administrator, appointed and controlled by the British government, who had veto powers over the local assembly and power to implement policies without consultation. Caymanians resented the arrangement, and in 1962 Jamaica transferred power to the Administrator, whose title was changed to Governor when a new constitution came into effect in 1972.

Montserrat

Montserrat has been a British colony since the 1630s. In 1866, the British government introduced direct rule with the implementation of Crown colony government. In 1871 the island was incorporated into the Leeward Islands administration and in 1958 into the West Indies Federation. In 1967 the population opted to retain colonial status. Economic misfortunes, hurricane Hugo in 1989 and the volcanic eruption of 1995 have made the island dependent on Britain to the present day (Figure 8.10.2). In 2002 Montserratians regained full British citizenship. The island remains a colony in spite of the desires of some islanders for independence.

Figure 8.10.2 Volcanic eruption, and economic misfortunes, have made Montserrat dependent on Britiain to the present day.

> **ACTIVITY**
>
> On a blank map of the Caribbean mark and name the Dutch possessions, the French *département* and the British Overseas Territories.

SUMMARY QUESTIONS

1. What is the nature of Puerto Rico's constitutional relationship with the United States?
2. Why were some European countries reluctant to decolonise their Caribbean possessions?
3. Compare the methods used by France and The Netherlands to avoid decolonisation in the Caribbean, and their outcomes.
4. Why have some British colonies chosen to remain in a colonial relationship with Britain?

KEY POINTS

- Puerto Rico sought independence from Spain but this was replaced by a unique relationship with the US.
- France did not want to give up its overseas possession and found ways to avoid the decolonisation process.
- The Netherlands faced difficulties in its attempts to retain its Caribbean territories.
- Some British Caribbean possessions preferred to maintain their colonial status.

Section C, Theme 9: Caribbean Society (1900–85)

9.1 Social and economic conditions 1: housing

LEARNING OUTCOMES

At the end of this topic you should be able to:

- Describe living conditions between 1900 and 1935.
- Describe social and economic conditions existing in the Caribbean between 1900 and 1935.
- Explain the relationship between living conditions and the social and economic conditions.

EXAM TIP

Remember to make the connection between economic conditions and the development of the different types of housing.

Post-emancipation housing

Post emancipation housing was of three types:

- Those which had housed enslaved Africans during enslavement. These housed freed Africans who remained on the estates and indentured sugar workers, and were of poor quality.
- Houses built by the freed Africans. These were on lands rented from the estates or in the free villages which sprang up after Emancipation. These were usually cheaply constructed and lacking in infrastructure. In Jamaica one-room shacks housing whole families became centres of disease and crime. Most of the houses rested on bare earth without flooring and were made of unsound boarding and rusty corrugated iron.
- Houses built in organised or communal settlements. These were usually established by the communal efforts of groups or with the assistance of missionary groups, or both. They were of a better quality than the other two types and included drainage and sanitary provisions.

Generally housing was of a poor quality. For most of the freed African population In Guyana overcrowding was the norm. Families were crowded into single rooms in tenements where roofs leaked, cesspits overflowed and yards flooded. Rents for these consumed at least a quarter of weekly earnings. Many sugar workers continued to live in run-down overcrowded barracks surrounded by stagnant water and without adequate sanitation or water supplies.

Ranges of single rooms rested on bare earth, some on the verge of collapse lacking every amenity and frequently surrounded by stagnant water. The dirty and verminous insanitary environment gave rise to malaria, worm infestation and bowel and rat-borne diseases. Leaking roofs, rotten floors and overcrowding facilitated tuberculosis, venereal diseases, leprosy, respiratory diseases, worm infestation and jigger lesions.

Urban slums

Urban slums developed because of the rapid migration of workers from rural areas and other territories searching for better employment opportunities and higher wages. The high demand for housing offered unscrupulous landlords the opportunity to profit. Although rents were high, housing accommodation was poor. Ill-constructed barracks were divided into small, poorly ventilated rooms which were not equipped with water or sanitation. Units were overcrowded with whole families and sometimes extended families as well. In Barbados

Figure 9.1.1 A characteristic chattel house in Barbados.

several families would often share a stand pipe and a bucket latrine in the street. Health conditions were poor and diseases rampant. The insanitary conditions contributed to high mortality rates in the slums.

Tenantries

Tenantries developed because freed Africans needed land and planters needed labour. There were several different tenantry systems, many of which were complicated. Where cash was short, tenants paid rent in the form of their labour, which did meet the needs of both employee and worker, but there were no laws governing the system, and many disputes arose between landlords and tenants. Landlords could evict their tenants unfairly.

Tenants were allowed to take items on credit from plantation shops and pay for them with their labour. This kept them in debt to their employers.

Chattel houses

Chattel houses were first used on the plantations but gradually built in the towns as well. They developed in post-emancipation Barbados on land rented by planters to freed Africans. Chattel houses are characteristic of **vernacular** architecture in Barbados.

They usually began as a two-roomed unit built on a loose foundation of coral stones with wooden walls and galvanised roof. As the family increased extensions could be added to the rear.

The wall, roof and floor could be dismantled, loaded onto a cart and re-assembled in a new location within a day. This was useful when conflicts between workers and landowners were common and workers needed to relocate their homes.

As fortunes improved they began to be decorated with styles of the plantation house—porches, fretwork and galleries.

DID YOU KNOW?

Even simple houses such as chattels would have jalousies—slatted shutters to help ventilation.

KEY TERMS

Vernacular: concerned with one's native country, not foreign. Vernacular architecture concerns ordinary, domestic buildings.

ACTIVITY

Collect pictures of each type of housing and make a poster that shows housing in the post-emancipation Caribbean.

SUMMARY QUESTIONS

1. What were the main features of post-emancipation housing in the Caribbean?
2. Why did slums emerge in urban areas in the Caribbean up to 1935?
3. Why did problems develop in the system of tenantries?
4. What were chattel houses and why did they develop in the post-emancipation period?

KEY POINTS

- Post-emancipation housing conditions were very poor.
- Free people were forced to become tenants as they were unable to buy land.
- Tenantries were varied and complicated and caused many conflicts.
- Chattel houses developed so that when there were disputes with landlords, tenants could dismantle their homes and relocate them quickly.

9.2 Social and economic conditions 2: cost of living and working conditions

LEARNING OUTCOMES

At the end of this topic you should be able to:

- Describe the social and economic conditions existing in the Caribbean between 1900 and 1935.
- Explain the factors which contributed to the existence of these conditions.

DID YOU KNOW?

In Berbice, Guyana Salamea, an indentured Indian immigrant woman, was one of the leaders in the 1903 protest of indentured workers on Plantation Friends for better wages.

EXAM TIP

Make sure that you can explain the factors which caused increases in the cost of living.

Cost of living

All the Caribbean territories relied on imports for basic food and essential items. The price of these imports was a major factor affecting the cost of living in the region. Prices were determined by external and internal transportation costs, import taxes and charges by importers, distributors and vendors. In the 1900s the cost of living increased significantly. This was due to:

- Changes in consumption patterns created dependence on imported items, so the prices of these items increased significantly.
- Shortages of some items caused by trade disruptions led to price increases.
- Wartime conditions led to price increases, causing strikes in several territories.
- Post-war depression conditions also stimulated a surge in prices of essential items, for example salt fish, salt beef and cotton items.
- Increased costs of rents, transportation, medical and building services

Many workers relying on wages to support their families saw little improvement in their earnings even up to the 1940s. Employers reduced wages, while prices climbed. Attempts to reduce wages of sugar workers in Antigua led to protests in 1935.

Working conditions

Poor working conditions stimulated protests across the region during the first four decades of the 1900s.

Wages

Wages could be deducted for trivial matters. In St Kitts the rate for cutting canes was reduced to 1881 levels and later in the 1930s the work force was reduced (Figure 9.2.1). There was no relationship between earnings and cost of living: wages were set arbitrarily by employers. In Guyana wages remained unchanged for over 30 years.

Hours

Working conditions in the Caribbean between 1900 and 1935 were characterised by long working hours—there was no fixed length.

Conditions

There were no safety procedures in jobs where workers faced danger, and no compensation for injuries. There were no overtime provisions, no pensions, no other benefits. The scarcity of jobs and large numbers of unemployed made it easy for employers to replace workers. This led to lack of job security, as workers could be easily dismissed and replaced. Casual workers might be employed for one or two days per week. Numbers employed and size of tasks increased as employers faced price reductions or increased costs.

Workers often faced racism. No attention was paid to grievances. In the 1900s breach of contract was a criminal offence. In 1935 in St Vincent protesting leaders lost their jobs, and others were denounced as agitators and troublemakers.

There was no representation and no negotiation—trade unions were not recognised (except in Jamaica and Guyana where they were recognised in the 1920s).

Unemployment

Unemployment was a major problem in all Caribbean territories in the 1900s. Unemployment was caused by several factors, outlined below.

Industry and economic conditions

Agriculture, especially the sugar industry, remained the major employer. As its fortunes fluctuated, wages and the size of the work force were reduced. Mechanisation of the sugar industry reduced the demand for labour, which was also seasonal, leading to higher unemployment at certain times of the year.

The oil and mineral sectors did not employ large numbers of workers. In Trinidad the cocoa industry crashed in 1922, and in 1929 the world was in an economic depression. In Belize mechanisation of the timber industry required fewer workers than before. In 1931 hurricane damage made matters worse for working people.

Population factors

Continuation of immigration schemes in Guyana and Trinidad caused significant growth in the population, and the work force. Within territories migration from rural areas to the towns and cities swelled the population and added to unemployment figures. In 1934 in Trinidad the National Unemployment Movement established a register which recorded 1200 unemployed persons in Port of Spain in 2 weeks. There were thousands of unemployed in Georgetown in the 1930s, which an official described as 'providing fodder for agitators'.

Figure 9.2.1 In St Kitts, as elsewhere, wages were reduced and many faced hardship.

ACTIVITY

Imagine you are a worker in an unemployment office. Make a journal of the types of people who register with your office during the course of a week. State their age, gender, type of jobs sought, previous jobs and the date of last employment.

SUMMARY QUESTIONS

1. What problems did working people face in the first three and a half decades of the 1900s?
2. What were some of the safety problems that workers faced in the Caribbean in the period 1900–35?
3. Why was there so much unemployment in the Caribbean between 1900 and 1935?

KEY POINTS

- Working people faced many problems in the early 1900s.
- Administrators and employers showed no concern for people's welfare.
- Working conditions were poor.
- Unemployment continued to grow over the period.

9.3 Social and economic conditions 3: health

> **LEARNING OUTCOMES**
>
> At the end of this topic you should be able to:
>
> - Describe the health problems existing in the Caribbean between 1900 and 1935.
> - Explain the relationship between health problems and the general social and economic conditions.

Early 20th century health conditions

During the first three decades of the 20th century health conditions in the Caribbean were poor. Deplorable living conditions and overcrowding in urban areas led to the spread of many diseases. There was little or no sanitation and sewage disposal—human waste was left on river banks or on the beach. Lack of clean water supplies contributed to the high incidence of water-borne diseases.

Most working people had poor diets, existing mainly on carbohydrates. Many suffered from deficiency diseases. Medical services were inadequate, with limited public health services, especially in rural areas. Working people could not afford doctors' charges.

Child mortality

The high infant mortality rate caused great concern to administrators. By 1935 infant mortality ranged from 150 deaths per thousand in Jamaica to 320 per thousand in Barbados.

Lack of health facilities meant that pregnant women, nursing mothers and babies did not receive adequate care. There were no separate hospital facilities for expectant mothers, sick babies or newborns. Overcrowded living conditions caused exposure to infection.

As with the adults, many babies' diets were inadequate. Baby food would be mixed with polluted water. Many mothers were poorly educated and had poor parenting skills.

Training for healthcare

Most doctors in the Caribbean were foreign-born. Only those formally trained at British or European institutions were officially recognised as qualified to provide health care in the colonies. Although this training did not prepare them for some of the ailments they encountered in the region, they dismissed the traditional healing methods and cures as superstitions. In many instances the treatments they offered just hastened the death of the patient.

Doctors who were indigenous were in many instances poorly trained and worked by trial and error. Until 1935 doctors worked for fees which were too high for most people. Most only worked in urban areas. In rural areas people depended on the village herbalist or 'obeah man' or woman for prescribed remedies. Obeahs had received their knowledge from the previous generation and would in turn pass it on to the next; people relied on them.

The London School of Tropical Medicine was established in 1899 to conduct research and provide training for work in the colonies. As scientific knowledge advanced, there was a better understanding

> **DID YOU KNOW?**
>
> The London School of Tropical Medicine (later renamed The London School of Hygiene and Tropical Medicine) was established in 1887 by Sir Patrick Mason, medical adviser to the Colonial Office.

of diseases and their causes. More emphasis was placed on preventative methods and the provision of training in a wider arrange of areas to include nutrition and hygiene alongside medical and nursing skills.

Improving the state of clinics and hospitals

Colonial administrations preferred to invest their resources in the ailing sugar industry rather than improve human welfare — until disease outbreaks threatened the upper class. Fears of particular diseases led to the early provision of special treatment facilities for mentally ill patients and people with yaws and leprosy.

In the 1900s more attention was paid to providing medical services because of the frequency of epidemics, overcrowding at colonial hospitals and protests against the poor conditions. Specialist clinics were established to treat patients with particular diseases, often with the assistance of charitable groups. Dispensaries were set up in communities where people could obtain medicines without having to come to the hospitals. Isolation wards were created in hospitals to separate patients with communicable diseases during epidemics. Medical departments were reorganised to provide more services.

In spite of these measures, there was little improvement. Hospitals could not cope with the number of people who needed them, and people in rural areas continued to have difficulties reaching medical services. In addition, some people preferred to be treated by the traditional healers as they had no faith in the public medical officers.

In most West Indian territories the planter class felt that there was no need for improvements in health care. The increase in infectious and communicable diseases and epidemics, as well as wider circulation of medical knowledge, led to attempts to make some improvements in the colonial medical services. New clinics and dispensaries were established but these were never adequate and by the 1930s political reformers and protesters demanded better health services. Despite these demands, by 1935 medical facilities and services continued to be substandard, especially in rural areas, and the mortality rate remained high in the region.

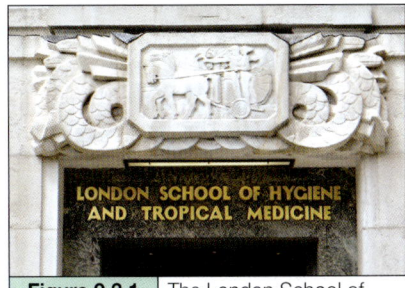

Figure 9.3.1 The London School of Hygiene and Tropical Medicine. The carving shows the ancient Greek god of medicine flanked by snakes, emblems of healing.

EXAM TIP

Understand the problems which limited the success of measures to improve clinics and hospitals.

ACTIVITY

Make a scrapbook of pictures of herbs used in traditional medicine and state the ailments they are used to cure.

SUMMARY QUESTIONS

1. What were the causes of poor health in the Caribbean up to 1935?
2. What caused the high infant mortality rate in the Caribbean up to 1935?
3. What problems did people who lived in rural areas face to obtain health services?
4. Who spearheaded health care improvements in the colonies and why?

KEY POINTS

- The population was affected by many diseases.
- Mortality rates, especially for infants, were very high.
- Governments did not treat the health problems as important.
- Progress to improve hospitals and clinics was slow.

9.4 Improving living conditions 1: organisations involved

LEARNING OUTCOMES

At the end of this topic you should be able to:

- Identify groups which attempted to improve social conditions in the Caribbean.
- Outline the efforts they made to improve social conditions.

Many people felt that governments were unable, or unwilling, to deal with the problems faced by the majority of the population across the region. In the face of this apparent indifference, other groups worked to improve social conditions. These groups included trade unions, women's groups, the UNIA and religious groups.

Trade unions

Trade unions were engaged in bargaining for better wages and working conditions for their members. They sought to establish fair wages which kept pace with the rise in the cost of living, job security and avenues for promotion so workers could improve their living conditions. Some, like the British Honduras Unemployed Association (BHUA), also functioned as friendly societies, helping to find jobs for the unemployed and providing death benefits and other forms of assistance to members. All the unions had welfare units which gave support to dismissed workers and to members during protests and strikes.

Women's groups

Several charitable women's groups operated in the Caribbean: these were formed by educated women whom custom did not allowed to work in paid employment, wives of officials and members of trade unions and church groups. In 1919 Lady Haddon-Smith, wife of the governor of the Windward islands, obtained donations to begin a district nursing service and started providing milk for needy children in Barbados.

Figure 9.4.1 The Black Cross Nurses were dedicated to improving the health and living conditions of black women.

The Black Cross Nurses, the women's arm of the UNIA, was organised along the lines of the Red Cross. It was dedicated to improving the health and living conditions of black women. The nurses provided health care through education, hygiene and training for expectant mothers. In Belize, where a branch had been established in 1920, an annual Baby Exhibition offered training in midwifery and child care, and demonstrated proper parenting practices, to reduce the territory's high infant and maternal mortality rate. A branch was established in Jamaica in 1922, where the nurses ran the Victoria Jubilee hospital and provided training. The nurses also operated in Cuba and Trinidad and Tobago.

EXAM TIP

Remember the contribution of the women's charitable organisations to improving social welfare in the Caribbean.

Audrey Jeffers established the Coterie of Social Workers in Trinidad and Tobago in 1921. This group ran hostels for working mothers, day nurseries in poor communities, a home for blind women and pioneered school feeding through its Breakfast Sheds. The group also advocated women's causes, such as equal pay for male and female teachers, the recruitment of women police and more scholarships for girls, and even the right of female clerks to remain seated when serving customers. Elma François advocated the improvement of conditions for both men and women.

UNIA

In addition to its political aims (see 8.2), the UNIA also aimed to improve the welfare of African people and remove their oppression and discontent. Through all its branches it was involved in social, humanitarian and educational activities which were intended to make life better for the working class. It promoted self-help and working together for the benefit of the African race.

The UNIA had several divisions through which it carried out its activities: for young people there was the Juvenile Division, for men the African Legion, and the Black Cross nurses and the Universal Motor Corps for women. It encouraged its members to come together to negotiate for better wages and working conditions. In Jamaica the organisation helped unemployed people to find jobs and organised programmes to assist the needy.

Religious organisations

In line with the teachings of their faith, many religious groups tried to help improve living conditions for poorer people.

The Christian churches' first contribution to Caribbean society was through education. The Anglicans, Roman Catholics, Baptists, Methodists, Presbyterians, Moravians, and Seventh Day Adventists all established primary schools throughout the region. The Roman Catholics and Anglicans also established secondary schools which became some of the premier educational institutions in the region. Qualifications obtained enabled young people to gain entry to higher-paying jobs and improve their living standards.

The churches also ran charitable institutions such as the St Vincent de Paul Society and the Living Waters Community of the Roman Catholic Church, which provided daily meals for the poor and homeless through soup kitchens. Church groups also established hostels for working girls, crèches for children of working mothers, and also ran orphanages and children's homes. The Salvation Army (established in Jamaica in 1887, Barbados in 1898 and Trinidad in 1901) devoted itself to social work among groups rejected by the established churches.

Hindu and Muslim groups offered assistance supporting the needy in their communities with food, clothes and money.

Friendly societies and fraternal lodges met a need where there were no trade unions and provided sick and death benefits and helped to develop organisational skills and a sense of self-reliance.

ACTIVITY

Make a chart of the organisations which helped to improve living conditions for the working classes. State the type of assistance each gave and the territory in which each was active.

SUMMARY QUESTIONS

1. In what ways did the unions assist Caribbean workers?
2. How did women's organisations contribute to social improvement in the Caribbean?
3. What was the UNIA and why did it become involved in the Caribbean?
4. What contributions did the churches make to social improvement in the Caribbean in the 1900s?

KEY POINTS

- Welfare services were not considered important by the ruling class.
- Religious groups, women's groups and trade unions contributed to the improvement of the working classes in the Caribbean.
- These groups fulfilled needs not met by colonial governments, who were seen as indifferent.

9.5 Improving living conditions 2: government policies

LEARNING OUTCOMES

At the end of this topic you should be able to:

- State the factors which caused Caribbean governments to institute policies to improve living conditions in the region.
- Describe the policies that were instituted.
- Explain the outcomes of these policies.

Government housing programmes

The report of the Moyne Commission (see 8.3) embarrassed the British Government. It drew attention to the deplorable housing conditions in the region. It recommended slum clearance, government acquisition of land for housing and the regulations to govern sanitation and water provisions. The colonial governments therefore undertook slum clearance programmes and set up government housing schemes to provide acceptable housing for people on low incomes.

Housing estates

Many governments later set up National Housing Associations (NHA) to develop areas where affordable houses could be built to provide for the housing needs of low and middle income families. Housing estates became a feature of government housing policy throughout the region.

Governments handled the entire development, hiring contractors to prepare the infrastructure (roads, drains, sewage systems, water and electricity supply) and construct the buildings. The units included single family homes, duplexes, town houses and apartment blocks. They were intended to create mixed communities so they were provided with recreation grounds, community centres and sometimes nurseries or early childhood centres. The application procedure for these homes involved an income qualification and a specified payment arrangement.

Figure 9.5.1 Swamp drainage was one of the measures taken to improve health in the region.

Health

The Moyne Commission reported that the main cause of disease in the region (for example hookworm, malaria, water-born diseases) was primitive sanitation. The commission concluded that most of the diseases in the region were preventable and recommended that each colony should reorganise their medical services and provide more facilities, especially in rural areas. Prevention should be through improved housing and sanitation, anti-malaria measures, provision of clinics such as for expectant mothers and child-care, venereal disease and school medical services.

Standards were higher in territories with established US bases. Swamp drainage, anti-malaria programmes, improved water and electricity supplies were already in place and populations near the bases benefitted from measures to eradicate mosquitoes and yellow fever, as well as vaccinations programmes.

DID YOU KNOW?

In 1931, Dr Joseph Pawan of Trinidad and Tobago identified the cause of rabies and the means by which it was spread.

EXAM TIP

Be familiar with reasons why the demand for education increased in this period.

The region did see more specialised medical clinics after the war: as well as clinics mentioned above, there were those for eye disease and tuberculosis treatment, and new educational institutions provided training for medical workers such as nurses, nursing assistants and sanitary inspectors The Rockefeller Foundation played an important part at this time in the drive to improve health and living conditions across the region.

Education

Administrators were concerned about reports on the poor quality of teachers, the dilapidated state of school buildings, irregular attendance and poor health of children in primary schools. People demanded improvements in four areas: secondary schools, vocational training, changes in curriculum and access to tertiary education.

- Secondary schools: the few established secondary institutions were intended to provide for the children of the upper classes and many parents could not afford the fees. More children needed access to higher paying jobs, especially in the civil service, and to be qualified for tertiary education.
School building and repair programmes were started after World War II. School meals were provided to encourage regular attendance and better nutrition and school medical and dental services were introduced.
- Vocational training: parents did not want their children to be restricted to agricultural labour. Vocational training would lead to higher-paid skilled jobs that were more respectable.
- Changes in curriculum: there were complaints about the limited primary curriculum which offered a heavy religious content, basic reading, writing and arithmetic but in contexts that were not relevant to the region's learners. The attempt to make education more suited to regional needs led to the establishment of the Caribbean Examinations Council.
- Access to tertiary level institutions in preparation for careers in the professions: scholarships were offered to the highest performers at secondary schools for attendance at a university in Britain. These were very competitive as they were limited to one or two awards each year, but they provided the only opportunity for middle and low income children to attend university. The University College of the West Indies, which became The University of the West Indies, was established in 1962, offering university education in the region itself on several campuses in the various territories.

More teacher training facilities were established and teacher salaries were fixed. Bonuses were paid to teachers whose students maintained high attendance. When Ministries of Education were established in the 1960s focus was placed on government control of the education system, training and employment of teachers. This led to rivalry between the government and the churches (mainly Roman Catholic) over control of education.

ACTIVITY

Do some research on the secondary schools in your area. Try to state whether the schools are denominational or secular, and if denominational, of which religious group, whether for boys or girls or mixed.

SUMMARY QUESTIONS

1. Explain the factors which caused governments to introduce welfare policies in the colonies.
2. How did governments attempt to deal with the problem of housing in the colonies?
3. In what areas were changes made to improve the colonial health services?
4. How effective were the changes made to the education system after the 1930s?

KEY POINTS

- Government social programmes were set up in response to the Moyne Commission.
- The programmes included housing, health and education.
- Properly planned subsidised housing units were constructed on housing estates.
- Health programmes included increased provision of health services.
- Changes were made in the education system.

9.6 Aspects of social life 1: community

LEARNING OUTCOMES

At the end of this topic you should be able to:
- List the festivals, celebrations and recreations in Caribbean social life.
- State their origins.
- Describe the main features of these festivals, celebrations and recreations.
- Have an understanding of their importance in Caribbean life.

Figure 9.6.1 The festival of Crop-over in Barbados originated in 1688, and was revived in 1974.

DID YOU KNOW?

From Trinidad and Tobago Carnival has spread through the Caribbean and to North America and Europe wherever Trinidad and Tobago nationals have settled, including New York, Toronto, Miami and London.

Festivals and celebrations

Caribbean festivals and celebrations revolve around religious observances and traditional cultural expressions. These different cultures merged in the context of the Caribbean historical experience to shape a distinct Caribbean culture.

Carnival

Trinidad Carnival evolved from the pre-Lenten masquerades and balls organised by the white French planters. From 1783–1838 it was an exclusive ball from which blacks and coloureds were excluded. White people dressed up as black people and re-enacted the *Cannes Brulées* (burnt canes), the practice of rounding up slaves to put out fires in the cane field. After 1838, Africans dominated the carnival and the upper classes withdrew. *Cannes brulées* became *canboulay*, which included dances and traditions from West Africa. This was the beginning of the street carnival.

Legislation banned many of the carnival activities which were considered noisy and obscene. Riots resulted in protest but in 1896 the most objectionable aspects were removed. Canboulay was abolished in 1884, stick fighting was driven underground and carnival celebrations were restricted to the two days before Ash Wednesday. The outlawed African drums were replaced by tamboo bamboo, and in the 1900s, by steel bands. The festival had developed into the carnival parade of bands, calypso and steelband competitions which it remains today.

Crop-over

Crop-over was a harvest festival in Barbados to mark the end of a successful sugar crop, originating in 1688. There would be singing and dancing with musical accompaniment. The festival was celebrated until the 1940s. It was revived in 1974 when it culminated on the first Monday in August with The Grand Kadooment, Calypso competitions and the Bridgetown market (Figure 9.6.1).

Holi

Holi, or Phagwa, is a Hindu festival which was introduced to the Caribbean by indentured Indians around the 1850s. It is a rite of purification to promote good health and is celebrated in Guyana, Jamaica and Trinidad and Tobago in March each year. It includes joyful singing and dancing when folk songs are sung with musical accompaniment. Participants are sprayed with coloured dyes.

Divali

Also called Diwali or Deepavali, this Hindu festival of Light, was brought to the region by indentured Indian workers in the 1850s and is celebrated in Guyana, Jamaica, Suriname and Trinidad and Tobago. It is marked by lighting small clay bowls filled with oil to symbolise the light of goodness, wisdom and godliness.

Hindus clean and decorate their homes, fast, hold prayers, share food, give charity to the needy and host a range of community-building activities.

Eid-ul-Fitr

Muslims celebrate the end of the fast during the holy month of Ramadan with Eid el Fitr when they give alms to the poor and serve special foods. The festival takes place after the sighting of the crescent moon which signals the end of the month of Ramadan. It is a time of spiritual regeneration when Muslims give thanks to Allah for all the blessings they have received. They celebrate the forces of good over evil. In preparation for the festival Muslims clean and decorate their homes and distribute greeting cards and gifts, give charity to the needy and visit friends and family.

Hosay

Hosay, or Tadjah, is an Islamic festival observed by Shi'a Muslims throughout the world which was brought to Trinidad by Indian indentured workers around 1845. It is a four-day festival of processions, which commemorate the martyrdom of the Prophet Mohammed's grandsons Hassan and Hussein at the Battle of Kerbala in Persia.

Jonkonnu

Also called John Canoe, John Kooner, and Junkanoo, Jonkonnu is a Christmas festival that is celebrated in Jamaica, the Bahamas, Belize, St. Kitts-Nevis, Guyana and Bermuda. The festival developed from English and African influences. African drumming, dancing and masquerades, and Christmas traditions are evident in the street parades.

Recreation

The upper classes introduced popular European sports such as cricket, horseracing, gambling, hunting, cockfighting, sailing and card games. For enslaved Africans there was little time for recreation other than occasionally swimming at the beaches and in the rivers. Once free, Africans created their own versions of European games. They used any available material such as coconut branches to shape cricket bats and wickets, young fruit as balls. They made pitches out of any available space—roads, beaches and clearings. They enjoyed **vernacular** sports: racing donkeys, goats and crabs instead of horses. Recreation continued to be differentiated by class.

Cricket

Cricket was first introduced into the Caribbean when soldiers played in their grounds. Planters played, but Africans and coloured people were not allowed. All-white cricket clubs were formed.

In free society Africans developed their own teams and cricket became one of the most popular sports in the Caribbean. In the 1900s there were inter-island competitions and by the 1930s black and Indian players were included. The West Indies team became a source of pride and a symbol of Caribbean unity.

EXAM TIP

Be familiar with the ways different social classes spent their recreation.

ACTIVITY

Make a list of outstanding members of the West Indies Cricket team and identify the territories from which they came.

SUMMARY QUESTIONS

1. Why did the ruling class try to ban Carnival and Hosay activities?
2. Describe two non-Christian religious festivals that are celebrated in the Caribbean.
3. Compare the Jonkunnu and Cropover festivals.
4. Why did cricket become an important feature of Caribbean life?

KEY POINTS

- Caribbean social life revolved around a variety of celebrations, which were religious and cultural.
- Celebrations reflected the many cultural influences in the region.
- The ruling class passed laws to prevent non-European cultural expression.
- Cricket assumed great importance in Caribbean life although it was initially racially exclusive.

9.7 Aspects of social life 2: visual and performing arts

LEARNING OUTCOMES

At the end of this topic you should be able to:

- Identify outstanding Caribbean painters and sculptors.
- State the key areas in the performance arts.
- Have an understanding of the early aims of Caribbean writers.

DID YOU KNOW?

Trinidadian artist, Carlisle Chang designed the Coat of Arms for the West Indies Federation and for independent Trinidad and Tobago.

Figure 9.7.1 'Negro Aroused', by Edna Manley.

Painting and sculpture

Early paintings produced in the Caribbean were created by visiting European artists, some of whom were commissioned by planters. Indigenous painters often studied in Europe and paintings of the period reflect that influence. In the early 20th century nationalist sentiments were reflected in art, as artists broke free from traditions and began to express themselves more freely.

The Trinidad Art Society was formed in the 1940s, with the assistance of the painter Sybil Atteck. The National Gallery of Jamaica was established in 1974.

One of the most distinguished sculptors of the region was Edna Manley (1900–87). Her 1935 sculpture 'Negro Aroused' (Figure 9.7.1) is famous for its political symbolism and celebration of black working people.

By 1985 artists across the region were working not just as painters and sculptors, but making pottery, jewellery, designing fabrics, working with wood and other materials. As with other art forms, Caribbean art reflects the influences of Africa, Europe and the indigenous peoples to produce vibrant and attractive work.

Performing arts: song and dance

Music and dance are closely linked in Caribbean culture. Influences came from Africa, Europe, Central and South America, India and the indigenous cultures themselves. Enslaved Africans, under repression, used what means they could to keep their musical traditions alive. Indentured workers from India brought their own musical traditions, as did immigrants from many parts of the world. The following paragraphs summarise a few of these styles.

Calypso
Calypso developed in Trinidad and Tobago from West African and French influences. First sung in French creole by *griots* or *chantuelles*, the calypso style emerged after Emancipation. People could express themselves when criticism was dangerous. Calypsos made fun of plantation owners and the authorities, exposed the scandals of the elite community, corruption of officials and cases of injustice. Calypsonians were distrusted by the upper classes and many attempts were made to silence them under sedition laws which remained in force until the 1960s. Women have entered what began as a male territory and have become very popular performers.

Reggae
Reggae music developed from Ska in Jamaica in the 1960s. The single most important influence on its international growth was Bob Marley, whose songs reflected social issues of the time. Examples of international success by other artists are Johnny Nash's 'Hold me Tight' in the US and the Beatles 'Ob-La-Di, Ob-La-Da' in the UK.

Its international popularity was increased by films such as the 1973 film 'The Harder They Come', documentaries such as Root Rock reggae and British and international radio shows.

Chutney

Chutney music was created by Indian indentured workers, a fusion of Indian religious songs using folk instruments with a dance beat. It appeared in Guyana in the 1940s but was first recorded in Suriname in 1968. In the 1970s Sundar Popo modernised the music with a fusion of western instruments. A Chutney Soca competition is now a part of Carnival celebrations in Trinidad and Tobago. The genre reflects American rhythm and blues, with lyrics a combination of English, Caribbean Hindustani and other Indian languages.

Other styles of Caribbean music include zouk, a rhythmic carnival fusion of French and African music, punta rock, originating in Central America and soca and salsa.

Dance

As with music, Caribbean dance is a fusion of cultural dances reflecting African, European and creole forms. Many traditional dances are rooted in celebrations and religious rituals. Well known dance styles in Jamaica are maroon, Bruckins, kumina, revival and hosay. The jonkonnu is a story-telling folk dance, a fusion of African mime and European folk theatre.

The folk dances of Trinidad also reflect African influences and religious origins. Some dance styles are adaptations of colonial-era European dances, for example the quadrille, polka and waltz. Ritual dances from Africa merged with English folk dances such as the reel and jig. The punta from Belize is a unique folk dance which is a mixture of indigenous and African traditions.

Many distinguished individuals and organisations have worked to preserve Caribbean folk dance traditions. In Jamaica, the National Dance Theatre was formed in 1962.

Literature

The earliest black Caribbean writers, such as Mary Prince and Olaudah Equiano, were writing when white people still believed that they were of superior intellect. In the first half of the 20th century some writers were also journalists and newspaper owners. Some, like Marcus Garvey and T. A. Marryshow, were political leaders as well, using their newspapers as a forum for black thinkers.

Other distinguished literary figures were C.L.R. James from Trinidad, Frantz Fanon from Martinique and politician Aimé Césaire (see 8.5).

After World War II, there was a massive increase in the number of outstanding literary writers, for example George Lamming, Samuel Selvon, Olive Senior of Jamaica, Pauline Melville of Guyana and Earl Lovelace of Trinidad and Tobago (who twice won the Commonwealth Prize) and Jamaica's Miss Lou — Louise Bennett-Coverley.

Nobel Prize winners from the region are Derek Walcott of St Lucia (1992) and V.S. Naipaul of Trinidad (2001).

EXAM TIP

Make sure that you know the names of some of the most outstanding figures in Caribbean artistic life.

ACTIVITY

Find the YouTube recording of Bob Marley's 'No Woman No Cry'. Listen to the lyrics and describe the various social issues faced by the lower classes.

SUMMARY QUESTIONS

1. What difficulties did calypsonians encounter in the performance of their craft?
2. Why did reggae music attain international popularity?
3. Describe four examples of traditional dance forms in the Caribbean.
4. What factors assisted the development of a literary tradition in the Caribbean?

KEY POINTS

- Art forms reflect influences from other groups in society and from colonial history.
- Earlier influences have combined to produce art forms that are distinctively Caribbean in style.
- There is a strong literary tradition in the region which has produced award-winning writers.

9.8 Aspects of social life 3: architecture and housing

LEARNING OUTCOMES

At the end of this topic you should be able to:

- State the different functions of architecture.
- Describe the factors which influence the use of particular architectural styles.
- Explain the role of architecture in the social life of Caribbean.

KEY TERMS

Jalousie: a slatted shutter or blind that lets air circulate, but keeps rain out.

DID YOU KNOW?

Grenada, St Lucia and Dominica were all at some point controlled by France; as a result French influence is still evident in their architecture, and fish scale tiles are used for roofing.

Figure 9.8.1 Technological developments in the 20th century made it possible for open, airy and light buildings to be built across the world.

Environment and architecture

All architecture reflects the building traditions of the population, the availability of materials and the climate. In the colonial era buildings matched the styles of the governing country and materials were shipped in to construct them. The high temperatures, humidity and heavy rains, hurricanes and insects influenced the provision of features such as **jalousied** windows, wide verandas and high roofs. **Vernacular** buildings would use local material and be adapted to suit local conditions and availability of materials. In Barbados, prone to hurricanes, buildings are squat. Indigenous materials such as mahogany would be used. The result was the development of a unique Caribbean style of vernacular architecture.

Traditional architecture

Traditional indigenous and African architecture was based on the social, cultural and religious needs of the community. Their architecture was based on wattle and clay with thatched roofs made of palm leaves. We saw in 9.1 how chattel houses were designed for quick construction and relocation using cheaply available local materials.

In the Caribbean traditional African architecture was reflected in the huts constructed on the plantations and the homes built after Emancipation. African civilisations did have a tradition of elaborate architecture, seen in the palaces of West Africa, but this was not transferred to the Caribbean.

Housing

Housing has always reflected the class and status of the occupants. The homes of the upper classes were of grand design on the large plantations while the slaves were grouped in settlements on the edge, in very basic constructions.

Working class housing was, as we have seen, often poorly constructed. As improvements were made, public housing estates and other government-sponsored housing schemes led to simple low-cost housing, cheap rented cottages and apartments. There are still hovels, slum-housing and barrack yards in the urban areas and poor quality wooden cottages in the rural areas.

As prosperity gradually increased, people constructed more elaborate housing and adapted European styles to produce buildings distinctive to the region. Houses would feature, for example, louvred windows, shingled roofs, decorated bargeboards and balcony railings. There are still many of these attractive houses across the region, and societies exist that aim to protect and restore this part of the region's heritage.

Public architecture

Public buildings can be used to give people a sense of pride in their town or city, or they may be used to dominate and convey the message that the rulers are very much in charge. If you look at public buildings and churches of the colonial era in your territory, you will see the styles of the ruling countries. In the 20th century public buildings began to reflect modern styles as new materials and techniques became available. While some buildings reflected the colonial past, for many it was an era of new styles, with open spaces. The growth of the University of the West Indies was an opportunity for new building styles—the Philip Sherlock centre on the Mona campus is just one striking example.

Modern architecture

Modern architecture became popular in Europe after World War I and in the US in the 1930s. It rejected the old style of large, rigidly divided, heavily decorated buildings made of heavy materials and offered light, open, airy buildings instead. This style was based on the principle that beauty in buildings could be achieved without ornaments and that the form of buildings should be determined by their functions and the materials used in their construction. Technological developments such as pre-fabricated buildings, air conditioning and heating which made it possible to transfer the style across the world (Figure 9.8.1).

Architecture and tourism

The demands of the tourism industry affect the styles of buildings constructed to meet its needs. Many people dislike the massive hotels and apartments that seem to spring up on coastlines. Some **tourist complexes** try to build in vernacular styles, with smaller huts with thatched roofs. The challenge for today's architects is to maintain a balance between styles that are attractive to visitors and those that are modern and practical with all the facilities that the modern visitor requires.

ACTIVITY

Do some research on public buildings in your territory. Try to identify buildings from different eras and make notes on construction materials, size and any details that you can see.

SUMMARY QUESTIONS

1. In what ways does the environment influence architecture?
2. Of what significance is public architecture/
3. What factors assisted in popularising modern architecture?
4. What is the relationship between tourism and architecture?

DID YOU KNOW?

European traditions were visible in styles of plantation great houses. and in public buildings of the colonial era, such as churches hospitals, offices, bridges, courts and prisons, as well as industrial and military buildings.

EXAM TIP

Remember that architecture serves several different functions.

KEY TERMS

Tourist complex: provision for visitors that includes accommodation and leisure facilities all on one site. Some complexes cover extensive areas and transform the landscape.

KEY POINTS

- There is a relationship between architecture and the environment.
- There are several variations of traditional architecture in the Caribbean.
- The architectural style on Caribbean houses reflects the class and status of the occupants.
- Public architecture is important for making impressions on its users.
- The tourism industry places particular demands on architects.

9.9 Aspects of social life 4: transport and communication

LEARNING OUTCOMES

At the end of this topic you should be able to:
- Identify the problems of transport and communication in the Caribbean.
- Trace the development of the region's communication systems.

EXAM TIP

Remember the importance of shipping links, particularly to smaller territories.

DID YOU KNOW?

Caribbean roads were constructed by enslaved labour and then by prison labour after Emancipation.

Figure 9.9.1 Pan American Airways began operating a service in the region in 1929.

Shipping links

Until the early 20th century sea transport was the only form of travel and communication in the Caribbean. The main shipping lines connected the colonies to London and other European cities for the transport of mail, people and goods. It was easier at the time to get to London than to any of the neighbouring territories. Since Emancipation there had been small vessel contact between the territories of the southern Caribbean, but most smaller territories had to depend on transhipment through the larger territories to access shipping links.

During the late 1800s and early 1900s important shipping links were established with North America to serve the new the US and Canadian markets.

While still a slow means of communication, shipping remains attractive for its cost, and the popularity of cruising has been maintained. The development of the container trade and the tourism industry has led to the expansion of shipping links and the development of ports in many territories.

Ports and roads

As plantations expanded, so did the need for efficient ports to export the produce, and receive necessary imports. As elsewhere in the world, ports are chosen for the natural protection they offer, and their central location, and they often become major urban centres in their territory. They become vital in times of conflict: it was essential for the ports serving the oil-bearing regions in South Trinidad, for example, to continue to function smoothly.

Early roads were mainly dirt tracks and bridle paths which led from plantation to port and connected estates. Transport would be difficult during the rainy season. While roads in urban centres would have been better, the Moyne Commission (see 8.3) recommended construction of proper roads in the region. Other factors driving this change were the transport demands of World War II, the location of new housing settlements and the needs of business operations. Increasing numbers of cars, the growth of urban centres and the expanding tourist industry were additional driving factors.

The development of responsible government and, later, independence, allowed administrators to focus on planned road development, with provisions for maintaining them. This led to the creation of public transportation systems, essential for the overall development of the territories.

Air service

Pan American Airways began operating a mail and passenger service in the region in 1929. The major carriers followed, competing for the region's tourist transport business. Pan Am's service was taken over by British West Indian Airways which began flying in 1940. From its centre in Trinidad and Tobago BWIA made flights to UK, Canada, US as well as to other Caribbean destinations.

Governments in the region wanted to encourage airline services for business and tourism development and airports and runways were constructed. Piarco airport was opened in 1931, the originally named Palisadoes in Jamaica in 1941. As with roads, these developments were stimulated by preparations for the war that eventually broke out in 1939.

Leeward Islands Transport (LIAT) was formed in 1956 to provide for the smaller island communities. By 1986 there were many daily flights across the region.

Air Jamaica began operating in 1969 with flights to the US. During the 1970s flights to Canada and other Caribbean destinations began. Long-haul services to Europe began in 1974. By 1985 domestic and international flights had become routine for many business travellers and visitors, an essential contribution to the development of the region.

Telecommunication

An efficient telecommunication system was slow to develop in the Caribbean. Up to the late 1800s mail and news were delivered by The Royal Mail Steamship Company which had its regional headquarters in Barbados. This means of communication was extremely slow. There was limited use of telegraph and telephone services in the territories from the 1880s, primarily in the urban areas. Until World War II, there was no significant improvement, although the demand for these services was increasing.

In the era of independence, governments nationalised the telecommunications services but they could not afford to maintain and expand the systems to meet demand and technological advances.

DID YOU KNOW?

BWIA (now Caribbean Airlines) began operating in 1940 with daily flights between Trinidad and Barbados.

EXAM TIP

Be aware of the challenges faced by governments to provide efficient telecommunications in the region.

ACTIVITY

Do some research to produce an illustrated poster that shows the history of any Caribbean airline.

KEY POINTS

- There were many problems in the shipping services to the Caribbean.
- Caribbean roads, which were created for the needs of the 1800s, were unsuitable for society in the 1900s.
- World War II stimulated the establishment of airports, runways and national airlines in the region.
- Caribbean governments nationalised telecommunication services but they were not able to provide the upgraded services the population demanded.

SUMMARY QUESTIONS

1. What were the shipping problems faced by Caribbean countries in the late 1800s and early 1900s?
2. What factors shaped new approaches to road development in the Caribbean in the 1900s?
3. Why did Caribbean countries find it necessary to establish national airlines since the 1940s?
4. Why was the Caribbean Association of National Telecommunications Organisations established?

9.10 Aspects of social life 5: ethnic and race relations

LEARNING OUTCOMES

At the end of this topic you should be able to:

- Identify any three races that occupied the Caribbean in the post-emancipation era.
- Examine the challenges faced by the lower classes
- Describe the impact of history on Caribbean race relations.

KEY TERMS

Ethnic: concerning a race or group, often one in a minority.

DID YOU KNOW?

In 1930 education became the largest item of public expenditure in Barbados long before this occurred in any other British Caribbean colony.

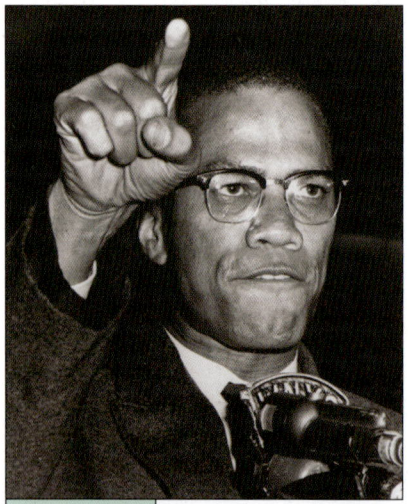

Figure 9.10.1 Malcolm X, originally from Grenada, was a key figure in the US Civil Rights Movement.

The effects of history—the plantation system

Caribbean society has been shaped by the plantation system. Plantation labour needs determined the composition of the population as the Caribbean became the home to a diverse population of Europeans, Africans and Asians.

The distribution of the population reflected plantation needs for a large labour force so Africans and Asians came to dominate the population.

The plantation created a complex system in which colour and wealth determined social position. Whites, the property owners, claimed that it was divine will for them to be at the top, enjoying social and political privileges. The mixed race people were in the middle segment of society. Because of their colour and blacks were at the base, expected to perform the most menial tasks, and associated with servile labour.

Ethnicity and power

The claims of white people to social, political and economic power were based purely on the notion that white people were superior and entitled to hold power in all spheres of life. The notion was supported by laws and regulations which emphasised the importance of **ethnic** differences in the allocation of power in society. These laws excluded blacks, coloureds and other non-white groups from holding political office, engaging in particular economic activities, owning land beyond a certain size and participating in the social activities of white people.

The laws and regulations ensured white domination of society because all the means to obtain power were closed to non-whites until the protests of the 1900s led to change. Despite acquiring property, owning businesses and obtaining the right to vote, social exclusion continued through the white-only clubs which continued to exist in the Caribbean up to the 1980s.

Education and social mobility

Education was the main means for blacks and other non-white groups to improve themselves and gain respect in society. In order to move up in society the first requirement was to change from manual labour to a more respectable form of employment; education was the means to achieve this.

During enslavement Africans took advantage of opportunities to learn and used Sunday school as a stepping stone to further education. After Emancipation, many freed people took advantage of the schools established by the churches and by the 1880s an educated class of journalists, pharmacists, teachers, lawyers and other professionals emerged from the freed African population.

By the end of the 1800s parents were demanding more and better schools, and in the 1900s, for secondary schools and vocational institutes. From these institutions some went on to the professions and a middle class of educated Africans and Indians was created.

Education empowered black people in the Caribbean and allowed them to attain social mobility in a very colour-conscious society.

The US Civil Rights Movement and the Caribbean

After years of oppression under segregation laws, African Americans fought discrimination through the civil rights movement. In 1956 Rosa Parks was jailed for not giving up her seat on a bus to a white man. This led to a bus boycott by the African American community, the transformation of the Civil Rights Movement and the emergence of Martin Luther King as a leading figure. These developments impacted on the Caribbean because of the key involvement of several Caribbeans, including the originator of the term 'black power', Stokely Carmichael (Kwame Ture) of Trinidad, and Malcom X, 'The Black Shining Prince', who had Grenadian roots (Figure 9.10.1). Caribbean immigrants were among the participants. Stokely Carmichael was banned from Trinidad for 20 years.

Black Power

The Black Power movement in the Caribbean developed out of local conditions. It was a cry for change in the living and working conditions, unemployment and poverty in the region, and an expression of frustration by people who were disappointed at the lack of significant change since independence. It was also an attempt to encourage pride in being black.

Although there were changes in the political administrations, economies were controlled by white foreign corporations which drained their resources, enjoyed all the profits and did not pay satisfactory wages. These frustrations occurred when global African consciousness was intensifying and foreign individuals and overseas developments influenced events in the Caribbean. Some of these events were the visit to the region by the Emperor of Ethiopia Haile Selassie in 1966, the activism of Walter Rodney, the writings and speeches of CLR James and the publication of Frantz Fanon's *The Wretched of the Earth*.

Protest marches and demonstrations in Trinidad in 1970, continued persecution of the Rastafari of Jamaica, bans on black power advocates and the growth of the black power movement in the United Kingdom and Canada, all contributed to an intensification of the movement: university students, trade unions, workers, young and unemployed demanded black power.

> **EXAM TIP**
>
> Note how the US Civil Rights Movement demonstrates how international events affect developments in the Caribbean.

> **ACTIVITY**
>
> Prepare a questionnaire of 10 questions on the Black Power demonstrations. Use these to interview a relative, friend or neighbour who was in one of the affected territories to obtain information on their experiences during the period.

> **KEY POINTS**
>
> - Plantation society created a society of resistors.
> - Ethnicity determined class status and power in Caribbean social relations.
> - Education was the only means through which black and other non-Europeans could improve their social status.
> - The Black Power movement was the culmination of a long history of oppression and discrimination in the Caribbean.

> **SUMMARY QUESTIONS**
>
> 1. How did plantation society affect Caribbean social relations?
> 2. Explain the relationship between ethnicity and power in Caribbean societies.
> 3. What permitted some black and Indian people to gain social mobility in the Caribbean?
> 4. What caused the Black Power movement of 1970?

9.11 Religious groups 1

> **LEARNING OUTCOMES**
>
> At the end of this topic you should be able to:
> - Identify some of the main religious groups in the Caribbean (indigenous, Christian, African-based religions and Rastafari).
> - Explain the reasons for the emergence of various religious groups in the Caribbean.

> **EXAM TIP**
>
> Remember that although there were many different denominations, the Christian churches had similar aims.

Indigenous

Look back to 1.4 and 1.4 to remind yourself of the beliefs of the Tainos and Kalinagos. The indigenous religions were based on nature worship and spirits. Historians and archaeologists believe that the people did not survive the arrival of the Europeans, who brought their religion with them and established Christianity across the region.

Christianity

The Christian church was an important agent of colonisation and Christianity was used as a means to control the indigenous and later the enslaved African populations. The Spaniards began the process by imposing the Roman Catholic faith on people. The pattern set by the Spaniards was followed by the other European colonisers. The French established Roman Catholic churches in their colonies, Moravians in the Dutch territories and the British established the Anglican Church.

Other Protestant Christian churches became active in the British colonies during the 1800s: Methodists, Baptists, Quakers, Scottish Presbyterians and Canadian Presbyterians who worked among the indentured Indian workers. During the 1900s other religious denominations arrived: Seventh Day Adventists, the Salvation Army, Pentecostal and Jehovah's Witnesses and the Evangelical churches and the Ethiopian Orthodox church. Some of these religious organisations established schools which were used to spread their faith and increase the numbers of their congregations.

African

African religions were condemned by Christians as pagan superstitions and banned both during and after enslavement. Africans were not allowed to give open expression to their religious beliefs—but they practised in secret. Since the African population came from different parts of the continent a variety of religious practices and names evolved, so there is no one African religion, but some common elements. Religions with this mix of elements are called **syncretic** religions.

These elements are reflected in the practices of Obeah, Kumina, Vodun, Myal and Santeria. The religious content of African art forms should also be noted. Their religious music generates values and ideals of the people, religious art creates statues of divinities and ancestral figures placed in shrines, dolls with ritual and healing function convey strong moral and spiritual values and masks transform and conceal power; bells and drums of celebration and resistance were important for the secrecy and survival in the new world. African religious rites for planting and reaping crops, safety, births and deaths, success in hunting and fishing, deliverance from plague, pestilence and famine, constructing new buildings and support for family and community are still practised in the Caribbean today.

Orisha

Africans wishing to practise their banned religion had to disguise the fact that they were doing so. Elements of Christianity would be blended with African beliefs, and gods and goddesses identified with saints of the Christian church.

Orisha, a religion of the Yoruba people of West Africa, is an example of such a religion, identifying Yoruba gods and goddesses with Roman Catholic saints: Oya, goddess of speed and wind, is identified with St Catherine, Osain, Yoruba god of medicine, healing and prophecy, with St Francis and Ogun, warrior god of iron and steel, with St Michael.

Rastafarian

Rastafarianism began in Jamaica in the 1930s as a resistance movement. Ethiopia's victory over the Italy at the battle of Adwa in 1896 was an important symbol of African strength in the face of colonialism. Mussolini's invasion of Ethiopia in 1935 generated both outrage at Italy and a growth in Ethiopianism. The Rastafari name was taken from **Amharic** words *Ras* meaning chief and *Tafari*, creator, the title of the venerated Emperor of Ethiopia.

The Garvey movement, which stimulated African consciousness in the Jamaica population, taught that Africans must have their own religion and worship their own God. The earliest Rastafarian preachers, such as Leonard Howell and Joseph Hibbert, preached of a black God and urged black people to return to Africa (Figure 9.11.1). They gave the poor and oppressed in Jamaica an Afro-centric world view and lifestyle. Haile Selassie was their god, and Africa was the promised-land to which Africans should return. Rastafari developed a new language, gave the world reggae, Africanised art, popularised Ital (vegetarian) foods and dreadlocks, the symbol of their strength, smoked marijuana to meditate and challenged the core concepts of Christianity. Upper and middle class Jamaicans ostracised the Rastafarians, who were opposed by the Jamaican government and were targeted by the Jamaican police.

Figure 9.11.1 Leonard Howell preached of a black God and urged black people to return to Africa.

KEY TERMS

Amharic: the language of Ethiopia.

ACTIVITY

Make a list of the religious ideas of the early Rastafarians.

KEY POINTS

- The early indigenous faiths did not survive the arrival of the Europeans
- Many Christian churches operated in the Caribbean. They had a strong missionary purpose
- African religions faced legal bans on their operations in the Caribbean in the time of enslavement.
- The Rastafarian movement resisted the domination of European belief systems.

SUMMARY QUESTIONS

1. What caused the presence of so many different Christian denominations in the Caribbean?
2. Why did African religions develop syncretic forms in the Caribbean?
3. What factors caused the development of the Rastafarian movement in Jamaica?

9.12 Religious groups 2

LEARNING OUTCOMES

At the end of this topic you should be able to:

- Explain the reasons for the presence of Judaism, Hinduism and Islam in the Caribbean Judaism
- Describe the implications of membership (social, ceonomic and political) of the different religions groups.

Judaism

The first Jewish people are thought to have arrived in the Caribbean at the time of the Spanish expeditions in the 1500s. They had been banned from Spain, and were not officially allowed in territories under Spanish rule. In the early days of conquest Jamaica, for example, was under the authority of Christopher Columbus's family rather than the Spanish Crown and their presence was tolerated. Nevertheless, Jewish settlers were often in fear of being exposed. Some would use different names and some converted to Catholicism.

The Jewish communities in the region are small, but have influenced the economies of their communities and its social artistic life. Many synagogues are also community centres as well as places of worship (Figure 9.12.1).

Hinduism

You will remember that many workers came from India to work on the plantations to supply labour needs after Emancipation in second half of the 19th century. Once called 'East' Indians, to distinguish them from the indigenous 'West' Indians, these indentured workers brought the Hindu faith to the Caribbean. The ruling powers were unfamiliar with the Hindu faith and the early arrivals faced some challenges as they sought to practise their faith. In some territories Hindu marriages were not recognised until 1957.

Hinduism is actively practised in many territories. Guyana and Trinidad and Tobago have large Hindu communities and celebrate the Hindu festivals. These include Divali (the Festival of Light), Holi and Ramlila.

Islam

Islam is also called the Muslim faith and its followers are Muslims. The first followers of Islam in the Caribbean came as enslaved Africans. The religion requires worshippers to pray five times a day and many Muslims found this impossible in their work on

EXAM TIP

Remember that discrimination against Hindus and Muslims was based on ideas of their religious and racial inferiority; followers of Judaism faced discrimination challenging their claims of superiority.

Figure 9.12.1 Many synagogues are also community centres as well as places of worship.

the plantations. The holy month of Ramadan would have been particularly difficult with its fasting requirement. Many Muslims from Africa were forced to use Christian names.

Muslim numbers were increased by the Indian indentured workers. In the 1960s the Black Power movement (9.10) created an awareness and a sense of pride in being black and Muslim.

Muslims celebrate Eid ul Fitr the Festival at the end of the holy month of Ramadan. Shi'a Muslims also celebrate Hosay.

Implications for membership

While Muslims and Hindus primarily belonged to the non-white labouring class and the Jews to the white planter and merchant class, both groups faced religious discrimination. The Hindu and Muslim religions were viewed as pagan, their practices frowned upon by the colonial authorities and the Christian churches. Although mosques and temples were established in the region from the 1850s, Indian immigrants were discouraged from practising their religion in public and were viewed as prime targets for conversion. Opportunities for social mobility and education were tied to acceptance of Christianity, so immigrants would outwardly convert, but many continued to follow their ancestral religion in the privacy of their homes.

Although there were large communities of Hindus and Muslims, numbers of Jews were small and they were mainly planters and merchants. While the Hindus and Muslims suffered discrimination because their religions were seen as inferior, the Jews suffered because the other white groups challenged their claim to superiority as the chosen people. They did not receive full civil rights until 1820 in Barbados and 1826 in Jamaica. In the Dutch colonies, however, they formed a majority in the white population.

The Jewish community in Barbados began as sugar specialists from Brazil and by 1750 the population had reached about 500. Special taxes were imposed on Jews and they were barred from employing Christians as their plantation workers. After an attack by a mob in 1739 and the destruction of their synagogue, the Jews migrated to Nevis, New York and UK. With the rise of Nazism in Europe about 30 families resettled in Barbados from Trinidad and Eastern Europe.

When the British occupied Jamaica the Jews were permitted to own land and to practise their religion openly so Jewish communities spread across the island, came to control sugar plantations and were leaders in foreign trade and shipping. After 1831 they began to play a prominent role in the social and political and cultural life of Jamaica. The population was increased by migrants from Syria and Germany in the 20th century but economic decline reduced numbers to less than 300 in the late 1960s.

The Jewish population of Nevis were plantation owners and merchants in Charlestown and they formed a quarter of the island's 300 white inhabitants until the disastrous hurricane in 1772 when most migrated.

Discrimination against Hindus, Muslims and Jews has been reduced in modern Caribbean societies where independence constitutions respect UN human rights regulations and guarantee freedom of worship to all groups.

DID YOU KNOW?

Islam is one of the largest religions in the world with over 1 billion followers.

ACTIVITY

On a map of the world, locate the place of origin of Hinduism, Islam and Judaism.

SUMMARY QUESTIONS

1. What factors made life difficult for early Jewish settlers in the Caribbean? What factor helped them?

2. State the reason that early Hindu arrivals in the Caribbean found it difficult to practise their faith.

3. What part of the Muslim faith would an enslaved believer have found particularly difficult to practise?

KEY POINTS

- Early Jewish settlers often had to disguise their faith
- Islam was brought to the Caribbean by enslaved Africans but its numbers were increased significantly by the indentured immigrant population.
- Muslims in the time of enslavement found practising their faith very difficult.

Section C Practice exam questions

SECTION C: Multiple-choice questions

1. After World War II the US invested in these two industries in Trinidad, Jamaica and Guyana:
   a sugar and cocoa
   b cocoa and coffee
   c oil and bauxite
   d banana and rum

2. ALL of the following incidences below occurred during the reign of which Cuban leader?

   The Cuban Missile Crisis, The Bay of Pigs Invasion, The Cold War, Expulsion from the OAS
   a Fulgencio Batista
   b Jose Marti
   c Antonio Macéo
   d Fidel Castro

3. The Cold War was the direct result of which of the following?
   a ideological differences between the United States and Russia
   b disagreements over global warming by European officials
   c economic sanctions against Cuban entrepreneurs
   d the sending of CIA agents into Nicaragua

4. Which two territories achieved independence in 1979?
   a Antigua and Belize
   b St Lucia and St Vincent
   c St Kitts and Nevis
   d Dominica and Montserrat

5. Identify the two countries that were early signatories to both CARIFTA and CARICOM.
   a Barbados and Trinidad
   b Dominica and Grenada
   c Jamaica and St Kitts
   d Antigua and St Vincent

6. The Netherlands Antilles consisted of how many islands in the Caribbean?
   a 4
   b 5
   c 6
   d 7

7. Which of the following buildings would NOT reflect European architectural styles?
   a great houses
   b mosques
   c chattel houses
   d administrative buildings

8. Which statement BEST explains the high unemployment in the Caribbean?
   a Depression in the sugar industry caused a reduction in the size of the work force.
   b Mechanisation of the sugar industry reduced the demand for labour.
   c The demand for labour in the sugar industry was seasonal, so fewer people were employed in the off-season.
   d The supply of labour exceeded the demand for workers.

9. Which of the following was NOT a positive impact of tourism on the Caribbean?
   a Improved air and sea links.
   b Increased food imports
   c An increase in numbers of hotels and guest houses.
   d Improved telecommunications.

10. All of the following were problems of communication experienced in the Caribbean EXCEPT:
    a It was easier to get to Britain than from one Caribbean territory to another.
    b Roads were located to serve the needs of the sugar industry.
    c Many rural areas were very isolated.
    d Mail deliveries were regular.

SECTION C: Additional practice questions

1. Explain why Puerto Rico was very important to the safety of the United States.

2. Two attempts were made to unify some British Caribbean territories during the 1870s.
   a. State the years and the territories which were involved.
   b. What caused the early attempts at unification of the Caribbean colonies in the 1870s?
   c. What were the outcomes of these attempts?

3. a. What factors contributed to the social and economic condition of the British Caribbean territories during the period 1900–35?
   b. What evidence indicates that these conditions were declining?
   c. What methods were used to relieve these conditions?

Further practice questions and examples can be found on the online support website.

Glossary of key terms

This glossary gathers in one place the key terms definitions that appear where the terms first occur. Subsequent occurrences are also highlighted in bold for students who wish to refer to the meanings given here.

Students should also note that the glossary defines words and phrases as they are used in this book.

Age of Enlightenment: a term describing the period in which people began to think that democratic values were more likely to achieve a fairer society than systems based on power and privilege. People began to place more value on the individual as a human being.

Alleviate: to lessen or make less severe.

Amelioration: making something better; for enslaved people it meant improving living and working conditions.

Amharic: the language of Ethiopia.

Arable: used to describe land that is suitable for ploughing and growing crops.

Artisan: a skilled, often manual, worker.

Associated statehood: the semi-independent stage during which states had control over internal affairs, while the colonial power was responsible for external affairs such as defence.

Bicameral: a parliament with two law-making parts, an elected 'lower' house, and non-elected 'upper house'.

Bull: often in the term 'papal bull': an edict or law issued by the pope. The term comes from the Latin *bulla*, a seal.

Chattel: personal property. Chattel slaves, along with their children and grandchildren, were regarded as the property of the owner.

Coercive: applied by force or with the use of threats.

Coffle: an Arabic word meaning a line of captive people fastened by the neck or feet.

Communism: political system that supports common ownership and sharing of wealth. There is a history of US opposition to communist movements in the Caribbean.

Custos: from the Latin, meaning a guard, a magistrate appointed by the governor of a territory. Today the post is mainly ceremonial.

Deculturisation: the attempt to make people give up a culture that is considered inferior and accept one that is projected as superior.

Demography: the study of a population.

Depression: a long-term downturn in economic activity.

Dynasty: a series of rulers who have inherited the title from a relative.

Embargo: a ban on trade with a foreign power.

Emulate: to copy with the aim of excelling.

***Encomienda*:** a grant by the crown to a conquistador or official enabling him to demand tribute from the Indians in gold, in kind, or in labour. In turn he was required to protect them and instruct them in the Christian faith.

Entrepreneur: a person who sets up a business.

Ethnic: concerning a race or group, often one in a minority.

Federation: a group of states that form a unity but remain independent in internal affairs.

Flora and fauna: plants and animals of a region.

Foreclosed: foreclosure is seizure of property by owners or financial authorities when contractual payments have not been made.

Franchise: the right to vote.

Genocide: the killing of a whole people. The Spanish committed genocide against the Taino.

Griot: a West African storyteller and musician who keeps the oral tradition alive, telling stories and histories to music.

Guerrilla: from the Spanish 'little war', a fighter in a small independent group.

Huckster: a person who sells small articles, either door-to-door or from a stall or small store.

Ideologoical: relating to the ideas and ideals of a political theory.

Imperial: describing countries that extended and exploited power over other states and acquired colonies, using military means to defend and control their interests.

Indentured: bound by a written and signed contractual arrangement, applied to workers to provide labour on estates for a stipulated time under specific terms.

Indigenous: belonging by birth, or occurring naturally in a region.

Inflation: a general increase in prices.

Jalousie: a slatted shutter or blind that lets air circulate, but keeps rain out.

Mandatory: compulsory.

Manumission: the act of setting an enslaved person free.

Maritime marronage: use of the sea as the means to escape to freedom.

Maroons: derives from *cimarron*, a Spanish word which originally meant an escapee. It then came to mean 'living on a mountain top'.

Matrilineal: descent through the mother's line.

Mercantilism: an economic theory of the 1500s and 1600s emphasising wealth and the belief that a nation increased its wealth and became economically independent by increasing exports and restricting imports.

Metayers: a French term for workers on the land who received a share of the produce.

Negritude: a cultural movement to awaken black consciousness and pride in African heritage. It was founded in protest against French colonial rule (*nègre* is French for black).

Paternalistic: behaving like a father, in a way that is well meant but that limits a person's freedom.

Patrilineal: descent through the father's line.

Plebiscite: a vote by all eligible voters in a state on an important issue, for example a change to the country's constitution.

Prohibition: a ban imposed in the US on producing, importing, transporting or selling alcoholic drinks. The ban lasted from 1920 until 1933.

Propaganda: information and opinions deliberately put about by a group or organisation to support their cause.

Proprietary: held in private ownership

Puppet administration: a government that appears to be independent but is in fact controlled by an outside power.

Reciprocal: in return for. A reciprocal agreement ensures benefits for both parties.

Representation: having a chosen person to speak on one's behalf in a court or assembly.

Royal Commission: a formal public enquiry set up by a government into a specific issue.

The Renaissance: a movement of the 1300s that saw the revival of classical art, architecture, literature, and learning. It originated in Italy and later spread throughout Europe.

Shaman: a priest who claimed to be the only being in contact with a god.

Stipendiary magistrates: officials who supervised the apprentices. A stipend is a salary.

Suffrage: the right to vote in political elections.

Sugar revolution: the transformation that came over Caribbean society as a result of the change from tobacco to sugar production.

Syncretic: a combination of different cultural forms to create something entirely new. Syncretic religions have integrated parts of other religions into their rituals.

Tariff: the duty or tax to be paid on imported or exported goods. The term may also mean the law that imposes the tax.

Tertiary: third. Tertiary education refers to colleges and universities for students who have completed secondary schooling.

Tourist complex: provision for visitors that include accommodation and leisure facilities all on one site. Some complexes cover extensive areas and transform the landscape.

Vernacular: concerned with one's native country, not foreign. Vernacular architecture concerns ordinary, domestic buildings.

Index

A
Abolition of Slavery Act, 64, 69, 72
Adams, Grantley, 144
adobe, 16, 17
African immigration, 80–1, 82, 83
Africans, status, 38
Afro-Caribbean folklore, 36
Age of Enlightenment, 64
Agrarian Reform Law, 122
agriculture, alternative, 100–1
agriculture, Taino, 9
agricultural education, 100
aid to former colonies from Cuba, 127
air services, 170–1
Akara, 54, 55
Allfrey, Phyllis, 145
Alliance for Progress, 124
aluminium industry, 106
amelioration, 66–7, 75
American War of independence, 110
Amerindians, migration, 59
Angola, 127
Anguilla, 131, 151–2
Antilles, Netherlands, 150–1
animals, domesticated, 17
animals, introduced, 15
Antigua, 73
anti-slavery movements, 64–5, 72, 84
apprenticeships, 69, 70–1
arable, 28
architecture, 168–9
arguments for and against slavery, 62, 63
arms race, 124
arson as resistance, 44
art forms, indigenous, 8, 10–11
artists, 166
Aruba, 151
asphalt, 104
Assembly, 90, 91
Associated States, 146, 151
Atta, 54, 55

B
banana industry, 96, 101
banks, 102, 118, 148
Baptist War, 57
Barbados, 131, 144
Barbados Defence Association, 130
Barbados riots, 55, 89, 91
Batista, President Fulgencio, 118, 122
bauxite, 104, 128
Bay of Pigs, 124–5
beliefs, indigenous people, 8, 10
Berbice revolt, 54–5
Bermuda, 150, 152
bicameral system, **90**
Big Stick Policy, 111
Bishop, Maurice, 117
Black Cross nurses, 160

Black Power movement, 173, 177
Bogle, Paul, 90
boiling house, 28–9, 30, 76
border disputes, 110, 112, 113
Boukman, Dutty, 51
boyez, 10
British Overseas Territories, 151
British Virgin Islands (BVI), 152
buccaneers, 18, 19
bull, 18
bus boycott, 173
Bustamante, William A, 144, 145
Butler, Uriah, 138
Buxton, Thomas Fowell, 68

C
caciques, 6, 7, 8, 9
calendar, Mayan, 5, 16
calypso, 37, 166
Caribbean Common Market (CARICOM), 147, 148
Caribbean Free Trade Area (CARIFTA), 148
Carmichael, Stokely, 173
Carnival, 164, 167
cassava, 3, 9, 10, 16–17
Castro, Fidel, 118, 122, 123
Castro revolution, 122–7
    impact of, 126–7
    US response, 124–5
Cayman Islands, 131, 152
centrifugal dryer, 97, 98
Césaire, Aimé, 140
chattel houses, 155
chattel, 28, 29
'Che' Guevara, Ernesto, 123, 127
Chinese immigrants, 81, 82, 83
Christian churches, 63, 161, 174
Christianity, spread of, 12–13, 14, 174
chutney music, 166
Civil Rights Movement (USA), 172, 173
civil war, 67, 120
Clarkson, Thomas, 64
clothing, 4, 6, 7, 34
Cockpit Country, 47
cocoa as a drink, 20–1
cocoa industry, 17, 80, 88, 101, 157
Code Noir, 42
coercive policies, **78**
coffee production, 21
coffle, 25
Cold War, 124, 126
Colonial Development and Welfare Act, 136
colonial government, role, 141
colonial unions, 131
colonisation, 14–15
coloured people, 38, 40, 173
Columbian Exchange, 14–17
Columbus, Christopher, 20, 176
communications, 105
compensation to planters, 69, 74–5, 76
control of slaves, 27, 42, 43

cost of living, 156
cotton crop, 20, 21
Council, 90, 91
counter-attacks by whites, 55
crafts of indigenous people, 3, 5–10, 16
craftsmen, 83
credit system, 76, 77, 94–5
creole language, 36, 40
creolisation, 40
cricket, 165
Critchlow, Nathaniel, 140
Cromwell, Oliver, 19
crop-over, 164
crops, alternative, 100–1
crops for export, 20–1, 88, 101
crops grown by indigenous people, 3, 5, 9, 11, 16
crops planted by slaves, 34
Crown Colony Government, 90–1, 93
Crusades, 12, 13
Cuba, 111, 118, 122, 123–5, 128
    loss of sovereignty, 111, 114, 118
    struggle for independence, 75, 114
    sugar industry, 81, 98–9, 114, 118
    and the USA, 112, 114, 118
Cuban Adjustment Act, 126
Cuban missile crisis, 125
Cuban revolution, 122–7
Cuban slave system, 67
Cubans in the USA, 124, 126
Cudjoe of Jamaica, 46–7
culture, 3, 27, 40, 83, 166
currency crisis, 76
curriculum changes, 163

D
dance, 37, 166, 167
decolonisation policy, 147
deculturisation, 43
Demerara, 55, 56
demographic collapse, 14
demography, 40
depression years, 92, **112**
Dessalines, Jean-Jacques, 52
developments post war, 92–3
diet, 9, 158
diseases, 14, 17, 80, 134, 154, 158, 162
disputes, border, 110, 112, 113
Divali, 164–5, 176
doctors, 158
dog tax, 89
Dollar Diplomacy, 111
domestic slaves, 29, 42
Dominica, 133, 145
Dominican Republic, 52, 116–17, 120–1
Drake, Sir Francis, 18, 19
drought, 94
duhos, 3, 8, 9
Dutch and the sugar industry, 23, 32
Dutch West India Company, 19
dyes, 8, 10
dynasty, 5

E
'East' Indians, 2, 176
Eastern Caribbean Central Bank (ECCB), 148–9
education, 86, 163
    and social mobility, 172–3, 177
'effective settlement', 18–19
Eid ul Fitr, 165, 177
Eisenhower, President, 124

emancipation, 60–1, 72–3, 74–5
Emancipation Act, 68–9
embargo, **99**, 123, 124
employment of women, 106–7
encomienda, **14**, 15, 17
Encumbered Estates Act, 77, 95, 96
entrepreneurship, 98–9, 101
epidemics, 54, 86
Equiano, Olaudah, 26
estate tasks, 31
estates, failure of, 92, 94
estates, falling value, 77
Ethiopia, 127, 133, 175
ethnic, **172**
ethnic groups, 38
ethnicity and power, 172
Europeans and indigenous people, 14–15, 16–17
exploration, age of, 12–13

F
factories, sugar, 28–9, 31
federation, attempts to establish, 140, 141, 142–3
Ferdinand and Isabella, 13
festivals, 7, 11, 164
financial services, 102
fishing, commercial, 104
flogging, 43
food, introduced, 34–5, 83
food prices, 134
Foraker Act, 114, 118
foreclosure, **95**
foreign industries, 104
franchise, **93**
Free Birth system, 75
free trade, 76–7, 92, 93
free villages, 73, 84–5, 88
French Revolution, 50–1, 61, 62
French territories, 151
friendly societies, 160, 161

G
garment industry, 106, 107
Garvey, Marcus, 132, 133, 167
Garvey movement, 175
gender, status, 38–9
genocide, **14**
German threat, 119, 120
gold, 8, 12, 104
Good Neighbour Policy, 111
government, representative, 90, 91, 93
Great House, 29
Greater Antilles, 6
Grenada, 89, 117, 121, 127, 147
griot, **37**
Guadeloupe, 151
guerrilla warfare, 46, **116**
Gunboat Diplomacy, 111
Guyana, 54, 56, 88–9, 124, 130, 139

H
Haile Selassie, Emperor, 173, 175
Haiti, 50, 52, 74
    rebellions in, 50–3, 120
    US involvement, 116, 119–20
hangings, 43, 44
hardwoods, 3
Hawkins, John, 18, 19
healing, traditional, 158, 159
health conditions, 158–9

185

health services, 87, 159, 162–3
healthcare training, 158, 160, 163
higglers, 72, 106–7
Hinduism, 176
Hindus, 161, 164–5, 177
Hispaniola, 50
Holi, 164, 176
Hosay, 165, 177
houses, traditional, 6, 7, 8, 9, 10, 11
housing, 34, 134, 154, 162, 168
Howell, Leonard, 175
hucksters, 40, 41
human resources, 105
hunting, 3, 9
hurricanes, 94, 153, 157, 177

I

immigration, Indian, 81, 82, 83
immigration schemes, 80–1, 82, 157
immigration, white, 3, 80, 82
imperialism, 32, 90, 112
indentured, 20, 81
independence, alternatives to, 150–3
independence, moves towards, 93, 139, 146–7
Indian independence, 133
indigenous people, 14–15, 16–17, **20**
industrial revolution, 77, 97
industrialisation, 104, 105, 106–7
infant/child mortality, 158
infrastructure, 102–3, 105
initiation rites, 7, 10, 11
integration, 144–5, 148–9
international representation, 149
Islam, 12, 13, 176–7

J

jalousie, 168
Jamaica, 19, 49, 104
    politics, 139, 145
    rebellion, 56–7, 88, 90
Jewish community, 177
job security, 156–7
jobs, 106
Jones Act, 114
Jonkonnu, 165, 166
Judaism, 176

K

Kalinago society, 2, 3, 6–7, 10–11
Kennedy, President J, 124, 125
Khrushchev, Premier, 125
King, Martin Luther, 173
Knibb, William, 56, 57, 84
Kofi, 54

L

La Ferrière fortress, 52, 53
labour, 17, 73, 76, 85, 105
    attitudes to, 78–9
    division of, 29
    legislation, 136
land ownership, 40, 84
land price falls, 95
language, slaves, 36
Leeward Islands Federation, 130, 152
Leeward Islands, governing, 131
Less Developed Countries (LDCs), 148
Lesser Antilles, 6–7
L'Exclusif, 32

Limitation Act, 65
literature, 167
Little Eight, The, 146
living standard, 107
'located labour system', 85
logwood, 21
London School of Tropical Medicine, 158, 159
L'Ouverture, Toussaint, 51, 52

M

maboya, 10
Madeira, immigration from, 80, 83
mahogany, 21, 168
Malcolm X, 172, 173
mandatory, 46
'Manifest Destiny', 110, 111, 113
Manley, Edna, 166
Manley, Michael, 118
Manley, Norman, 142, 144, 145, 148
manumission, 41, **66**
maps, 2, 4, 18, 59, 64
maritime marronage, 48
markets, local, 41, 88
Marley, Bob, 166, 167
maroons, 44, 46–9, 64
marronage, 44, 46, 48
Marryshow, Theophilus A, 144, 145
Martinique, 151
matrilineal, 6
Mayan society, 4–5
medicinal plants, 17
medicine, traditional, 35
mercantilism, 12, 19, 32
metayers, 85
Middle Passage, 25
migrants, anti-Castro, 124
migration, effects of, 82–3
migration patterns, 2–3, 14, 59
migration, rural to urban, 157
migration schemes, 80–1, 128
militia, 41
mills, sugar, 28, 30, 97, 98, 99
missile warheads, 125
missionaries, 57, 63, 67, 78, 84, 87
mixed race people, 93, 172
molasses, 30, 31
Monroe Doctrine, 110, 111, 113
Montserrat, 147, 152–3
Moors, 13
Morant Bay Rebellion, 88, 90, 91
More Developed Countries (MDCs), 148
Moret Law, 67
Moyne Commission, 93, 135–6, 137, 138, 162, 170
mulattoes, 43, 50, 52
muscovado sugar, 30–1
music, 9, 36, 166–7
Muslims, 161, 165, 176–7

N

Nanny of the Maroons, 47
nationalisation in Cuba, 122, 123
nationalism, 122, 123, 132–3
NATO (North Atlantic Treaty Organisation), 126
natural disasters, 94
natural resources, 104
Navigation Acts, 32, 33, 110
negritude, 141
Netherlands Antilles, 150–1
New Jewel Movement, 117

newspapers for black people, 132
Nicaragua, 127
Nobel prize winners, 167
Norman Commission, 96, 100

O

obeahs, 35, 36, 158
OECS (Organisation of Eastern Caribbean States), 117, 121, 149
Ogé, Vincent, 51
oil industry, 104, 128
'one drop rule', 38
O'Neal, Charles Duncan, 139
oral traditions, 37
Organisation of American States (OAS), 124, 128
Organisation of Eastern Caribbean States (OECS), 117, 121, 149
Orisha, 175

P

painting, 166
Panama, 115, 119
Panama Canal, 111, 112, 115, 119
papal bull, 18
paternalism, 62
patois, 36
patriarchy, 4, 7
patrilineal, 6
Pawan, Dr Joseph, 162
peasant communities, 88–9
Pelée, Mt, 94
performing arts, 166–7
piracy and pirates, 18, 73
plantation design, 28
plantation system, 26–7, 39, 172
plantations in debt, 76
planters, 33, 39, 55, 67
    compensation, 69, 74–5, 76
    relations with workers, 73, 77, 78, 79
Platt Amendment, 98, 111, 114, 118
plebiscite, 150
political parties, early, 138–9, 144
polygamy, 6, 7
Pope-Hennessy, John, 130–1
population increase, 83, 157
ports, 170
Portugal, 18
Portuguese immigration, 80, 82
potatoes, 16
pottery, 6, 7, 8, 10
primer, 93
privateers, 18
Prohibition, 118
proprietary, 85
pro-slavery groups, 62
protests, 134–5, 173
Puerto Rico, 65, 75, 114–15, 118–19, 150
punishments, 27, 42, 43, 60
puppet administration, 116, 118, 120

Q

Quakers, 64, 174

R

rabies, 162
race and status, 172
racial class system, 27
Ramadan, 165, 177
Rastafarianism, 173, 175
ratooning, 30
Reagan, President Ronald, 117, 121
Reciprocal Trade Accord, 99
recreation, 165

Reform Act, 68
reform, attempts to stifle, 141
reggae music, 166, 175
regiments, 41
Reign of Terror, 62
religions, 4–5, 12, 13, 36, 174–5, 176–7
religious groups, 161, 174–7
Renaissance, 12
resistance attempts by slaves, 25, 44–7
revolts, 44, 54–7, 60–1
rice cultivation, 89
right to vote, 41, 93, 138
road development, 170
Roosevelt Corollary, 111, 113
Roosevelt, President Franklyn D, 111, 115
roucou, 10
Rousseau, Jean-Jacques, 50
Royal Mail Steamship Company, 171
rum production, 30, 31

S

sabotage, 45
sacrifice, human, 4, 5, 6
Saint Dominique, 50
Salamea, Guyana, 156
Sandinistas, 118, 127
sanitation, 158, 162
Santo Domingo, 50
Schoelcher, Victor, 65, 74
schools, 86, 161, 163
'scramble for Africa', 92
sculpture, 166
'seasoning process', 25, 26
self-rule, move towards, 93, 139, 146–7
service industries, 102
settlers, 2, 19, 50
shaman, 8
Sharp, Granville, 61, 64
Sharpe, Samuel, 57
shipping, 32, 170
ships, 12, 13
Sierra Leone, 78
Siete Partidas, 42
slash-and-burn, 3
slave journeys, 25
slave laws, Spanish, 42
slave quarters, 29
slave rebellions, 61, 64
slave trade, 24–5
    end of, 29, 61, 65, 74
    reinstatement, 74
    support for abolition, 61
slavery, arguments for and against, 62–3
slavery awareness in Britain, 60, 61
slavery, effects of revolts, 60
slaves, 21, 22, 23, 38, 39, 60–1
    control of, 27, 42, 43
    escaped, 48, 61
    estate tasks, 31
    personal experience, 26
slums, 154–5, 162, 168
smallholdings of freed slaves, 73, 78
smallpox, 14, 86, 134
Smith, Adam, 68, 92
Smith, Reverend John, 56
Soberalis, Antonio, 138
social class, 38
social conditions, 154–9
social control, 86–7
social life, 164–9

social mobility and education, 172–3, 177
social relations, 38–9
social status and freedom, 40
social structure, 39
socialism, spread of, 127
soil fertility decline, 95
soldiers, World War I, 132, 133, 134
Somerset, James, 61
Soufrière volcano, 94
sou-sou, 101
South Africa, 133
Spain, exploration by, 13
Spain's monopoly, 18, 19
Spanish cultural impositions, 15
St Croix, 75
St Domingue, 50, 51, 52
status, 38, 40, 42–3
steel bands, 164
stipendiary magistrates, **68**, 69, 70–1
storytelling, 37
strikes, 135
Sturge, Joseph, 71
Sturge Town, 84
subsistence farmers, 9
suffrage, adult, 138, **146**
Sugar Act, 99
sugar beet, 74, 92, 94
sugar cane varieties, 97
sugar, duties on, 77,
Sugar Equalization Act, 92, 94
sugar estate layout, 28
sugar factories, 28–9
sugar industry, Cuba, 81, 98–9, 114, 118
sugar industry problems, 76–7, 94–7
sugar, markets for, 32, 97
sugar mills, 28, 30, 97, 98, 99
sugar planting, 28, 30
sugar price, 33, 95, 98, 114, 118
sugar production, 22–3, 30–1, 32–3
sugar revolution, 22–3
Suriname, 49, 118, 151
syncretic, **40**, 174–5

T

Taino society, 2, 3, 6, 7, 8–9
task system, 85
teachers, 163
technology, 77, 94–5, 97, 105
    Kalinago, 11
telecommunications, 105, 171
tenantry system, 155
tobacco crop, 17, 19, 20, 22
tourism, 102, 103, 169
trade in captive Africans, 24–5
trade, international, 12, 110
trade regulations, 94
trade unions, 136, 138, 139, 160
traders, illegal, 19
transport, 102, 170–1
treadmill, 60, 71, 87
Treaty of Basseterre, 149
Treaty of Chaguaramas, 148
Treaty of Tordesillas, 18
Trelawny Town, 49
'triangular trade', 22, 24
Trinidad and Tobago, 104, 131, 139, 164
tripartite kingdom, 150
Turks and Caicos Islands, 131

U

ubutu, 7
unemployment, 134, 157
unification attempts, early, 130–1
United Fruit Company, 101
unity, reasons for, 140–1
Universal Negro Improvement Association (UNIA), 132, 133, 161
University of the West Indies, 97, 163, 169
urbanisation, 106
US aid, 126
US cultural effects, 128–9
US expansion, 110, 112
US fear of communism, 117, 121, 124, 126, 127
US foreign policy, 114–17
US intervention, 112–13, 116
US investment, 98, 111, 114
US involvement in Caribbean, 110–21, 128–9
US multinational companies, 128
US security, 110, 112–13
US spheres of influence, 126
US trade, 110–11, 112

V

vacuum pan, 97
vernacular, **155**
vernacular buildings, 168, 169
vernacular sports, 165
Virgin Islands, British (BVI), 152
Virgin Islands, US (USVI), 112, 150
vocational training, 163
volcanic eruptions, 94, 153
voting rights, 41, 93, 138

W

wages, 95, 107, 134, 156, 157
wars, 10, 19, 92, 116, 132–6
water availability, 103
weapons, 3, 11
weaving, 8, 10
Wedgwood medallion, 65
West African societies, 24, 34–7
white society, 38–9, 50
white-only clubs, 172
Wilberforce, William, 64, 65, 68
Williams, Eric, 142
Windward Islands Federation, 130–1
women in employment, 106–7
women slaves, 29, 45
women, voting rights, 93
women's groups, 160
working conditions, 134, 156–7
writers, 167